READING HISTORY

General Editor: Michael Biddiss
Professor of History, University of Reading

To Helen and Natalie

RETHINKING THE RUSSIAN REVOLUTION

EDWARD ACTON
Senior Lecturer in Russian History, University of Manchester

Edward Arnold
A division of Hodder & Stoughton
LONDON NEW YORK MELBOURNE AUCKLAND

© 1990 Edward Acton

First published in Great Britain 1990

Distributed in the USA by Routledge, Chapman and Hall, Inc.
29 West 35th Street, New York, NY 10001

British Library Cataloguing in Publication Data
Acton, Edward
  The Russian Revolution.
  1. Russian Revolution, 1917
  I. Title
  947.0841

  ISBN 0-7131-6609-6
  ISBN 0-7131-6530-8 pbk

Typeset in Linotron Times by Rowland Phototypesetting Limited
Bury St Edmunds, Suffolk
Printed and bound in Great Britain for Edward Arnold,
a division of Hodder and Stoughton Limited,
Mill Road, Dunton Green, Sevenoaks, Kent TN13 2YA by
Biddles Limited, Guildford and King's Lynn

CONTENTS

ACKNOWLEDGEMENTS

Among the many friends and relations to whom I am indebted for help in writing this book, I would like particularly to thank Richard Acton, Roy Davison, Peter Gatrell, Genia Lampert and John Parker for the time and trouble they took to read an earlier version of the manuscript and for their invaluable critical comments. The blemishes that remain are no fault of theirs. I would also like to thank Rory Miller for encouraging me to start the book, and Michael Biddiss and Christopher Wheeler for overseeing its progress with such patience. I am grateful to the British Academy and the Leverhulme Trust for their generous grants in support of my research; to Nick and Jill Lampert for their hospitality while I was using the excellent library at the Centre for Russian and East European Studies at the University of Birmingham; and to the London School of Slavonic and East European Studies for an Honorary Visiting Fellowship at a crucial stage in my work. Finally, I would like to thank Stella for keeping the home fires burning while I was delving into the past.

E.D.J.L.D.A.

University of Manchester

GENERAL EDITOR'S PREFACE

The aim of this series is to provide for students, especially at under-graduate level, a number of volumes devoted to major historical issues. Each of the selected topics is of such importance and complex-ity as to have produced the kind of scholarly controversy which not only sharpens our understanding of the particular problem in hand but also illuminates more generally the nature of history as a developing discipline. The authors have certainly been asked to examine the present state of knowledge and debate in their chosen fields, and to outline and justify their own current interpretations. But they have also been set two other important objectives. One has been that of quite explicitly alerting readers to the nature, range, and variety of the primary sources most germane to their topics, and to the kind of difficulties (about, say, the completeness, authenticity, or reliability of such materials) which the scholar then faces in using them as evidence. The second task has been to indicate how and why, even before our own time, the course of the particular scholarly controversy at issue actually developed in the way that it did – through, for example, enlargements in the scale of the available primary sources, or changes in historical philosophy or technique, or alterations in the social and political environment within which the debaters have been structuring their questions and devising their answers. Each author in the series has been left to determine the specific framework by means of which such aims might best be fulfilled within any single volume. However, all of us involved in 'Reading History' are united in our hope that the resulting books will be widely welcomed as up-to-date accounts worthy of recommendation to students who need not only reliable introduc-tory guides to the subjects chosen but also texts that will help to enhance their more general appreciation of the contribution which historical scholarship and debate can make towards the strengthening of a critical and sceptical habit of mind.

MICHAEL BIDDISS

Professor of History
University of Reading

European Russia: main regions, cities and minority nationalism in 1917

PROLOGUE

The purpose of this volume is to provide a fresh introduction to the Russian revolution. During the last two decades a wealth of research by a new generation of western scholars has cast much light upon the events of 1917. The political, ideological, institutional, military, economic, regional and above all social dimensions of the upheaval have been the object of detailed 'revisionist' analysis. The 'revisionists' adhere to no common philosophy of history and as yet have generated no comprehensive synthesis. What distinguishes them is their determination to subject received wisdom about the revolution to searching scrutiny, their commitment to social history and quantitative methods, and their use of sources hitherto barely tapped. They have exposed many inadequacies in traditional ideas about the revolution and have made possible a far-reaching reappraisal.

To bring home the full import of their work, I have sought to combine conventional narrative with an analysis of the controversy which has long surrounded the revolution. The nature of the controversy makes the case for adopting such an approach compelling. The Russian revolution occupies the strategic centre of contemporary history. It saw power in the world's largest country pass from the hands of traditional autocracy into those of Marxist revolutionaries. The Empire of the Tsars, for centuries a bastion of reaction, gave way to the Union of Soviet Socialist Republics. The repercussions were momentous. The new State that emerged challenged a world dominated by the West and by capitalism. It presented a prototype of economic, social and political development which was to exert a potent influence over the world's less privileged classes and less advanced nations. It transformed the international order. As a result, the revolution evoked and continues to evoke the fiercest enthusiasm and the most unqualified horror. For its admirers, it represents a milestone in human progress, for its critics a catastrophe of monstrous proportions. For both, the revolution has come to stand as a classic model in terms of which events far removed in time and place are judged. Conflicting explanations for it have served to mould, reinforce and entrench sharply conflicting views of the modern world and of the very nature of history. Rival interpretations of the Bolshevik victory constitute an important part of the intellectual baggage of subsequent generations, both eastern and western, Marxist and liberal.

Of several well-established interpretations of the revolution, I have chosen to concentrate upon three – the orthodox Soviet view, the liberal view, and the view of the 'libertarian' Left. The first of these is impossible to ignore. True, the advent of Gorbachev and *glasnost* may well herald a fundamental change in Soviet treatment of the revolution. A new generation may jettison the old orthodoxy with its triumphant celebration of Lenin's genius and the infallible leadership provided by the Bolshevik party. With each month that passes the willingness to reconsider even this most hallowed ground becomes more evident. But as yet professional historians have responded much more cautiously to the challenge of *glasnost* than have their colleagues in literature, journalism and cinema, and whereas the 1930s are rapidly being rewritten, the orthodox version of 1917 has so far largely withstood the tide of *perestroika*.[1] Moreover, even if during the 1990s the traditional Soviet view is destined to be discredited, the need to come to terms with it will remain. Not only have historians subscribing to it been responsible for most of the work published on the revolution, but it has left a powerful imprint upon the evidence on which knowledge of 1917 is based. From the earliest days, the Soviet State was anxious to ensure that its own version of events gained currency and had little time for evidence that ran counter to it, or seemed irrelevant. The great bulk of the archival material that has been published or made available to historians has been selected by the Bolsheviks and their heirs. An understanding of the Soviet view is therefore a prerequisite for studying the revolution.

The liberal view, too, is impossible to ignore. It has played a lesser but important part in shaping the record by colouring both the memoirs of many of the participants vanquished by the Bolsheviks and most western documentary collections. At the same time, its portrayal of the Bolshevik victory as the product of the organizational skill of a ruthless, conspiratorial minority has informed conventional wisdom in the West for so long that it has made an all but indelible impression on popular assumptions about the revolution. Although recent specialist work has cast doubt upon many of its propositions, studies adhering to it continue to appear and it still provides the common currency of western media commentary. Moreover, the spectacle of *perestroika*, of Communism repentant, promises to lend it a new lease of life. The graver the travails of the Soviet Union, the bolder the adherents of the liberal view seem likely to become.

The 'libertarian' approach has exerted much less influence than these two rivals. Its treatment of the revolution, depicting an epic struggle in which the attempt by the masses to create a novel social order devoid of all forms of hierarchy and subordination was betrayed by the Bolsheviks, represents a decidedly minority view. It offers a less

[1] For a wide-ranging discussion of Soviet historians in the *glasnost* era, see R. W. Davies, *Soviet History in the Gorbachev Revolution* (London, 1989); see also D. Spring, 'Soviet Historians in Crisis', *Revolutionary Russia* I (1988), pp. 24–35.

detailed and comprehensive analysis of 1917. In few academic institutions and history courses has it been regarded as being of sufficient importance to merit attention. Yet on several key aspects of the revolution it provides a valuable counterpoint to the better-known versions.

None of these three schools of thought is homogeneous. In the course of the seven decades since the revolution, each has undergone significant change and development. It has long been possible to point to major differences of emphasis separating one Soviet historian from another. An historian who typifies the liberal approach when treating one issue may well reject that approach when treating another. The measure of consensus among 'libertarian' historians is even more limited. The summary treatment involved in an introduction of this kind, therefore, pigeon-holes historians in a manner that does individuals less than justice. Yet the crudity of classification along these lines may be justified by Bacon's reassuring maxim that 'the truth proceeds more easily from error than confusion'. My concern is less to label individual historians than to illuminate the major contours of three distinct approaches and to identify the central issues on which controversy turns.

This historiographical background throws revisionist findings into sharp relief. It carries the reader who comes fresh to the subject to the heart of current debate. It may also prove of value to the reader who has already imbibed, more or less consciously, one or other traditional image of the Bolsheviks' route to power. A dispassionate analysis of these interpretations is the most effective way to bring home the implications of revisionist research. It is a sound adage that the protagonist best placed to win the argument is the one who can state the rival case as well or better than can its own adherents. Nowhere is this more true than in a field that raises such divisive issues as does the revolution.

Before considering the controversy in detail, it is essential to have in mind at least an outline of events. This poses an immediate problem. Any chronology, however basic, begs the question not only of what happened but of which 'facts' merit inclusion. It is almost a century since the first Lord Acton drew up the agenda for an account of Waterloo that would satisfy French and English, Germans and Dutch alike.[2] We still await its appearance. A Soviet chronology of the revolution will feature every move made by Lenin and the Bolsheviks; a liberal chronology will highlight the actions and decisions of leading political figures; a 'libertarian' chronology will give short shrift to both and stress mass initiatives instead. Even if consensus could be reached on a dozen different factors that contributed to the Bolshevik victory,

[2] J. Rufus Fears, ed., *Selected Writings of Lord Acton* (3 vols, Indianapolis, Ind., 1985) III, p. 676.

there would be no agreement on the weight to be attached to each.[3] No account can apportion equal importance to every factor: to explain is to prioritize different causal factors. One benefit of weighing the relative merits of conflicting interpretations of the revolution is the antidote it provides to the belief that 'neutrality' is an option, that it is possible to pronounce the *Alice in Wonderland* verdict that 'all have won and all must have prizes'. Yet to examine the controversy a frame of reference is necessary. For clarity's sake the survey offered in the first chapter dwells upon political landmarks rather than upon social and economic developments, upon events in the capital rather than those in the provinces. This is followed by an analysis of the assumptions that underly the three traditional schools of interpretation. The main body of the book examines the major bones of contention in the light of revisionist research.

---

[3] This was the illustration used by E. H. Carr in his classic Trevelyan lecture on causation in history, E. H. Carr, *What Is History?* (London, 1961), p. 23.

1 THE BATTLEGROUND

Introduction

The middle decades of the nineteenth century marked a watershed in Russia's modern history. The international pre-eminence the country had enjoyed since defeating Napoleon in 1812 was brought to an abrupt end by the Crimean War (1853–56). She was soundly defeated in her war against Turkey when Britain and France intervened for fear that Russia would establish her sway over Constantinople. The Tsar's forces were humiliated by land and sea and under the terms of the Treaty of Paris Russia was disarmed on the Black Sea. The defeat brought home in the most devastating fashion just how far the Empire's development had fallen behind that of her Great Power rivals in the West. It fully exposed her backwardness – military, economic, social, administrative. It served as a catalyst which greatly accelerated the pace of change within the Empire.

In the aftermath of the war the government of Alexander II (1855–1881) undertook a series of major reforms. The Tsar's authority remained unlimited but almost every area of public life was affected, and in preparing the reforms the government slackened censorship and gave unprecedented opportunity for different sections of society to air their grievances. The most far-reaching reform was the abolition in 1861 of serfdom, the supreme symbol of Russia's backwardness. The 22.8 million serfs privately owned by members of the nobility were emancipated. The principle of the statute was that the newly-freed serfs should retain their household plots and an allotment of land, but that they should pay for this land. The amount of land made available to them was, on average, less than that which they had tilled for their own subsistence under serfdom. The government provided compensation for the nobility, while the peasantry were to repay the government in annual redemption dues spread over a period of 49 years. Statutes of 1863 and 1866 enabled peasants on crown lands and state peasants to redeem their land on somewhat more favourable but broadly similar terms.

A series of other 'great reforms' recast much of the country's traditional institutional structure. Administratively, the most innovative measures were the local government statutes of 1864 and 1870 which established a network of elected provincial and district *zemstvos* and city *dumas* outside the regular bureaucracy. They were empowered to improve a range of local facilities from transport, credit, and insurance to health and education. Their autonomy, it is true, was carefully circumscribed. The chairmen of zemstvo assemblies were state appointees. The zemstvo franchise, while providing minority representation for urban and peasant proprietors, ensured the domination of wealthier members of the nobility, and the duma franchise was equally restricted. But the zemstvos in particular rapidly expanded their activities during the ensuing decades. They employed a growing number of teachers, medical workers, veterinary surgeons and other specialists, thereby introducing the so-called 'third element', often a radical one, into rural life.

The reform of the legal system (1864) was explicitly modelled on advanced western practice, and laid down that the law was to be overseen by an independent judiciary. Juries were to deal with serious criminal cases, elected justices of the peace were to hear minor criminal and civil cases, and trials were henceforth to be held in public. The appeals procedure was streamlined, court practice was refined, and the crudest forms of punishment were abolished. The reform of censorship (1865) was based on the principle that it was for the courts to decide when the press had broken the law, and pre-publication censorship was significantly reduced. Measures affecting higher education saw the universities granted greater autonomy in running their own affairs. In the 1870s, a series of military reforms gave new impetus to the professionalization of the officer corps, and sought to emulate the Prussian example by introducing universal conscription, building a reserve of trained men, and reducing the size of the massive standing army.

In each case, the reforms were hedged in with clauses designed to preserve leeway for the authorities. During the late 1860s and 70s, administrative powers were frequently used to override the principles of the reforms as the government took alarm at the critical attitude of a more assertive 'public opinion', at recurrent outbreaks of student protest, and at the emergence of a small but dynamic underground revolutionary movement. In 1878 diplomatic humiliation at the Congress of Berlin threw the government onto the political defensive at home, and during his last years Alexander II was subject to renewed pressure for further change. His own ministers even proposed the creation of machinery for a measure of consultation on national issues with representatives of 'society' drawn from the zemstvos and municipal dumas. In 1881, however, on the very day he had decided to accept some of these proposals, the Tsar was assassinated and his son, Alexander III (1881–1894), firmly reasserted the principle of autocracy.

From the 1880s the regime made plain its determination not only to halt any further movement in the direction of public participation but in some respects to reverse the reforms of the 1860s. There was a purge of ministers sympathetic to reform and office was entrusted to staunch conservatives. Emergency regulations empowered the government to declare virtual martial law at will. Steps were taken to restrict the autonomy of the zemstvos, to discipline the universities, to intensify censorship. In 1889 a new tier of provincial officials, the 'land captains', was created with both administrative and judicial powers to tighten the State's direct supervision of the peasantry. Police sections specializing in the prevention and exposure of underground political activity (the Okhrana) were developed. The regime attempted to impose narrow restrictions on the ability of the different classes and groups within society to organize and articulate their aspirations. This was the inheritance which Nicholas II (1894–1917) pledged to uphold when he ascended the throne. Yet while the last tsars sought to preserve the traditional order Russia was undergoing a process of profound economic and social change. Within a decade of his accession, Nicholas was to be confronted by a wave of social and political protest which shook tsarism to its foundations.

The Emancipation of the serfs made possible a gradual but sustained acceleration in the rate of economic growth, the development of the internal market, the division of labour, the accumulation of capital, technological innovation and urbanization. From the 1880s the State itself sponsored an upsurge in heavy industry. The focal point of the policy, most closely identified with the name of S.Iu. Witte, Minister of Finance from 1892 to 1903, was a massive programme of railway construction financed by foreign capital. A major stimulus in the industrialization of most countries, railways made a particularly powerful impact upon an economy uniquely handicapped by vast distances and poor communications. They linked the Empire's far-flung mineral resources with each other and with the centres of population; they enormously increased the volume of both domestic and foreign trade; and their construction generated a massive new demand for coal, steel, iron and manufactures. The social repercussions of Emancipation and accelerated economic development gave rise to a range of diverse pressures upon the regime.

For the landed nobility, the impact of Emancipation was deeply disturbing. The compensation granted them was not sufficient to prevent a steady decline in noble landownership during the decades that followed 1861. A growing proportion of the nobility lost their ties with the land altogether. This was reflected in a loosening of what had traditionally been a strong correlation between landownership and civil and military office, especially at the highest level. The privileged position of the nobility seemed threatened, too, by the growing professionalization of the bureaucracy and the army. Among those who remained attached to the land, the result was a new wariness in their attitude towards the government. Their resentment focused on the way industry seemed to be benefiting at their expense and they blamed the Finance Ministry's favouritism towards industry for the plight – and the restiveness – of the peasantry. Towards the end of the century their anger began to take political form. A politically active minority of provincial landowners voiced criticism of the arbitrary nature of the bureaucracy and the autocracy. They made maximum use of the forum provided by the zemstvos and drew them towards an alliance with the liberal and constitutional movement emerging in the cities.

Along with the development of the urban economy, the education system and public services, the decades after the great reforms saw a rapid broadening in the ranks of educated, urban-orientated society outside officialdom. The quickening pace of trade and industry provided new opportunities for industrialists and entrepreneurs, and generated a need for managers, engineers and clerks of every description. The development of the legal system, the press, education and public services saw sustained growth in the numbers of lawyers, doctors, teachers, journalists, writers, students, and specialists of various kinds. As different strata of the educated public became conscious of belonging to a substantial and articulate body of opinion, 'society's' self-confidence grew. And as the aspirations of the various professions, of students, of the 'third element' rose, so did their exasperation at continuing official inefficiency, corruption and oppression. Leading industrialists and businessmen, many of whom were involved in foreign-owned enterprises, generally remained as politically quiescent as the traditional merchant community. But the economically less powerful sections of the middle class became increasingly outspoken, exploiting to the full the limited opportunities for organization and public debate opened out by the great reforms. During the 1890s the demand for guaranteed civil liberties and public participation in state decision-making gathered momentum. The foundation in 1902 of the émigré journal *Osvobozhdenie*, edited by Peter Struve, was an important milestone in the emergence of a liberal movement. In 1903 a loosely structured organization, the Union of Liberation, was formed to unite all sections of opposition and to press for constitutional democracy based on universal, equal, secret and direct franchise. More radical sections of the educated élite looked beyond liberal and constitutional reform to socialist revolution. From the 1860s they created a succession of underground organizations culminating in the foundation, in 1898 and 1901 respectively, of the Marxist-inspired Russian Social Democratic Workers Party (RSDWP) and the rival, peasant-orientated Socialist Revolutionary Party (SR).

Discontent lower down the social scale was no less intense. For the peasantry, the terms of Emancipation, under which they were compelled to pay for the land, were a bitter disappointment. Moreover, in the following decades pressure on the land was constantly increased by explosive population growth. During the second half of the century the Empire's population rose on average 1.5 per cent a year, the total soaring from 74 million at Emancipation in 1861 to 126 million in 1897. The result was to force up the price both of renting and of buying land. The overall trend in peasant living standards during the period is hotly disputed. But recurrent harvest failures, the most notorious of which led to devastating famine in 1891, imposed severe hardship on many. Equally clear is the peasantry's sense of injustice over the Emancipation settlement, their resentment against the landowning nobility, and their yearning to see all noble land made over to them.

Village life and the peasant outlook were conditioned by the administrative arrangements adopted at Emancipation. Except in the most westerly provinces, the land was redeemed not by individual peasants but by the village commune. It was the commune that was to own the land and to be responsible for all peasant obligations, including the payment of redemption dues. In part to ensure that all households could meet their obligations, the traditional practice whereby the commune periodically redistributed the land between households according to the size of families was extended. These arrangements entrenched a distinctive land-owning pattern among the peasantry and perpetuated the peasantry's distance from other social estates. Despite increasing integration into the market, therefore, the village remained in large measure set apart from the world outside, regulating its own affairs through customary law under the tutelage of the police. Deprived of any effective legal mechanism through which to express their discontent, the peasants expressed it instead through rural disturbances. The incidence of rent and labour strikes and land seizures from private landowners rose during the 1890s. Serious crop failure in 1901 was followed by major peasant uprisings during 1902 in the Ukraine, the Volga area, and Georgia. Peasant protest, both in the countryside and among the rank and file in the army, played a major part in the revolution of 1905.

Although the peasantry continued to account for over 80 per cent of the population, discontent among the urban poor and especially the industrial working class was of scarcely less significance than the unrest in the countryside. By the turn of the century, some two million men and women, rather less than 5 per cent of the working population, were employed in mines and factories. As in the West, the early stages of industrialization were accompanied by harsh working and living conditions. Moreover, large-scale manufacture tended to be concentrated in a few industrial areas, of which St Petersburg, Moscow, and the major cities of Poland, the Ukraine and the South were the most significant, and the plants themselves tended to be markedly larger than in the West. The concentration of labour both facilitated organization among workers and heightened the political significance of labour protest. The government tended to intervene swiftly with police and troops when major plants or the railway system were disrupted. Although labour organizations were illegal, protest from the working class grew ominously from the mid 1880s. In 1896 and again in 1897 almost the entire textile industry of St Petersburg was briefly paralysed. From 1899 Russia was hit by a severe depression which temporarily weakened the strike movement but aggravated unemployment and urban discontent. Towards the end of 1902 and during 1903 there was a series of mass strikes in several important cities in the South, including Rostov-on-Don, Baku and Odessa. The Ministry of the Interior, anxious about the security implications of labour unrest, experimented from 1901–3 with police-run labour organizations through which it hoped to direct working-class energy from political towards purely economic and cultural aims. These 'Zubatov unions', so-called in honour of the police chief who sponsored them, tended to escape the control of their sponsors and contributed to the explosion of protest which shook the regime during 1905.

Mounting social tension was accompanied by the swift development of national consciousness among the Empire's ethnic minorities. At the turn of the century only 43 per cent of the population were Great Russians, and the tsarist government's overt identification with them and with the Orthodox Church alienated minority nationalities. A heavy-handed policy of Russification tended to push even relatively mild cultural movements, such as that in the Ukraine, in the direction of political protest. In areas such as the Baltic provinces and the semi-autonomous Duchy of Finland, the government's attempts to tighten its control and impose administrative and cultural uniformity created nationalist opposition where little had existed. Where there was a long history of nationalist resistance, notably in Poland, Russification provoked bitter resentment. Particularly harsh was the discrimination imposed against the Empire's 5.5 million Jewish minority. Nationalist unrest among the minorities in general, and the Poles in particular, constituted an important ingredient in the upheaval of 1905.

The revolution of 1905

This complex pattern of social and political agitation was brought to a head by the outbreak of war between Russia and Japan (January 1904–August 1905). The war, which arose over the two countries' rival ambitions in Manchuria and Korea, was widely regarded in Russia as the product of intrigue at court and among a handful of entrepreneurs, and aroused little patriotic enthusiasm. A series of military and naval defeats, culminating in the loss of the war, generated fierce criticism of government incompetence, ministerial confidence was visibly shaken, and smouldering discontent burst into flames. During 1904, with the government on the political defensive, there was an upsurge of liberal and revolutionary propaganda. A campaign of banquets and public meetings was mounted to demand reform, a zemstvo congress drew up specific proposals for constitutional change, and a series of politically-orientated professional unions was formed.

At the same time, working-class protest and strikes intensified and on 9 January 1905 a massive demonstration gathered to present a petition for reform to the Winter Palace. Troops opened fire on the unarmed, hymn-singing men and women. The events of 'Bloody Sunday' had a profound effect on the political consciousness of all classes. In the following months, government efforts to open a dialogue with workers failed as their representatives pressed for changes too radical for the government to consider. Attempts to extract expressions of loyalty from the peasantry also backfired. An All-Russian Peasants' Union was formed and at its first congress, which met in secret in July, it demanded the abolition of private property in land and the convening of a constituent assembly. By August the government was trying to pacify protest by undertaking to summon an elected consultative assembly. But the following month saw a renewed wave of strikes paralyse St Petersburg, Moscow and many provincial cities. The new Union of Railwaymen brought the railways to a halt, a liberal Union of Unions and leading liberal figures proclaimed full support for the strikes, and many employers showed sympathy by lenient treatment of striking workers. The disparate movements of protest were for a moment united in massive resistance. The government looked so vulnerable that even irreproachable traditionalists among the landowning nobility concluded that political reform was inescapable. In desperation the Tsar appointed Witte to handle the crisis, committed himself to creating a unified cabinet under Witte's premiership, and on 17 October issued an historic Manifesto. The autocracy undertook to guarantee full civil liberty, to give major legislative powers to the promised assembly (the State Duma), and to base it upon a broad franchise.

The Manifesto marked a major turning-point in the revolution. It divided the forces arrayed against the Tsar. Once it had been issued, moderate unions, including the Union of Railwaymen, called for a return to work. Employers brought maximum pressure to bear on workers in order to restore order: recalcitrant strikers faced lock-outs. Liberals generally considered the Manifesto less than satisfactory but sufficient grounds for a return to normality. They formed the Constitutional Democratic (Kadet) party, dedicated to using the concessions of 17 October as a stepping-stone towards full parliamentary democracy. More enthusiastic was the Union of 17 October (Octobrists), a loose political alliance led by landed nobility and a few prominent industrialists, which was formed to work with the Tsar on the basis of the Manifesto. On the extreme Right, disparate reactionary groups formed the violently loyalist, nationalist and anti-Semitic Union of the Russian People to rally support for the Tsar.

On the other hand, much of the opposition to the regime remained unpacified by the Manifesto. Unrest continued among the most militant national minorities, notably in the Baltic and in Poland. The period from October to December saw a rash of mutinies among soldiers and sailors. From the naval base of Kronstadt near St Petersburg to the Far Eastern Army came reports of large-scale insubordination. Peasant protest – labour and rent strikes, land seizures, and direct assaults on noble manors – peaked in the same period. A second congress of the All-Russian Peasants' Union in November was satisfied neither by the Manifesto nor by the announcement that redemption dues were to be phased out altogether, and peasant disturbances continued through 1906 and into 1907. The working class was hardly more impressed by the Manifesto and in the weeks that followed it the government faced an unprecedented challenge to its authority, centred on St Petersburg and Moscow. On the very day of the Manifesto a central strike committee in the capital proclaimed itself the St Petersburg Soviet (Council) of Workers' Deputies. Its deputies were elected directly at factory level and subject to immediate recall, while on its Executive Committee members of the socialist parties played prominent roles. This novel organization rapidly gained the confidence of the capital's work-force, and helped to inspire the creation of soviets elsewhere in the country – among peasants and soldiers as well as workers. The Petersburg Soviet took on quasi-governmental functions, including the setting up of an armed militia. Early in November it called a second general strike. This time, however, employers' resistance was rigid and the strike soon lost momentum. When on 3 December the government arrested the Executive Committee and suppressed the Petersburg Soviet, the immediate sequel was an armed uprising in several cities, headed by Moscow.

Yet the government survived. It retained the loyalty of a sufficient proportion of the army to stamp out the mutinies, impose martial law in Poland, deploy troops on a wide scale in the countryside, and crush both the soviets and the week-long guerrilla-style urban uprisings of December. Moreover, the threat of social upheaval increased the anxiety of the government's more moderate critics to see the restoration of order. In the months that followed October the government gradually regained the initiative.

Pre-war Russia

Although the period following 1905 saw an extension in the freedom of the press and of assembly, the civil liberties granted fell short of the promises made in the October Manifesto. Equally, although the popularly elected State Duma promised by Nicholas was duly established, the franchise discriminated heavily against peasants and workers, elections were to be indirect, and votes were to be cast and counted by class and property groups (*curias*). Moreover, the powers entrusted to the legislature under the Duma Statute and Fundamental Laws issued in 1906 were severely limited. Ministers were not responsible to it and continued to be appointed and dismissed by the Tsar. The traditional supreme body within the bureaucracy, the State Council, was expanded to form an upper chamber half of whose members were appointed by the Tsar and half elected from such relatively privileged institutions as the Holy Synod, provincial assemblies of the nobility, and zemstvos. The Tsar retained the power to veto all legislation and should an emergency arise while the Duma was not in session, Article 87 of the Fundamental Laws enabled him to legislate by decree.

When the First Duma met in April 1906 it was dominated by Kadets, led by P. N. Miliukov, and peasant deputies loosely bound together in the Trudovik (Labour) Group. Efforts by the Tsar's ministers to persuade Miliukov and other prominent Kadets and Octobrists to join the cabinet were unsuccessful. Instead the Kadets took the lead in issuing a series of demands for far-reaching reforms, including the appointment of a government responsible to the Duma and the redistribution of private land. The government rejected these proposals out of hand and after two months dissolved the assembly. The Kadets led other radical deputies across the border to Vyborg in Finland where they issued a manifesto calling for protest in the form of passive resistance. The 'Vyborg Manifesto' elicited little response and those who took part were debarred from election to the next Duma.

The dissolution of the Duma coincided with the appointment of a new Prime Minister, Peter Stolypin. During his five years in office he combined vigorous measures to suppress continuing disorder with efforts to promote a programme of reforms which he hoped would prevent a recurrence of the upheaval of 1905. The centrepiece of these reforms was addressed to the issue of peasant landownership. He rejected the idea of compulsorily alienating noble land, but tried to alleviate peasant land hunger by providing additional credit for peasants to buy land and by facilitating resettlement on vacant land in Siberia. Above all he sought to dismantle the traditional peasant commune. Peasants were encouraged to register their communal holdings as private property and to consolidate their scattered strips into coherent farms. Stolypin described the measures as a 'wager on the strong', hoping to see the emergence of a class of efficient yeomen farmers with a firm stake in the status quo.

Stolypin's reforms found little sympathy in the Second Duma, which met in February 1907. Although the Second Duma saw a small increase in the number of right-wing deputies, more striking was the decline in the number of Kadet deputies and the advance of the extreme Left, including Social Democrats and SRs who had decided to abandon the electoral boycott they had staged during the elections to the First Duma. The government was bitterly denounced for the emergency measures it was taking to enforce order. Unable to establish any common ground between his proposals and the radical demands of the Left, Stolypin dissolved the Second Duma on 3 June 1907 and drastically altered the franchise on which subsequent Dumas were to be elected. The representation of the urban population (especially the working class), the peasantry and the national minorities was cut to a fraction.

The make-up of the Third Duma (1907–12) was markedly more conservative than the first two Dumas. The Left was reduced to a small minority and the tone of Kadet opposition became more cautious. A majority of the deputies were landed noblemen and the Octobrists, led by A. I. Guchkov, now formed the largest parliamentary group. The Octobrist leadership were broadly sympathetic to Stolypin's proposals for legal and administrative changes, and shared his hope that co-operation between Duma and government would strengthen the State's authority, check the pretensions of minority nationalities and reduce social tension. Yet Stolypin proved unable to enact more than a fraction of the measures he proposed. Not only were many of his proposals radically altered by the Duma, but he encountered stiff opposition from the State Council and the Tsar himself gave him no more than lukewarm support. Stolypin's problems were epitomized by the constitutional crisis that arose in 1911 over a bill to establish zemstvos in the western provinces. To ensure that the zemstvos would be controlled by Russian rather than Polish landowners in the region, the bill envisaged a cautious lowering of the property qualifications and the creation of electoral curias based on nationality. The majority in the State Council feared that these proposals would set a damaging precedent and, with the consent of the Tsar, rejected the bill. Stolypin's frustration was intense. He consented to continue in office only on condition the Tsar suspended both chambers, disciplined his leading opponents in the State Council, and promulgated the bill under Article 87. The Tsar felt humiliated, the majority in the State Council were furious, and the Octobrists joined in bitter denunciation of Stolypin's high-handed use of Article 87. The premier's downfall was widely predicted before he was assassinated, by an anarchist but with possible police complicity, in September 1911.

After Stolypin's assassination relations between ministers and the Duma deteriorated further. The parties at the centre of the political spectrum became more outspoken in their criticisms of the government. The core of the Octobrist party, which had suffered major defections to the Right, and a new Progressive party, led by a group of Moscow industrialists, moved close to the Kadets, who in turn intensified their opposition to the government. In the Fourth Duma (1912–17) the government showed little concern to defuse opposition or to exploit the deep divisions between its more moderate critics and the small minority of radical Left deputies. The Tsar proved wary of replacing Stolypin with a leader committed to any firm legislative programme. By 1914, when he appointed the aged I. L. Goremykin, the premier had become a mere figurehead in charge of no major department, and individual ministers reverted to reporting independently and in haphazard fashion to the Tsar.

The lack of clear leadership was underlined by the increasing isolation of Nicholas himself. The anxiety of the Tsar and Tsarina to shield their haemophiliac son led them to withdraw into a narrow family circle, incurring the displeasure of members of high society. The royal couple's prestige was further damaged by their devotion to the 'holy man' Rasputin. To the Tsar, and especially to the Tsarina, he seemed a gift from heaven endowed with miraculous power to stem the Tsarevich's bleeding attacks. On the other hand, in the eyes of even the most loyal ministers and the foremost grand dukes and prelates, he was no holy man but a charlatan whose doctrine of 'redemption by sin' was but a thin veil for crude depravity. No amount of censorship could quell public curiosity and disapproval.

Following the revolution of 1905 Russia experienced a further period of rapid economic and social change. A recession brought on by the disruption of war and revolution lasted into 1908 but thereafter swift industrial growth coincided with a series of generally good harvests. The pace of urbanization accelerated as did the development of civil society visible before 1905. The education system expanded at all levels. There was a rapid increase in the output of journals and books and in the range of and demand for newspapers. The number and size of business, professional and other independent organizations rose swiftly. The legal limitations on organizations representing labour remained more severe. Legislation passed in 1912 to establish funds for accident and illness insurance for workers created councils to which workers elected representatives. Trade unions, on the other hand, after enjoying a brief period of vigorous growth in the immediate aftermath of their legalization in 1906, were subjected to a variety of restrictions and reduced to a skeletal and precarious existence. Until 1910 organized labour protest was subdued but as the industrial boom gathered pace, bringing the number of workers in mining and large-sale industry to over three million by 1914, the relative industrial calm was broken. In 1912 over half a million workers across the Empire went on strike to protest when government troops opened fire upon a large crowd of striking miners in the Lena goldfields in eastern Siberia, killing some 270. No city proved more strike-prone than the capital where there was a general strike in the summer of 1914.

The strike coincided with international crisis. As the Ottoman Empire in Europe disintegrated in the late nineteenth century, leaving a number of small successor states, hostility mounted between Russia and Austria-Hungary over their rival claims to influence in the Balkans. Between 1908 and 1913, while Austria-Hungary sought to check the growth of Serbia, the most ambitious and assertive of the successor states, Russia lent her fellow Slavs diplomatic support. The conflict played a key role in exacerbating tension between the Dual Alliance of Austria and Germany, on the one side, and Russia and France on the other. In July 1914, after Serbian nationalists had assassinated the Habsburg heir apparent, the Austrian government resolved to crush the Serbian menace once and for all. Fully confident of German support, Vienna issued Serbia an ultimatum which she could not fulfil, and declared war. Russia mobilized her army, Germany immediately followed suit, and the First World War ensued.

The revolutionary intelligentsia

A significant role in the disorder that plagued the last decades of the Russian Empire was played by the so-called 'revolutionary intelligentsia'. A watertight definition of the elusive social category 'intelligentsia' is difficult to frame. The term is generally taken to denote that section of the educated élite – an élite deliberately nurtured by the tsarist regime to man the civil and military establishment – which became critical of the existing order. A radical minority of the intelligentsia took their criticism beyond intellectual dissent, broke their ties with conventional society and made a conscious commitment to the revolutionary overthrow of the tsarist order. Emerging in significant numbers in the 1860s, this revolutionary intelligentsia established a tradition of revolutionary thought, organization, propaganda and agitation. Until the last years of the nineteenth century it was they who posed the most visible challenge to the status quo. It was they who introduced and developed the political vocabulary in terms of which protagonists of the Left interpreted the revolutionary drama. It was they who, at the turn of the century, founded the socialist parties which came to dominate the political scene in 1917. And it was from their number that the most prominent socialist leaders of 1917 were drawn.

In the decades before Emancipation only a few isolated individuals had carried dissent to the point of revolutionary commitment. The most prominent of these was Alexander Herzen who emigrated in 1847 and in 1853 founded a Free Russian Press in London which launched a tradition of radical émigré journals smuggled into the Empire. From the late 1850s, as censorship was slackened and expectations of imminent and major reform rose, a small but steady stream of intelligentsia, largely drawn from students in higher education, became involved in radical dissent. At first much of their energy was absorbed in rebellion against the values and conventions, the patriarchy and religion, of the educated world from which they sprang. During the 1860s, however, cultural revolt became overlaid by concern for broader social problems. They drew upon the émigré press and upon a steady flow of western social, political, economic and scientific works.

They drew, too, upon illegal literature put out by clandestine presses within Russia, and upon the legally published works of social critics who skilfully circumvented the censor, the most influential being the journalist N. G. Chernyshevsky.

The dominant theme of this literature was concern for the well-being of the peasantry. Castigating the terms of Emancipation as unjust and rejecting the prospect of Russia following the western path of capitalist development, they developed the 'populist' ideology adumbrated by Herzen and Chernyshevsky. At the centre of their vision of Russia's revolutionary transformation stood the peasant commune which, they argued, had preserved the peasantry from the corruption of private property. With its egalitarian tradition of periodic redistribution of the land it seemed to them to provide a basis on which Russia could bypass capitalism and make a direct transition to socialism. During the late 1860s and 70s a series of revolutionary underground organizations was formed. They attempted to propagate socialist ideas among the peasantry, and in 1874 two to three thousand young radicals 'went to the people' in the countryside. They made little impact and at the end of the decade some of them resorted to terrorist attacks on senior officials in an effort to destabilize the government. The most highly-centralized and coherent terrorist organization they created was the 'People's Will' formed in 1879. Despite the government's efforts, the People's Will succeeded in 1881 in assassinating the Tsar himself. The upshot, however, was not revolution but the destruction of the organization.

During the 1880s Marxism began to gain currency among the revolutionary intelligentsia. Its most influential spokesman was G. V. Plekhanov, who along with four other former populists founded the émigré 'Emancipation of Labour' group dedicated to spreading Marxist ideas in Russia. Plekhanov argued that Russia was bound to undergo capitalism and that the populist notion of direct transition from semi-feudalism to socialism was an utopian illusion. The commune was doomed by the spread of market relations and the peasantry were becoming divided between capitalists and propertyless rural labourers. Moreover, capitalism alone could generate the industrial base necessary for socialism and the class destined to overthrow the bourgeoisie and carry through socialist revolution, the industrial working class. The revolutionary intelligentsia, Plekhanov urged, must abandon its romantic and terrorist traditions, adopt the scientific perspective of Marxism, and devote itself to assisting in the development of a powerful revolutionary organization of the proletariat.

By the early nineties a significant proportion of young radicals had adopted Marxist ideas. At first they devoted themselves to self-education, fierce polemics against the populists, and propaganda among circles of selected workers. During the mid nineties, however, they began to turn to mass agitation at factory level. In 1895 the

'Union of Struggle for the Emancipation of the Working Class', among whose leaders were V. I. Lenin and Iu. O. Martov, was set up in St Petersburg and its members were active in the major strikes of 1896 and 1897. 1898 saw the foundation of the RSDWP. It was promptly shattered by police arrests, and following the economic downturn of 1899 there was a brief fall-off in strike action and contact between *intelligenty* and workers declined. But in 1900 Plekhanov's group, augmented by Lenin and Martov, set up *Iskra*, an émigré journal designed as a rallying point for like-minded Social Democrats. In 1903 a second founding congress, held in Brussels and London and dominated by delegates loyal to *Iskra*, re-established the party.

At this congress the delegates split into two factions. The initial bone of contention was the question of the terms on which sympathizers should be admitted to the party. One faction (the Bolsheviks – 'partisans of the majority') favoured a narrow definition which would admit only dedicated and disciplined activists, while another (the Mensheviks – 'partisans of the minority') envisaged a much broader party embracing wide sections of the proletariat. Lenin, who had spelled out his ideas on the need for a tightly-knit, centralized party of 'professional revolutionaries' in his major tract on party structure, *What Is To Be Done?* (1902), emerged as the leader of the Bolsheviks. The Mensheviks, among whom Martov played a leading role, rejected Lenin's vision of the party on the grounds that it would institutionalize the gap between intelligentsia and workers, between party and class.

The following years saw repeated attempts at reconciliation between the two factions, and local activists showed markedly less interest in ideological divisions than did leaders abroad. During the revolution of 1905, when many of the émigré leaders briefly returned to Russia, there was considerable co-operation between them. Yet after 1905 the rift widened. Mensheviks in general adhered more strictly to the traditional Marxist assumption that in so backward a country as Russia the impending revolution would bring the bourgeoisie to power. They were willing to envisage greater co-operation with liberal representatives of the bourgeoisie and tended to place more emphasis on taking advantage of the new opportunities of the Duma era for the development of a legal workers' movement. Bolsheviks, on the other hand, were more dismissive of the revolutionary potential of the Russian bourgeoisie, saw the peasantry as more likely allies of the proletariat, and regarded legal activity as no substitute for underground preparation for revolution. During the Stolypin years, when the SDs were hard hit by repression and membership fell precipitately, factional strife amongst émigré SDs was fierce. Lenin clashed with the most intransigent Bolsheviks, led by the philosopher A. A. Bogdanov, who were hostile to even minimal use of such legal outlets as Duma representation and favoured concentration upon preparation for a new armed uprising. In 1909 Lenin succeeded in having Bogdanov expelled from the Bolshevik faction. In January 1912 he organized a conference of like-minded Social Democrats in Prague. A new Central Committee was elected and the Bolshevik faction became a fully-fledged independent party. A rival meeting in Vienna the same year, at which the radical Menshevik L. D. Trotsky took a leading role, failed to forge unity among the non-Bolshevik Social Democrats. Trotsky subsequently became identified with the 'Interdistrict' Committee which was formed in St Petersburg the following year in an attempt to create a bridge between rival party groups.

In the immediate pre-war years, as working-class protest resumed, the parties created by the revolutionary intelligentsia enjoyed something of a revival. Bolshevik publications, demanding an eight-hour day, a democratic republic, and confiscation of all noble land, achieved wider circulation than those of the Mensheviks. In the Duma elections of 1912 the Bolsheviks won six of the nine curias reserved for workers and by 1914 the Mensheviks had lost control of the trade unions and social insurance councils in the Moscow and St Petersburg regions to their more radical rivals.

By no means all revolutionaries were converted to social democracy. Many refused to accept the notion that the peasantry must pass through the mill of capitalism and be divided between rural capitalists and rural proletarians. From the 1890s 'neo-populists', whose chief theorist was V. M. Chernov, placed less emphasis on the peculiar virtues of the peasant commune than had earlier populists, but argued that since the vast majority of peasants rejected private landownership and depended upon the labour of their own hands, they were already semi-socialist in outlook. While accepting that in the cities events would unfold much as Marx had envisaged, with a phase of bourgeois rule culminating in proletarian revolution, they insisted that in the countryside peasant revolution could achieve the immediate 'socialization' of the land and abolition of private ownership in preparation for the ultimate transition to socialist production. Several local groups came together in 1901 to form the SR party, and were joined the following year by the émigré Agrarian Socialist League.

The party addressed much of its effort to workers and it enrolled few peasant members, yet the peasant question was central to its programme and during the revolution of 1905 it exerted considerable influence in the All-Russian Peasants' Union. The SRs suffered divisions over tactics – the older generation tended to disapprove of the wave of terrorist attacks mounted by younger members between 1901 and 1907. The repression of the Stolypin years took as heavy a toll on the SRs as the SDs and the party suffered a major blow to both its morale and organization in 1908 when E. F. Azef, the leader of its 'fighting organization', was exposed as a double agent working for the Okhrana. The level of SR activity declined sharply and in the pre-war period they took less advantage than did the SDs of the opportunities for legal activity. When the franchise reform of 1907 virtually ruled out the possibility of exploiting Duma elections for propaganda purposes among the peasantry the party boycotted both the Third and Fourth Dumas.

The war and the February revolution

The initial public response to the outbreak of war was an upsurge of patriotic fervour, at any rate among the middle and upper classes: the Kadet leadership in the Duma called for a political truce and national unity against the common enemy. Yet the war proved far longer and more destructive than had been generally expected. The news from the front was grim. Although Russia scored major victories against Austria-Hungary in 1914 and again in 1916, she could not hold her own against Germany. An initial invasion of East Prussia relieved German pressure on the French but led to disastrous Russian defeats at Tannenberg and the Masurian Lakes. During 1915 the Russians were forced to evacuate a vast stretch of territory reaching beyond Poland into the western provinces and 1916 saw further defeats. The number of deaths, casualties and prisoners taken spiralled remorselessly upwards. In both the navy and the army, which enrolled a total of 15 million predominantly peasant men, morale deteriorated. By the winter of 1916–17 the High Command had become seriously worried by rank-and-file disaffection.

The war effort imposed heavy burdens on the civilian population. As production for the front was stepped up, the output of civilian manufactures fell, prices soared, and peasants found less and less incentive to sell their produce. The market mechanism linking city and countryside began to break down, and was further disrupted by the inability of the railway system to cope with the exceptional wartime demands made upon it. The flow of grain to the cities – and to the army – dwindled. Real wages for workers declined steadily and in the winter of 1916–17 even those of skilled metal workers in the capital (renamed Petrograd in line with patriotic sentiment) plummeted. The length of the working day was extended and the incidence of accidents in mines and factories rose. At the same time, the hectic expansion of war industries swelled the industrial proletariat by no less than a third, there was a massive influx of refugees from front-line areas, and the cities became increasingly overcrowded, insanitary and disease-ridden.

The regime was held responsible. The High Command, and the Tsar himself, especially after he took personal command in the summer of 1915, were blamed for military incompetence. The War Ministry was blamed for the desperate shortage of arms and ammunition during the first two years of the war, and for the tardiness with which domestic industry was harnessed to war production. Civilian ministries were blamed for failing to ensure adequate supplies of food, for chronic shortages of every kind, for the endless queues. National minorities were given particular cause for grievance by the High Command's disregard for their sensibilities, epitomized by the wholesale deportation of Jews from the Polish provinces. Rumours of treason, corruption and massive war-profiteering gathered pace, fed by the Germanic origins of the Tsarina, the notoriety of Rasputin, the frantic jostling for office among government ministers, and the relative comfort enjoyed by high society.

Initially, mobilization had served to increase government control of public affairs. Civil liberties were further curtailed, disruptive workers were drafted into the army, censorship was tightened, legal socialist publications suppressed, and the Bolshevik members of the Duma arrested. Underground socialist organizations were hard hit by arrests. Émigré socialist leaders had greater difficulty communicating with Russia. Moreover, the war intensified factional disputes as socialists divided between 'defencists' who were prepared to support the war effort and 'internationalists', among whom Lenin was most uncompromising, who condemned it. Yet the authorities were unable to silence the expression of political opposition. Within the Duma the small contingent of Menshevik and Trudovik Deputies, led by N. S. Chkeidze and A. F. Kerensky respectively, became increasingly strident in their attacks upon the regime. In August 1915 a broad spectrum of liberal and conservative Duma deputies formed a 'Progressive Bloc' under Miliukov's leadership and called upon Nicholas to appoint a government enjoying public confidence. In November 1916 a speech by Miliukov created a sensation when he punctuated a list of the government's shortcomings with the rhetorical question: 'Is this stupidity or treason?' The Tsar rejected the Duma's demands and permitted it only the briefest of sessions. Yet as the war dragged on it served not only to increase the regime's unpopularity but also to give new leverage to the forces of opposition.

The professional and business classes, anxious to support the army with auxiliary services and medical care for the wounded, and to increase military production, organized their efforts through public organizations – the Union of Zemstvos, the Union of Towns and a network of War Industry Committees (WICs). These provided a forum and focus for public criticism of officialdom. The holding of elections for worker representatives to the WICs from 1915 created new outlets for agitation and organization among the proletariat. While Bolsheviks and radical socialists urged a boycott of the WICs, the predominantly Menshevik Labour groups that were established secured a new platform. Moreover, the direct dependence of the war effort upon industrial output rendered workers' resort to the strike weapon even more devastating than in peacetime, and from the summer of 1915 there was a resurgence of industrial stoppages.

Equally, mobilization drew millions of peasants into closer contact with national affairs and, especially in the urban garrisons behind the lines, created a concentrated pool of peasant discontent far more threatening than that of scattered villagers.

In early 1917 the number of strikes in the capital rose and there was a series of demonstrations, notably on 9 January, the anniversary of Bloody Sunday, and 14 February, the day the Duma reconvened. News of impending bread rationing created panic buying and on Thursday 23 February, International Women's Day, female textile workers went on strike and demonstrated, closely followed by metal workers concentrated in the most militant and solidly proletarian quarter of Petrograd, the Vyborg district. In the following days the strike rapidly spread across the city and workers were joined by white-collar employees, teachers and students in mass demonstrations which converged on the city centre. Calls for the creation of a workers' soviet, including a summons by the Bolshevik Vyborg District Committee to form it at the Finland Station in the Vyborg district, became widespread. On Monday 27th many insurgents converged on the Tauride Palace, seat of the Duma, and that evening a group of predominantly Menshevik intelligentsia established a Provisional Executive Committee (EC) of the soviet in the palace and summoned factories and barracks to elect deputies to it.

The authorities failed to regain control of the situation. On Sunday 26th on instructions from the Tsar, troops opened fire on demonstrators and the Duma was prorogued. The following day General Ivanov was instructed to assemble loyal forces near the capital to restore order. On Monday and Tuesday, however, the government's forces in the capital disintegrated as soldiers in the garrison ignored orders and streamed from the barracks to fraternize with civilian demonstrators. By the Wednesday the revolution had spread to Moscow, Kronstadt and the Baltic Fleet and the High Command ordered a halt to Ivanov's expedition. On Thursday 2 March the military leaders recommended to Nicholas that he abdicate. He did so not only for himself but also for his son, in favour of his brother Mikhail, and when Mikhail declined the throne the monarchy disappeared.

On the same day that the Petrograd Soviet was set up, the Duma leaders, while accepting the prorogation ordered by the Tsar, held a private meeting and created a Provisional Committee. The Committee decided to form a government and by Wednesday 1 March Miliukov, who had emerged as the dominant figure, was drawing up a list of potential cabinet ministers. Radical socialists urged that the Soviet was in a position to establish a revolutionary government in defiance of the Duma Committee. Workers had rallied enthusiastically to the Soviet, and soldiers in the capital also seemed to have more faith in it than in the Duma leaders. This was borne out on the Wednesday when insurgent soldiers pressed the Soviet to issue an order – Order No. 1 –

which severely circumscribed the authority of officers both by sanctioning the election of soldiers' committees with control over weapons and by laying down that officers' orders were to be subject to the Soviet's approval. Yet the majority of the Soviet EC favoured a government drawn from the Duma. On Thursday 2 March they reached agreement with the Duma leaders and the Soviet plenum voted overwhelmingly to offer conditional support to Miliukov and his colleagues. The following day the formation of a Provisional Government was proclaimed, headed by Prince G. E. Lvov, chairman of the Union of Zemstvos, with Miliukov as Foreign Minister, Guchkov as War Minister and Kerensky, the only socialist member, Minister of Justice.

February to October

The Provisional Government committed itself to a wide range of reforms. All the classical liberal demands were rapidly satisfied by decree: a political amnesty and full freedom of the press, speech, association and religion; an end to all discrimination based on class, nationality or religion; the abolition of the death penalty and the creation of a fully independent judiciary. Church and State were to be separated, local government democratized, and a Constituent Assembly elected by universal, direct, equal and secret franchise was to be summoned to settle the future form of the country's constitution and to resolve major social problems such as that of the land.

The early weeks of the new era saw far-reaching institutional change throughout the country. The tsarist police force disintegrated and was replaced by local militias. New commissars replaced the provincial governors. Zemstvos and city dumas co-opted new members in preparation for democratic elections and meanwhile had to contend with 'Committees of Public Organizations' which sprang up in most localities. Within the army, a hierarchy of committees was elected to represent the soldiers. Peasant representatives were incorporated into committees established to organize food supplies and make preparations for land reform. New bodies emerged to represent and press the claims of the more assertive national minorities. Workers established their own militia, factory committees and trade unions, and a complex network of regional, city and suburban soviets was elected to represent workers and in some areas soldiers and peasants. In March an All-Russian Conference of Soviets met in Petrograd and created a Soviet Central Executive Committee.

At the centre the authority of the new government was limited by the rival authority of the Petrograd Soviet, a situation dubbed 'dual power'. The issue which initially caused greatest friction between the two was that of the war. On 14 March the Soviet issued an appeal to the world for a democratic peace based on renunciation by all sides of annexations and indemnities. The Foreign Minister Miliukov, however, was determined to pursue war to victory. Demonstrations against his policy, which took place from 18–21 April, precipitated a cabinet crisis. Miliukov and the War Minister, Guchkov, resigned and the whole cabinet threatened to follow suit unless the socialist leaders of the Soviet agreed to form a coalition. A majority of the EC, in which the Georgian Menshevik I. G. Tsereteli had emerged as a leading figure, had by this time adopted 'revolutionary defencism', accepting that until peace had been secured they must uphold the front. Reluctantly, and after much soul-searching, they decided to respond to Lvov's invitation. On 5 May six socialists led by Tsereteli formed a coalition with Lvov and his liberal colleagues. The SR leader Chernov became Minister of Agriculture and the Menshevik M. I. Skobelev became Minister of Labour.

The First Coalition pursued two lines in the search for peace. Working through the Soviet, the Mensheviks and SRs tried to organize an international socialist conference in Stockholm, designed to rally anti-war feeling in all countries. M. A. Tereshchenko, the non-party liberal who succeeded Miliukov as Foreign Minister, proposed to the Allies that they revise their war aims to bring them closer to the peace proposals enunciated by the Soviet. While both approaches were being pursued with little success, the government made preparations for a new offensive against Germany and Austria-Hungary. The new War Minister, Kerensky, made a series of highly-publicized tours of the front to raise the men's fighting spirit. The offensive was launched on 18 June but was deeply unpopular with much of the rank and file and collapsed in the first week of July.

Meanwhile, the government was confronted by an array of problems. The incipient trade breakdown which had helped to spark the Petrograd insurrection accelerated after February. This exacerbated the growing shortage of food, fuel and raw materials. Industrial output was cut, prices soared, and urban conditions deteriorated. Conflict between employers and workers intensified, and the number of strikes rose. In addition, peasant unrest in areas where there was significant private landholding had reached serious proportions by May. Moreover, there was an upsurge in nationalist agitation: demands for varying degrees of autonomy were made by minorities from the Baltic to the Caucasus.

To make matters worse, the government was faced by increasingly strident opposition from the Bolsheviks. On 3 April Lenin returned from exile, travelling from Switzerland on a sealed train provided by the German Foreign Ministry, and denounced 'revolutionary defencism' as tantamount to supporting a 'predatory imperialist war'. In his 'April Theses' he called for a revolutionary government based on the Soviets and empowered to control the banks, production and distribution. He demanded the confiscation of all private estates, the nationalization of the land, and its management by local peasant soviets. At the Party Conference held at the end of April the Bolsheviks officially repudiated even the most heavily qualified support for the Provisional Government and adopted Lenin's programme which was disseminated in crisp, clear, and hard-hitting language. Until the late summer the Bolsheviks were outnumbered by moderate socialists in most popular forums. Menshevik and SR sympathizers dominated the soldiers' committees; among the peasantry the SRs enjoyed far more support than any other party; the Mensheviks were most prominent in the trade unions; together the two parties won large majorities in municipal duma elections which began in May; and in June they dominated the First All-Russian Congress of Soviets and consolidated control of its Central Executive Committee (CEC). Yet the size of the Bolshevik party increased, it gained widespread support in the factory committees, and developed a network of military organizations in the army and navy. On 18 June the CEC was taken aback when a demonstration in the capital which it had itself summoned featured Bolshevik anti-government slogans.

At the beginning of July, this array of social and political problems induced a renewed cabinet crisis. The Kadet ministers considered their socialist colleagues were pre-empting the decisions of the Constituent Assembly by making partial concessions to Ukrainian demands for autonomy and to peasant demands for the redistribution of private land. On 2 July the Kadets resigned. On 3 and 4 July mass demonstrations in which workers, garrison soldiers, and sailors from the Kronstadt naval base were prominent, converged on the Tauride Palace. Demonstrators urged the socialist leaders of the EC to break with their liberal allies and form a purely socialist, Soviet-based government. The EC refused and with the help of loyal troops restored order. The Bolsheviks were blamed for the 'July uprising', and Lenin was publicly denounced as a German agent. Leading Bolsheviks, including Trotsky who now joined the party, were arrested, their press was attacked, and Lenin was driven into hiding in Finland.

After prolonged negotiations, a Second Coalition government headed by Kerensky was formed on 25 July. Kerensky sought to consolidate the position of the government by holding a State Conference in Moscow (12–15 August). The Conference was met by a protest strike in Moscow and the Bolsheviks boycotted the proceedings. The middle-class organizations and parties who dominated the Conference gave a rousing reception to General Kornilov, the new Supreme Commander. Kornilov urged the government to take decisive measures to restore discipline in the army and quell disorder at home. The upshot was the 'Kornilov affair'. At the end of August Kerensky abruptly denounced Kornilov for plotting to overthrow the government. He gained a free hand from his ministerial colleagues to reconstruct the cabinet and called upon the Soviet to help defend the

capital against 'counter-revolution'. Bolsheviks and moderate socialists alike joined garrison troops, sailors from Kronstadt and workers'
militia ('Red Guard') detachments in heading off the force despatched
by Kornilov. Railway workers halted the troop trains, rank-and-file
soldiers abandoned the expedition and Kornilov was arrested.

Kerensky's prestige was badly tarnished, the government was left in
disarray, and the call for 'All Power to the Soviets' became more
popular. The moderate socialists remained opposed to the formation
of a Soviet-based government, but rejected co-operation with the
Kadets whom they considered implicated in the Kornilov affair. After
a Democratic Conference summoned to resolve the membership of the
new government had failed, Kerensky was allowed to form a Third
Coalition which took office on 27 September. The Kadets were again
included. The moderate socialists who took office alongside them were
lesser-known figures and included neither Tsereteli nor Chernov. The
new government was to be responsible to a Provisional Council of the
Russian Republic, or 'Pre-Parliament', drawn from democratic elements which convened on 7 October and was still in session when the
Provisional Government was overthrown.

The Kornilov affair boosted the fortunes of the Bolsheviks. Trotsky
and other party members arrested after the July Days were released.
The Petrograd Soviet endorsed the call by their spokesman, L. B.
Kamenev, for an exclusively socialist government. By the end of
September the Bolsheviks had gained majority support in both the
Moscow and Petrograd soviets, where Trotsky had become chairman.
The moderate socialists still controlled the CEC elected by the first
All-Russian Congress of Soviets in June, but acceded to demands that
they summon a Second Congress which, following a series of regional
soviet congresses, eventually met on 25 October.

On 14 September Lenin, still in hiding, began to urge his colleagues
on the Bolshevik Central Committee to organize an immediate seizure
of power. The Central Committee was at first unsympathetic but on 10
October, at a meeting which Lenin attended, it was resolved to make
armed insurrection the order of the day. The decision was confirmed
on 16 October at an expanded meeting which included representatives
from the Petrograd city committee and other regional bodies. The
decision was vigorously opposed by some sections of the party,
including two of Lenin's leading lieutenants, Kamenev and G. E.
Zinoviev. Meanwhile the Petrograd Soviet had voted to establish a
Military Revolutionary Committee (MRC) to co-ordinate measures
both against any German assault on the capital and against any attack
on the Left by the Provisional Government. The MRC contained
radical SR members but was dominated by Bolsheviks and it was
through it that the October uprising was planned. On 21–22 October
the MRC asserted its own control over the garrison. On 24 October its
forces rebuffed efforts by the government to close Bolshevik news-

papers and seal bridges linking working-class districts to the city centre. That night Lenin travelled incognito to Soviet and party headquarters and in the early hours of 25 October strategic points in the city were seized. Kerensky left the capital and tried with little success to raise loyal troops. At 10 a.m. Lenin drafted a proclamation announcing the fall of the Provisional Government, and that evening, shortly after the Second All-Russian Congress of Soviets had assembled, the Winter Palace was taken and the cabinet arrested.

The minority of moderate socialists at the Congress denounced the seizure of power and walked out. The majority, made up predominantly of Bolsheviks with a substantial bloc of radical SRs, approved the formation of a Bolshevik government, the Council of People's Commissars. Cadets from military schools and a force of 1000 cossacks from outside the capital tried without success to overthrow the new government. Moderate leaders of the railway and postal workers attempted to force the formation of an all-socialist coalition, a 'homogeneous socialist government'. Several Bolshevik commissars favoured such a compromise, but Lenin and Trotsky were adamantly opposed and negotiations broke down. In November the Left SRs, now formally established as a separate party, entered negotiations for the formation of what proved a short-lived coalition with the Bolsheviks.

The first steps of the new government included decrees on land, peace, the rights of national minorities and workers' control in industry. The peasants were authorized to parcel out the private estates while legal ownership of all land was vested in the State; factory committees were given broad powers to vet the actions of management; the minorities were granted the right of self-determination; each regiment was authorized to negotiate armistice terms. A general armistice was signed on 4 December and by the treaty of Brest-Litovsk the war was brought to an end. Urban soviets in many parts of Russia quickly declared their allegiance to the new government. Opponents were harrassed, an All-Russian Extraordinary Commission for Combating Counter-Revolution and Sabotage (Cheka) was created, and Kadet and non-socialist newspapers banned. Elections to the Constituent Assembly, which the Provisional Government had eventually scheduled for November, went ahead. But when the Assembly met for its first session on 5 January 1918 it immediately became clear that a majority of the deputies were hostile to the government and the Assembly was forcibly disbanded. The economic situation worsened dramatically in the months that followed October as soldiers flocked home and military orders to industry abruptly halted. Industry was nationalized and steps were taken to tighten discipline in the factories and extract food from the countryside. During 1918 the Right, the Mensheviks, the SRs, various minority national groups, and foreign powers sought to reverse different aspects of the revolution and in June 1918 large-scale civil war broke out.

2 THE THREE TRADITIONS AND REVISIONISM

The Soviet view

For Soviet historians, the October revolution is the greatest event in history. It ushered in a new era in the history of mankind, inaugurating the construction of socialism in an area covering one sixth of the globe. It dealt a stunning blow to an international order based on the exploitation of man by man and provided a powerful base of support for progressive movements across the world. It represented the prototype of the transformation for which the whole of the capitalist world is destined.

Soviet historiography is rooted in an amalgam of the ideas of Marx and Lenin. To understand the Soviet interpretation of the revolution it is essential to grasp the cardinal tenets of Marxism–Leninism. First, history is a coherent story of progress. Its central theme is the development of man's productive power. The forces of production – the combination of human labour, tools and raw materials with which men produce – condition the social structure: over time the distribution of power and wealth in society is that most conducive to the development of the productive forces. As the forces of production change and develop, as men acquire new skills, fashion new implements, discover new raw materials, a point is reached at which the existing structure of society becomes an obstacle to further development. One social formation gives way to another. Second, central to each social formation (except the final one) is a division between those who control productive power and those who do not, between exploiters and exploited – a division, in other words, between antagonistic classes. As the productive forces develop so the struggle between classes intensifies. And it is the climax of this struggle which precipitates social revolution and the transition from one social formation to another. Third, the supreme expression and direct reflection of class struggle is political struggle. The power of the State represents the interests of the ruling class in any given era. The interests of the other classes find more or less coherent expression in movements of opposition and protest. When the productive forces outgrow a social formation, the ruling class is confronted by a revolutionary challenge from the class destined to succeed it. Having seized political power, the new ruling class presides over the transformation of the social structure. After passing from the most primitive stage of development, through the Asiatic, ancient and feudal stages, mankind enters the capitalist stage, the immense productive power of large-scale factory industry, and the division between the bourgeoisie and the proletariat. The final revolution, the socialist revolution, sees the proletariat overthrow the bourgeoisie, abolish private property, and construct a socialist society based on public ownership, a planned economy and the satisfaction of the needs of all.

To these fundamental propositions of Marx, Lenin added three more. First, capitalism in the advanced countries had, by the end of the nineteenth century, reached its highest and last stage – imperialism. The contradictions between bourgeois society based on private ownership coupled with the market economy, on the one hand, and the enormous productive power of large-scale factory industry, on the other, reached explosive proportions. The class struggle between bourgeoisie and proletariat became ever more intense; mounting economic crises followed in rapid succession and spilled over into the catastrophe of world war. The necessary economic and social conditions had been created for the overthrow of capitalism and the construction of socialism.[1] Second, Lenin showed that revolution was likely to break out initially not where imperialism was most strongly developed but 'at the weakest link in the imperialist chain': Russia. In Russia imperialism had developed alongside a semi-feudal agrarian structure and the bourgeoisie had proven too feeble to overthrow the absolute monarchy. The first revolution on the agenda, therefore, was the bourgeois-democratic overthrow of tsarism and abolition of feudal remnants. But by taking the lead in the bourgeois-democratic revolution, the proletariat, in alliance with the poor peasantry, could push straight forward to the socialist revolution.[2] Third, the success of the revolution depended on the presence not only of the appropriate 'objective' social and economic conditions, but of the necessary 'subjective' conditions: the organization of the proletariat into a class-conscious revolutionary movement. The critical role here belonged to the Social Democratic party. The formation of 'a party of a new type', democratic but disciplined and centralized, composed of the vanguard of the workers' movement, and united by conscious commitment to revolutionary Marxism, was indispensable. Without the leadership of such a party, the proletariat would be subordinate to bourgeois ideology, accept the premises of capitalism, and go no further than trade-unionism. Only a party guided by Marx's scientific understanding of the historical process and the objective interests of the proletariat could instil socialist consciousness into the working class,

[1] Lenin's major work on imperialism was *Imperialism, the Highest Stage of Capitalism* written in 1916, V. I. Lenin, *Polnoe sobranie sochinenii* (55 vols, Moscow, 1958–65) XXVII, pp. 299–426.

[2] See in particular Lenin's 'Letters from Afar' and 'April Theses' of 1917, *op. cit.*, XXXI, pp. 9–59, 113–18.

organize the revolutionary movement, and provide it with unerring tactical and strategic leadership.[3]

For Soviet historians, the Russian revolution was the supreme vindication of the general laws of history discovered by Marx and creatively developed by Lenin. The revolution was in the fullest sense 'law-governed'. By the late nineteenth century, Russia had indeed entered the imperialist stage. The insoluble contradictions and brutal exploitation of advanced capitalism, further aggravated by the semi-feudal exploitation of the peasantry, generated repeated revolutionary crises – in 1905–7, in 1914, and in 1917. The proletariat established its 'hegemony' over the mass movement which overthrew tsarism. The attempts of the Provisional Government to consolidate the rule of the bourgeoisie duly failed. During 1917 the proletariat detached the mass of the petty bourgeoisie from their earlier allegiance to the Mensheviks, SRs, and bourgeois nationalist movements of the minority nationalities, and in October, in alliance with the poorest peasantry, carried through the epoch-making socialist revolution. And throughout, the leading role was played by the Bolsheviks. From its inception Lenin's party worked tirelessly to forge the 'spontaneous' protest of the proletariat into 'conscious' revolutionary action. It took the initiative in each revolutionary situation. It provided the leadership in February, it succeeded in opening the eyes of the more backward sections of the proletariat and the working masses to the reactionary nature of the petty-bourgeois and liberal parties, it welded the proletariat into an invincible revolutionary force and, drawing the poor peasants into alliance with them, it led the October revolution.

The Marxist–Leninist interpretation of 1917, moreover, seems to Soviet historians to have been borne out by the whole sweep of the history of the USSR. The establishment of Soviet democracy placed state power in the hands of the working masses, led by the Bolshevik (in 1918 renamed Communist) party. And despite massive obstacles – the destruction caused by the First World War, the ravages of a civil war brought on by the support that foreign capitalists lent the savage counter-revolutionary efforts of Russia's defeated classes, international isolation in the inter-war period, the appalling destruction wrought by Hitler's rapacious invasion, the sustained hostility of the capitalist West – a socialist society was built. Under the leadership of the party the working masses constructed the material base for socialism, replaced primitive private farming with collectivized agriculture, and carried through an industrialization programme which astonished and alarmed the bourgeois world. Unemployment was abolished, class struggle overcome, and the living standards and cultural level of even the most backward of the country's peoples

[3] Lenin's classic statement on the role of the party, *What Is To Be Done?*, was published in 1902, *op. cit.* vi, pp. 1–183.

transformed out of all recognition. The USSR provided inspiration and support for the liberation of the masses of eastern Europe, for the overthrow of imperialist exploitation in Asia and Africa, and for progressive forces throughout the world. Russia in 1917 had indeed been ripe for socialist revolution; Lenin had applied the science of society with brilliant precision; and under the guidance of Marxism –Leninism the party had provided unfailing leadership of the working masses from that day to this.

From the Soviet viewpoint, the propagation of the authentic, Marxist–Leninist interpretation of the revolution was integral to the construction of socialism. History constituted a vital part of the class struggle. A proper understanding of the revolution would play a central role in developing the socialist consciousness of the working masses, in inspiring the people with confidence and pride in the construction of socialism under the leadership of the party. Champions of the vanquished classes, at home and abroad, would inevitably seek to distort the truth. It was the duty of the party to guard against bourgeois distortions, and the duty of loyal Soviet historians to deepen, to enrich, to expound the Marxist–Leninist understanding of October. As early as 1920, therefore, a special commission on the history of the party and the October revolution was set up and empowered to gather all relevant documentary material – from party archives to the records of the tsarist secret police and the memoirs of participants in the great events. Access to the archives was jealously guarded, and censorship of counter-revolutionary distortions was instituted. During the 1920s the party line was far from monolithic. The memoirs and documentary editions published reflected a relatively wide range of Marxist approaches. Rival views of the revolution became an important part of the struggle over power and policy between the 'Left Opposition' identified with Trotsky, the 'Right Opposition' identified with Bukharin, and the ultimately victorious line identified with Stalin. The record of October cast light both on the validity of the rival policies advanced by each faction, and on the credentials of the leading figures as true revolutionaries and allies of Lenin. With Stalin's victory, however, centralized control over histori-cal interpretation became progressively tighter. Dissentient voices, castigated as 'hopeless bureaucrats' and 'archival rats', were silenced.[4] The simplistic and rigid line of interpretation laid down from above culminated in the publication in 1938 of the authorized *History of the Communist Party of the Soviet Union (Bolsheviks), Short Course.*[5] The

[4] For further discussion see J. Barber, *Soviet Historians in Crisis, 1928–1932* (London, 1981), and G. M. Enteen, *The Soviet Scholar-Bureaucrat. M. N. Pokrovskii and the Society of Marxist Historians* (Pennsylvania, 1978).
[5] *History of the Communist Party of the Soviet Union (Bolsheviks), Short Course* (Toronto, 1939).

Mensheviks and SRs were portrayed not only as counter-revolutionaries but as vicious saboteurs, the treachery of Stalin's various rivals was traced to their earliest participation in the party, and Stalin's role in and before the revolution was inflated out of all recognition. It was unthinkable to cast doubt on the authorized version; major facets of the revolution became too dangerous for scholars to touch; the flow of documentary publications dried up.

The Stalinist phase did all but irreparable damage to the international reputation of Soviet historiography. So simplistic an approach, and a body of 'scholars' that tolerated such flagrant abuse of documentary evidence forfeited all credibility. With Stalin's death in 1953, however, historiography shared in the general 'thaw'. As the regime reduced reliance on overt coercion and sought to win greater support, and as international tension began to ease, the scope for genuine research widened. The *Short Course* was withdrawn. In his famous denunciation of Stalin's 'personality cult' in 1956, Khrushchev positively invited substantial revision of the Stalinist version of October. Access to archives became easier, and a flood of new documentary collections began to appear. Between 1957 and 1967 eight times as many such collections appeared as in the previous decade, and thereafter the flow continued, if at a slower rate. Moreover, these collections became increasingly scholarly. 'Thematic' collections tended to be replaced by the publication of coherent archives from party, state and soviet institutions, and there was more open and critical discussion of editorial methods. The fifth edition of Lenin's collected works (1958 –65) contained three times as many items as the fullest version published in the Stalin era. Memoirs from the twenties, for long consigned to oblivion, began to be used again. The number of historians in higher education increased rapidly, from some 17,000 in 1962 to 27,000 a decade later, and their professional training and competence rose markedly. Historical conferences became regular and much more lively. Contact with western scholars increased, as did knowledge of the work being done in the West. True, bolder challenges to orthodoxy, especially when they touched upon the role played by the party, provoked fierce resistance. And many of the positive trends slowed during the late 1960s and 70s, in the Brezhnev period now damned as the period of 'stagnation'.[6] Constraints upon historians tightened, one symptom of this being a sharp decline in the number of scholars entering the profession and in the output of new books and articles on the revolution in the early 1980s. Yet by the time Gorbachev became General Secretary in 1985, the historical profession had advanced a long way from the crudities of Stalin's era.

---

[6] On Soviet historiography in the 1950s and 60s, see N. W. Heer, *Politics and History in the Soviet Union* (Cambridge, Mass., 1971). There is also a useful review in W. Z. Laqueur, *The Fate of the Revolution* (London, 1967).

Neither the post-Stalin 'thaw', nor as yet Gorbachev's *perestroika*, has led the historical establishment to depart from the basic propositions of the Marxist–Leninist interpretation. The historical legitimacy of the Great October Revolution, and the direct line of succession running from the victorious Bolsheviks to the Central Committee of today, remains fundamental to the way in which the Soviet establishment views itself and wishes to be viewed. Until the late 1980s, Soviet historians remained under close party supervision. Their career prospects, their contacts with foreign scholars, their publication outlets – all were controlled by a complex web of party bodies ultimately responsible to the Central Committee. The published documentation improved out of all recognition, but Lenin's 'complete works' remained manifestly incomplete and access to the more sensitive archives remained restricted, and obvious distortions, such as the underrating of the role of Trotsky, are only now being overcome.[7] The major collective syntheses were invariably supervised by the most senior figures in the profession and bear the imprint of authority. Historians lower down the hierarchy were expected to work within the guidelines advanced by their superiors. Monographs treating potentially contentious areas have tended to be published in very restricted editions, and until the most recent times an individual historian who strayed onto dangerous ground or advanced unwelcome ideas ran the risk of public reprimand and expulsion from the profession. Historians took Lenin's ideas as their point of departure and model. Lenin was quoted time and again in every article, in every monograph. His works were regarded as a primary source of overriding significance for the study not merely of his own activity but of any and every aspect of the history of the revolution.

Nevertheless, the relationship between politics and historiography was incomparably more complex than it had been in Stalin's day. On all but the most fundamental issues, the party line became much less forthright and clear-cut. For one thing, absurd as the respect paid Lenin may seem in the West, his works in fact constitute a much looser strait-jacket than did Stalin's *Short Course*: composed in the heat of political struggle and fierce polemics, Lenin's works are far from unambiguous and he can be quoted in support of conflicting interpretations of many secondary issues. For another, the torrent of documentation, however carefully edited, led to ever more nuances and qualifications. Evidence introduced to bolster orthodoxy in one field frequently carried unforeseen implications for conventional wisdom in another. Once published, documents are not easily suppressed. Above all, Soviet historiography became more sophisticated. The account

---

[7] For a discussion of the number of letters, telegrams and articles excluded from Lenin's collected works, see R. C. Elwood, 'How Complete Is Lenin's *Polnoe Sobranie Sochinenii*?', *Slavic Review* 38 (1979), pp. 97–105.

given had to satisfy an increasingly professional and self-confident body of scholars. It had to carry conviction with a better educated, more discriminating public. It had to provide a solid base for review articles and monographs devoted to the exposure of 'bourgeois falsifications' emanating from the West. Flagrant disregard for the evidence freely available in libraries at home and abroad was self-defeating.

As a result, the invitation to overcome the distortions introduced under the influence of Stalin's 'cult of personality' opened the way for re-examination of much of the revolutionary record. Since 1956, not only has Stalin's role been sharply revised downwards, but new studies have been undertaken on every aspect of the revolution.[8] There has been much more detailed study of the pre-revolutionary economy, of Russia's claim to have entered the imperialist phase of capitalism. Quantitative methods have been applied to social developments not only at the centre but in individual provinces, towns and villages. There has been more careful analysis of the relative weight of 'spontaneous' and 'conscious' party-organized protest, of the change of political consciousness among workers in different cities and individual factories, among soldiers in different sections of the front and rear, and among peasants in different regions of the country. The SRs and Mensheviks have received more detailed treatment, and come to be regarded less as cynical saboteurs and traitors than as misguided champions of the petty bourgeoisie. More careful attention has been paid to the Kadets and to political developments on the Right. The part played by the Bolshevik party has remained hallowed ground, but immense energy has been devoted to substantiating the claims made on its behalf, to tracing its growing influence across the country, and there has even been somewhat more critical discussion of divisions within it. Differences between one specialist and another have been openly aired. By the end of the 1970s it was possible to find a Soviet historian proclaim that 'It is precisely through controversy that the truth emerges.'[9] Successive new syntheses have been published both of the history of the party and of the revolution, and with each edition they have tended to become more detailed, more finely nuanced, more subtle. While Soviet historiography continues to celebrate the revolution as the supreme vindication of Marxism–Leninism, the case has been developed with sufficient scholarly skill to merit new attention.

---

[8]Translations from a number of major new Soviet publications may be found in the journal *Soviet Studies in History*.
[9]V. P. Naumov, *Sovetskaia istoriografiia fevral'skoi burzhuazno-demokraticheskoi revoliutsii* (Moscow, 1979), p. 172.

The liberal view

The traditional liberal interpretation has rejected outright every major tenet of the Soviet view. To liberal scholars, the Soviet version is a manifest distortion based not on scholarly analysis of historical evidence but on the political requirements of the post-October regime. They reject not only the Soviet claim that October and the overthrow of capitalism blazed the trail for which all humanity is destined, but the very notion of laws governing the historical process. Far from being the ineluctable outcome of intensifying class struggle in Russia, they see the revolution as fortuitous, arising from the coincidence of catastrophic war, abysmal monarchist leadership and liberal ineptitude in a country which had only recently begun to move towards liberal democracy. The Bolshevik claim to represent the true interests of the masses they regard as an arrogant illusion born of a fundamentally false doctrine. And rather than viewing the party's triumph in October as an expression of the will of the Russian masses, they see it as the product of manipulation of an unstable situation by an élite group of fanatical revolutionaries.

The traditional liberal interpretation is rooted in an approach to history fundamentally at odds with that of Soviet historiography. In the liberal view, the historical process is altogether too rich and complex to be reduced to class struggle. Few would deny the existence of class differences. There is bound to be a certain tension between employer and employee over wages and conditions. There is likely to be tension between landlord and tenant, between large landowners and impecunious peasants. At moments of economic dislocation, these tensions may well become acute. But they are by no means the prime determinant of history. They exist within the context of a complex social reality which belies the simplicities of the Soviet view. For one thing, the 'classes' so beloved of the Marxist analysis are neither homogeneous nor tidily defined. Individuals within each may well diverge from the norm. The differences between educated, skilled and highly-paid workers on the one hand and unskilled, illiterate or unemployed workers on the other may well outweigh what they have in common. Progressively-minded professionals may well have values and priorities entirely different from those of their fellow 'bourgeois' industrialists. Peasants in grain-short areas may well be at loggerheads with those in grain-surplus areas. The concerns of the landless rural labourer and the urban proletarian may be fundamentally at odds. Moreover, even if the existence of distinct social classes is conceded, their 'objective interests', by which Soviet historians set so much store, are far from self-evident. The interest of workers may well be higher wages – but not so high that their employer is driven from business. In theory they may stand to benefit from the nationalization of property;

in practice state ownership may provide less liberty and less efficiency than private ownership. By the same token, there is no discernible law according to which class differences are bound to intensify with time. The century since Marx's death has belied his expectation that advanced industrial society would witness ever sharper polarization between bourgeoisie and proletariat.

In any case, in the liberal view, the significance of class struggle must be weighed against other divisions which cut across this struggle and limit its importance. Primary amongst these are national divisions. In a multinational empire such as that of the tsars, the divisions between Great Russians, Ukrainians, White Russians, Poles, Georgians, Armenians, Jews and the hundred other national minorities may at different times be of infinitely more significance than the divisions between classes. Equally, the interests common to the different classes of a given nation or state may override what divides them. This is most graphically illustrated by their co-operation in time of war, and despite Marxist faith in the common interests of the proletariat of all nations, time and again national loyalties have proved stronger than those of class. Again, no society evolves in a vacuum: the supposed logic of class struggle is repeatedly vitiated by intervention from outside – be it by war or by foreign support for one group or another. Moreover, since there is no irreducible kernel of class interest which in the last analysis guides all else, the ideas, the culture, the religion of a given society may well play a critical role in explaining social and political development. The force of traditional deference, of apathy, of ignorance and habit may well override strictly economic interests and make nonsense of any interpretation based solely upon class interest. Finally, and by no means least important, even where class division is intense, and popular discontent acute, the forces of order, of the State may well contain and suppress revolt until conditions have changed and conflict eased. Their success or failure in doing so may depend on factors bearing a minimal relationship to class struggle.

Liberal emphasis on the complexity and indeterminacy of history entails an approach to the political process again at variance with that of Soviet historiography. In the liberal view, the notion of class interest offers no satisfactory explanation for the policies either of the State or of opposition parties. Political organization represents a more or less autonomous factor in the historical process. Rather than seeing political struggle as ultimately reflecting class struggle, the liberal tradition credits the leading actors in the historical drama with an independence and causative importance of their own. Indeed, there is a strong tendency to attribute primary causal importance to the actions of political leaders. It is those at the summit who make the decisive moves in history. To quote Bernard Pares, a founding father of the study of the revolution in Britain, writing in 1939, 'The cause of the [tsarist] ruin came not at all from below, but from above.'[10] The same approach can be found in successive studies published between the 1950s and 80s by Leonard Schapiro, for long the doyen of Russian studies at the London School of Economics and one of the most influential western historians of the revolution. His aim, Schapiro explained, was 'to look at the principal characters concerned as human beings, and not as exponents of this or that theory, or as representatives of this or that class interest. I have tried, without, I hope, ignoring economic and social factors, not to let them obliterate what is after all the key to any historical situation – the men who thought or acted in this way or that.'[11] It is the decisions, the policies, the judgement, motives, principles and ambitions, the skill and lack of it of the leading political actors which are decisive. They are not to be reduced to mere puppets responding to influence from below. They are, no doubt, conditioned by the environment in which they live, they act in a given time and place. But their actions can only be explained by the infinitely complex interaction between general causes – economic, social, cultural and ideological – and their individual personalities, moulded by a particular experience of childhood and maturity.

The corollary of this emphasis on the crucial importance and autonomy of the political leadership is the liberal tendency to see the role of the masses as essentially subordinate. In a backward, largely illiterate society such as late Imperial Russia, the subordinate role attributed to the lower classes is particularly marked. They oscillate between passivity and elemental violence. This approach by no means necessarily reflects lack of sympathy for the lot of the least privileged in society. But their actions tend to be anarchic and destructive, the product of intense resentment and wild, irrational hope. Ignorant, politically immature, with no grasp of the real issues at stake, they are guided not by rational goals of their own but by the vagaries of rumour, the skill of rival political leaders, rabble-rousing, propaganda and demagogy. In the liberal view, harsh material conditions may have predisposed the Russian masses to revolt, but the occasion and the direction of their intervention depended upon the actions of the leading figures on the political stage. In 1917 they were 'caught up in great events over which they had no control.'[12] The Bolshevik victory is to be explained in terms of the most skilful exploitation of chaos.

From a liberal perspective, the subsequent history of the regime established in October bore out the ruthless, doctrinaire and fundamentally undemocratic nature of the Bolshevik party. On coming to

[10] B. Pares, *The Fall of the Russian Empire* (London, 1939), pp. 24–5.
[11] L. Schapiro, *The Origin of the Communist Autocracy* (London, 1977, 2nd edn), p. vii; *1917. The Russian Revolutions and the Origins of Present-Day Communism* (Hounslow, 1984), pp. ix–x.
[12] J. L. H. Keep, *The Russian Revolution. A Study in Mass Mobilization* (London, 1976), p. viii.

power, Lenin and his colleagues promptly deserted the Allied cause in the First World War and repudiated the massive loans which western investors had made in good faith to the tsarist government. Worse still, they openly proclaimed their support for violent and seditious movements designed to overturn the political, social and diplomatic bases on which world order rested. To these offences were soon added the brutal measures which the Bolsheviks took to cling to power, the barbarous excesses of the 'Red Terror' during the Civil War (1918–20), the suppression of all rival parties, the curtailment of liberties as basic as freedom of speech and conscience. Stalin's collectivization and industrialization drive launched at the end of the 1920s was accompanied by untold horrors: acute deprivation of workers and peasants alike, epitomized by a catastrophic famine in 1933 to which the government turned a blind eye; repression and imprisonment on a truly mass scale; and the blood-letting of the Great Terror of 1936–38. With Moscow still actively seeking to destabilize the western democracies during the thirties, Soviet calls for collective security (1934–39) against Nazi expansionism were viewed with acute suspicion and the Nazi–Soviet pact of 1939 seemed to confirm the worst.

Soviet behaviour after Hitler's defeat (1945) did nothing to change liberal opinion. At home ex-prisoners of war swelled the population of the labour camps, while abroad the Soviet secret police and Red Army were used to impose Communist regimes on the bitterly hostile peoples of eastern Europe. Worse still, Moscow appeared willing to exploit to the full the unstable post-war conditions, probing western defences in Germany and the Middle East, blessing the Chinese revolution (1949), supporting the invasion of South Korea by the communist North (1950), and seeking through force, demagogy and sabotage to spread Communism across the undeveloped world. Even when, after Stalin's death in 1953, the regime edged towards détente, ran down the labour camps, and showed a new concern to reduce overt terror, the Soviet system remained anathema to liberal opinion. The premises of liberal political philosophy appeared fully vindicated. The abolition of private enterprise in Russia had proved a disaster. Centralized state control of the economy had proved grossly inefficient, fostered privilege and corruption, and given rise to a 'totalitarian' party dictatorship whose terrifying powers of coercion controlled even the innermost thoughts of its citizens. The whole Soviet record seemed to confirm the undemocratic origins of Bolshevik power in Russia: glasnost and perestroika suggest that the regime itself is on the point of admitting as much.

Much of the early work on the revolution carried out in the West was by émigré victims of the Bolshevik victory. February, October, the Civil War, and the consolidation of Bolshevik rule provoked a massive exodus to the West. The émigrés, ranging from monarchists to anarchists, were of course bitterly divided and carried on a fierce polemical battle over the responsibility for their common defeat. But a number of able scholars, most of them of liberal sympathies, were drawn into western academic life and played a leading role in guiding western research. The domination of the liberal view was reflected in the relatively narrow range of sources on which western scholars worked. Attention was focused overwhelmingly on the political and ideological antecedents of the revolution, on the ideas and activities of the government and the liberal, moderate socialist and Bolshevik parties, rather than on social and economic developments. Much use was made of the memoirs which began to pour forth in the 1920s from figures at court and in the army, from foreign diplomats and correspondents, and from political leaders across the political spectrum. And it was those of liberal and moderate socialist leaders, men like Miliukov and Kerensky, which exerted greatest influence. In part, of course, the problem was simply that the Soviet archives were inaccessible to western scholars, while during the Stalin era the documents and memoirs published in the Soviet Union were sparse and manifestly tendentious. But even the much richer Soviet collections issued in the twenties were given scant attention in the West. A number of documentary collections, some of them drawing on Soviet publications, were compiled by western scholars, but they tended to bear the strong imprint of liberal editorship and to concentrate on political rather than socio-economic material.[13] Moreover, even when access to primary materials began to improve from the late 1950s and early 60s, the major contours of the liberal approach remained unchanged. Although the western consensus based on the traditional liberal interpretation has now broken down, many of the most distinguished scholars in the field remain firmly committed to it and it continues to inform conventional wisdom among non-specialists in the West.

The libertarian view

A third view of the revolution has been developed by writers on the far Left of the political spectrum. For them, the Bolshevik triumph marked not the fulfilment but the failure of the revolutionary promise of 1917. The mass movement which had swept away tsarism and the Provisional Government was mastered, curbed and ultimately crushed by Lenin and his party. Bolshevism proved, ultimately, counter-revolutionary.

In the immediate aftermath of the revolution this point of view was most clearly articulated by Russian anarchist writers. Before October

[13] See for example J. Bunyan and H. H. Fisher, *The Bolshevik Revolution, 1917–1918, Documents and Materials* (Stanford, Cal., 1934), and R. P. Browder and A. F. Kerensky, *The Russian Provisional Government 1917* (3 vols, Stanford, Cal., 1961).

the anarchists had stood closest to the Bolsheviks, and had been every bit as radical in their determination to overthrow the Provisional Government. But after October they rapidly became disillusioned with their erstwhile allies. Whereas the revolutionary upheaval of 1917 had seemed to them to foreshadow an entirely novel social order in which power would remain firmly in the hands of the masses themselves, the Bolsheviks proceeded to restore hierarchical and coercive control in every field. Behind a veil of revolutionary rhetoric, the Council of People's Commissars suppressed the masses' striving for liberty. Instead of relying upon the workers' militia and the election of officers, Trotsky and his acolytes created a Red Army modelled on thoroughly traditional lines. In place of the major role which workers were demanding in running the factories, Lenin presided over the centralization of economic power and the establishment of managerial structures divorced from the rank and file. Instead of fostering the peasants' bid for liberty, the commissars emasculated local peasants organizations and, by forcibly requisitioning grain, did all they could to subject the peasantry to the dictates of the State. It was not only the press and organizations of the Right and of moderate socialist parties which were repressed: the anarchists, too, were ruthlessly hounded by the Cheka.

Proof of the growing estrangement between the masses and their new rulers was not long delayed. It was the manifest failure of the Bolsheviks to retain the confidence of the masses, their resort to brutal coercion, which enabled the openly reactionary Whites to come so close to overthrowing them. The appearance of large-scale peasant resistance in Tambov, and even more the sustained independent peasant movement led by the Ukrainian peasant Nestor Makhno during the Civil War, pointed to an irreconcilable clash of principle. And in the cities, the strikes and demonstrations of the winter of 1920–21 reached a crescendo with the Kronstadt uprising which openly demanded from Lenin and his party a return to the free soviets of 1917. The regime reacted violently and furiously. Kronstadt was savagely suppressed; the mass movement which had swept all before it until October was finally subdued; and the way was cleared for the brutal state coercion associated with the name of Stalin.

At first, studies of the revolution written in this spirit were impressionistic rather than scholarly and the voice of criticism from the Left was barely audible. Bolshevism appeared to dominate that pole of the political spectrum; success had rendered Marxism–Leninnism almost synonymous with revolutionary ideology and made Lenin and Trotsky household names. The defeat of the Mensheviks and the decomposition of the Second International deflated the confidence of moderate Marxists. Their strictures on the 'maximalism' of the Bolsheviks, on the 'premature' nature of the October revolution, and on the backwardness of Russia gave them a broad area of common ground with the liberal view. At the same time, the eclipse of the SRs, with their primary emphasis on the peasantry, appeared complete when within two decades of the revolution the Soviet Union was launched upon a massive industrialization programme. Moreover, radicals with reservations about the socialist credentials of the USSR confronted the dilemma that every word of criticism aligned them with the 'reactionary' views dominant in the West: to attack Moscow, the acknowledged centre of international revolution, was tantamount to sympathy for her capitalist enemies. There were of course bitter disputes among the Bolsheviks themselves over the direction of Soviet policy after the immediate threat to their power receded, with furious denunciation from those who fell foul of the regime – most notably from Trotsky. But they left largely unchallenged the Bolshevik view of October 1917 itself as the greatest achievement of the world revolutionary movement. The horrors associated with collectivization and early industrialization, it is true, increased left-wing qualms about the revolutionary credentials of the USSR. But the spectre of international Fascism, the Nazi invasion, and the herculean efforts of the Red Army in driving Hitler's forces back to Berlin helped to sustain the USSR's image as the standard bearer of the forces of the Left.

After 1945, however, that image rapidly became tarnished. The xenophobia and repression associated with Stalin's last years and the culmination of the personality cult belied the Soviet Union's internationalist pretensions. Even those who saw the extension of Moscow's control over her eastern European neighbours as primarily a response to American expansion objected to the oppressive form of Soviet rule. The successive rebellions against Soviet-backed regimes – in East Germany in 1953, in Poland and Hungary in 1956, in Czechoslovakia in 1968 and in Poland in the early 1980s – progressively undermined the allegiance of foreign radicals to the USSR. This bristling empire built on the bones of peasants and political prisoners and denying the most fundamental rights to the workers themselves seemed more and more a mere mirror image of the capitalist system rejected by western radicals. Moreover, the emergence of countries pursuing rival paths to socialism – the relatively decentralized economy of Yugoslavia, the peasant-based movement in China, and the variety of socialist experiments in many of the newly-independent countries of Africa and Asia from the late 1950s and early 60s – stirred new criticism of Moscow's claim to be the infallible source of the socialist creed. From within eastern Europe a number of significant critiques of the bureaucratic and oppressive nature of Soviet-style 'socialism' began to appear. At the same time, developments in the West encouraged a resurgence of non-Soviet radicalism. Disenchantment with the fruits of modern industrialization and a sense of alienation from the impersonal structures of the modern capitalist state found increasingly articulate expression. It was this mood, interacting with unease over the superpower arms race and the chorus of international protest provoked by American involvement in the Vietnam War, which nurtured the variety of radical currents dubbed the 'New Left'.

A by-product of the resurgence of the Left has been a far-reaching reappraisal of the Russian revolution. For radicals of all persuasions, the 'Soviet experiment' exercises perennial fascination: the validity of any alternative radical strategy must be measured against the theory and practice of the Bolsheviks. And the corollary of disillusionment with the USSR has been a new readiness to subject the hallowed events of 1917 to criticism. There has been no sign of a radical consensus. The far Left is riven by fierce factional divisions both between Marxists and non-Marxists, and between different schools of Marxist thought, and the chiliastic vision of anarchism has remained a distinctly minority current. A summary synthesis of radical views on 'what went wrong' in 1917 is bound to provoke dissent from one faction or another at every turn. Yet it is possible to discern running through the work of a variety of radical historians a measure of common ground which amounts to a distinctive 'libertarian' discourse. The view of the revolution it offers has raised questions that challenge the basic assumptions of both Soviet and liberal orthodoxy.

The driving force behind the libertarian interpretation is an approach to history which, though related to that of Marxism–Leninism, differs from it fundamentally. Like Marxism–Leninism, it entertains a sublime vision of human potential for social harmony and individual fulfilment. Man is capable of a measure of creativity and mutual co-operation of which history has witnessed no more than the faintest inkling. The essential condition for realizing this potential is the overthrow of all forms of oppression. Economic oppression, the exploitation of man by man, is the source from which all other forms of oppression flow. Unlike Marxism–Leninism, however, the libertarian approach implies no all-embracing historical theory, no tightly-knit analysis of class struggle. While recognizing the importance of technological advance and man's increasing interdependence, it places no overriding causal emphasis on the level of the productive forces. Both the tempo and the degree of success of man's striving for freedom depend upon a host of political, cultural and moral as well as economic factors. The root of economic oppression, in the libertarian view, lies not in a given level of the productive forces, but in the 'relations of production', in the way in which individuals and groups relate to one another in the process of producing wealth. The critical question, the acid test of socialism, is the distribution of power at the point of production. Wherever those who produce are subordinated to those who manage production, society will be marked by division and individuals will be subjected to humiliation and their potential stunted. Oppression can only be overcome when the producers themselves manage production, when workers and peasants exercise self-management. Liberty cannot be delegated, it cannot be enjoyed at one remove.

For libertarian historians, therefore, the centre-stage of the revolution was occupied by the masses, by ordinary men and women, anonymous peasants and workers. They were responsible for the revolution and their rejection of the authority of Tsar, bourgeoisie and moderate socialists alike, and their sustained assault upon the State and private property, is celebrated as one of the greatest expressions of man's striving for liberty. Protest which Soviet historians disparage as 'spontaneous' and unreflecting, and which liberal historians see as mindless and destructive, libertarians regard as the very stuff of history. The central drama of the revolution was precisely the attempt of the Russian masses to assert direct control over their own lives; its tragedy was their subordination to Bolshevik domination. October marked the moment at which power began to move from the hands of the mass movement, then at full tide, into the hands of an organization determined to exercise control from above. The popular vision paled, dimmed and faded away.

Rather than providing a rounded history of the revolution, historians with libertarian sympathies have concentrated on various specific themes in the revolution. Two such themes stand out. The first concerns the issue of self-management by workers and peasants. Attention has focused in particular upon the factory committees established during 1917 and 1918. These grass-roots organizations which began to be formed immediately after February represent, in their view, the aspiration of the Russian proletariat to take command of the productive process. But the Bolsheviks were determined to frustrate them and immediately after October a bitter struggle ensued between the workers and the party. Given Bolshevik interest in obscuring the truth about this struggle, libertarians see no cause for surprise that 'we know less today about the early weeks of the Russian Revolution [i.e. after October] than we do, for instance, about the history of the Paris Commune.'[14] The crucial power was torn from the hands of the proletariat, and within months the Bolsheviks found themselves on the other side of the barricades. Whereas for Marxist–Leninists, the nationalization of property in the hands of a workers' State ensured that through the institutions which represented them – the State, the party, the soviets and the trade unions – the working masses were now in command, for libertarians this represented little more than a 'change of guard'. Management had merely passed from private hands into those of state appointees; society continued to be divided between those who rule and those who must obey. In the libertarian view self-management by no means precluded the establishment of co-ordinated planning and distribution. But socialism was doomed unless power remained on the factory floor and flowed upwards, rather than downwards. It was the refusal of the Bolsheviks to countenance this, their insistence upon hierarchical control, in agriculture and industry alike, which opened the door to bureaucratization and the degeneration of the entire Soviet experiment.

Directly related to this theme is the second major concern of libertarian writers: the roots of what they regard as the élitist, coercive nature of the regime established by the Bolsheviks. The most arresting libertarian thesis holds that far from constituting the vanguard of the proletariat, as it claimed, the party had from the start represented an entirely different class, that of 'intellectual workers'.[15] This new class embraced on the one hand the 'marginal intelligentsia' of Imperial Russian society, and on the other the middle-ranking officers and bureaucrats of the old order. While these two strata took different paths, one working from within the tsarist regime and the other confronting it, their aim was the same: both sought forceful economic modernization of backward Russia, and both aspired to monopolize power over the distribution of wealth in the new society. Sincere though the ideals of Lenin and his allies may have been, Marxism served as a mystifying ideology, masking even from themselves the real ambitions of the intelligentsia. And after the revolution the two strata coalesced to form a ruling class which repressed and exploited workers and peasants as brutally as did the capitalists of the West.

The libertarian view is still barely acknowledged by Soviet historians and is treated by most western historians as not wholly academically respectable.[16] Its dynamism is derived from faith in the potential for human transformation which beggars the imagination of a disillusioned generation. Yet for its adherents the common hostility it attracts from the orthodoxies of East and West is no cause for surprise. It is evidence rather of the common interest of the Soviet and the capitalist establishments in suppressing a revolutionary vision which threatens both.

The revisionists

So sharply have the battle lines been drawn between Soviet, liberal and libertarian historians that fruitful debate between them has been all

[15] This idea can be traced back to the nineteenth-century Russian anarchist Bakunin and was developed at the turn of the century by the Polish-born revolutionary Jan Machajski, whose main work *The Intellectual Worker* is skilfully analysed in M. S. Shatz, *Jan Waclaw Machajski. A Radical Critic of the Russian Intelligentsia and Socialism* (Pittsburgh, Pa., 1989).

[16] Libertarian studies of the revolution have tended to be published by specialist radical presses such as Black Rose Books in Montreal and Freedom Press in London.

but impossible. Each has tended to discount the work of the others as the product of brainwashing, special pleading or wishful thinking. Yet since the 1960s a number of scholars working in the West have begun to break the mould. They have carried out a wealth of painstaking research while consciously seeking to resist the presuppositions of these established camps. Their work provides the necessary material to assess the strengths and weakness of the three traditional approaches.

The emergence of a 'revisionist' school among western historians was made possible by the easing of tension between East and West from the late 1950s. A number of western historians of Russia, among whom the American professors Leopold Haimson and Reginald Zelnik were prominent, began to break out of the attitudes encouraged by the Cold War. To question the liberal account was no longer tantamount to condoning communist rule. Disenchantment with the liberal establishment characteristic of the 1960s began to find expression in the work of a new generation of scholars at major universities and research institutes. They began to apply to the revolution the techniques and approaches, the concern with social history and with quantitative methods, already being widely applied in less sensitive fields. Moreover, following the Second World War, there was a great expansion of Russian studies in the West – in the USA, Britain, France, Germany, and rather later, in Israel and Japan. In no country was a concerted research plan adopted, but there was a rapid increase in the number of Russian and Soviet specialists. In the USA alone the output of doctoral theses on Russian subjects increased from a grand total of 45 before 1950 to four times that number in the decade from 1965 to 1975. Western researchers gained the resources for more detailed study of social, economic and institutional aspects of the revolution. Revisionist scholars began to make full use of the primary material published in the Soviet Union in the 1920s; the cultural thaw and the opening up of debate among specialists within the Soviet Union increased readiness to take seriously new research by Soviet scholars; from the late 1950s a series of cultural exchange agreements between the USSR and the major western democracies facilitated western scholars' access to Soviet libraries and, to a much more limited extent, to archives.[17]

The major thrust of this recent research has been in four directions. First, it has begun to examine the revolution 'from below', to penetrate beneath the world of high politics to developments in the factory, in the village, in the barracks and trenches. A wide range of sources has

---

[17] See R. F. Byrnes, *Soviet American Academic Exchanges, 1958–1975* (Indiana, 1976). Since the early 1970s, an important forum for the development of revisionist work has been the annual conference organized by the British-based Study Group on the Russian Revolution. The Group's annual publication, *Sbornik*, was replaced in 1988 by a biannual journal, *Revolutionary Russia*.

been sifted to reconstruct the changing ideas and goals of the masses: private correspondence and letters to the press, contemporary reports in the metropolitan and local press and the myriad publications put out by the new organizations which sprang to life after February, memoirs and official reports, conference protocols and records of the countless resolutions passed in grass-roots meetings in the villages, at the factory gate, in soldiers' committees and local soviets. Inspired by western social historians such as E. P. Thompson, and by the *Annales* school in France, detailed monographs have appeared on the way in which the revolution was experienced by workers, peasants, soldiers and sailors.[18]

This challenge to the assumption that the revolution can be understood primarily by studying the major actors on the political scene leads to the second major theme addressed by revisionist work: the impact made by ordinary men and women upon political developments. Rather than analysing 'social' history in isolation from political developments, as social historians are at times accused of doing, they have dwelt upon the interaction between popular experience and mentality, on the one hand, and the struggle for power on the other.[19] They have taken seriously the aspirations of the masses themselves and credited them with an independence, sense of direction and rationality of their own. They have concentrated on the newly-formed mass organizations – soviets, soldiers' committees, trade unions, factory committees, peasant committees, Red Guards. They have explored the extent to which they reflected mass aspirations and their role in the political outcome of the revolution. In contrast to the traditional liberal view, they have suggested that during the revolution the masses acted upon the political leaders as much as they were acted upon by them.

Illumination of the social dimension of the revolution has at once encouraged and been complemented by the work of revisionist economic and political historians. Traditional assumptions about the development of the pre-revolutionary economy have been subjected to detailed re-examination. So too has the received wisdom about the structure and policies of the tsarist State, the Provisional Government, and the major political parties – Kadet, moderate socialist and Bolshevik. Taken together, the studies carried out by social, economic and political revisionists have opened the way to a far-reaching reassessment of the dynamics of popular unrest during Nicholas II's reign, the role of the revolutionary intelligentsia, the prospects of stable capitalist and western-style democratic development

---

[18] See E. P. Thompson's seminal study, *The Making of the English Working Class* (London, 1963).
[19] For a valuable introduction to the debate on the Left over the virtues and pitfalls of social history see P. Anderson, *Arguments Within English Marxism* (London, 1980).

in the period before the First World War, and the drama of 1917 itself.

The final focus of revisionist research is upon the sequel to October. For their analysis of 1917 highlights a profound discontinuity between the democratic and egalitarian movement which underlay the October revolution, and the rapid emergence of a monolithic Bolshevik dictatorship. Revisionist work in this area is less advanced than on the events of 1917 itself, but it has begun to unravel the process which led to the rapid breakdown of the broad popular alliance of October, the metamorphosis of the Bolshevik party, and the transformation in the nature of its power.

Recent Soviet reviews have treated this new species of western historiography with more respect than earlier western studies.[20] The deeper the impact of *glasnost*, the closer Soviet historians appear to be moving towards constructive debate over the issues raised by revisionist research.[21] Indicative of this has been the appearance of a soviet translation of the major revisionist account of October and further translations are planned.[22] Among western specialists many revisionist arguments have begun to gain a wide measure of acceptance. Their work features prominently in a new international encyclopedia of the revolution.[23] Libertarian historians have warmly welcomed the measure of common ground between their approach and revisionist concentration on the view from below.[24]

Yet partisans of the traditional schools have, predictably enough, reacted with hostility. One implication of revisionist work is that the root cause both of the fall of tsarism and of the failure of the liberals and moderate socialists lies much deeper than the liberal interpretation would have it. Another is that the view of October as the product of a truly mass-revolutionary movement is not so wide of the mark. Accordingly, for champions of the traditional liberal view, the main aim of this recent scholarship 'is to re-establish the old pro-Bolshevik

[20] G. Z. Ioffe, 'Velikii Oktiabr': transformatsiia sovietologicheskikh kontseptsii i ego klassovo-politicheskaia sut'', *Voprosy istorii KPSS* (1985) 6, pp. 72–86; V. P. Buldakov, A. Iu. Skvortsova, 'Proletarskie massy i Oktiabr'skaia revoliutsiia. (Analiz sovremennoi zapadnoi istoriografii)', *Istoria SSSR* (1987) 5, pp. 149–63.

[21] See for example the conference of Soviet historians held in May 1989 on discussions within the Bolshevik party between March 1917 and 1920 described in *Voprosy istorii KPSS* (1989) 10, pp. 144–8 and the series of discussion articles on the revolution and its immediate aftermath appearing under the rubric of 'New approaches to the history of Soviet society' in *Voprosy istorii* (1989) 10, 11, 12.

[22] An article by A. Rabinowitch on the relationship between the Bolshevik party and the masses in the October revolution was published in *Voprosy istorii* (1988) 5, pp. 14–27, and his monograph *The Bolsheviks Come to Power* appeared in translation in 1989.

[23] H. Shukman, ed., *The Blackwell Encyclopedia of the Russian Revolution* (Oxford, 1988).

[24] See for example C. Sirianni, *Workers' Control and Socialist Democracy. The Soviet Experience* (London, 1982).

legends about the period.'[25] It is seen as a latter-day product of the naïve romanticism of the 1960s, the decade in which many of its practitioners acquired their interest in the revolution. Equally, revisionist conclusions conflict with many of the central tenets of Soviet orthodoxy. They deflate the leadership role of the Bolshevik party and the 'genius' of Lenin. By demonstrating why workers, soldiers, and a minority of peasants came to support the Bolshevik party in 1917 they bring to light the limitations of the party's popular mandate, and the speed with which that mandate was forfeited. Champions of the traditional Soviet view have therefore condemned the bulk of revisionist work as a variation on an anti-Bolshevik theme, a more sophisticated form of 'bourgeois falsification'.

Revisionist work has still to be drawn together into a full-scale synthesis, in part no doubt, because the quantity of new doctoral research in the field slowed down in the early 1980s.[26] But the revisionists have set about dismantling separate aspects of each of the traditional versions. This cannot in itself resolve the philosophical questions which underly the controversy. But the conviction which Soviet, liberal and libertarian approaches to the historical process carry does rest in part upon the veracity of their respective portrayals of 1917. Revisionist work points to an understanding which, while drawing specific features from each school of thought, supersedes them all.

---

[25] R. Conquest, 'The inherent vice', *The Spectator*, 5 May 1984, p. 20.
[26] See A. Buchholz, ed., *Soviet and East European Studies in the International Framework. Organization, Financing and Political Relevance* (Berlin, 1982) for a useful discussion. Two recent introductory studies which include brief treatments of 1917 and draw on revisionist work are R. Service, *The Russian Revolution 1900–1927* (London, 1986) and B. Williams, *The Russian Revolution 1917–1921* (Oxford, 1987). See also the introduction by Sheila Fitzpatrick, a pioneer 'revisionist', who treats the 'revolution' as a process extending into the 1930s, *The Russian Revolution* (Oxford, 1982). On a much larger scale is the earlier and somewhat idiosyncratic, but innovative, two-volume study by the French historian M. Ferro, *The Russian Revolution of February 1917* (London, 1972); *October 1917. A Social History of the Russian Revolution* (London, 1980).

3 PRE-WAR RUSSIA: 'LAW-GOVERNED REVOLUTION' OR LIBERAL EVOLUTION?

The immediate prelude to the revolution was Russia's involvement in the First World War. For two and a half years the Empire was subjected to heavy casualties on the battlefield, acute economic austerity, and massive social dislocation. All sides in the debate over the revolution accept that the war served to heighten discontent, intensify social conflict and destabilize the political regime. But should the war be regarded as the cause or merely the precipitant of the revolutionary transformation of Russia? Whereas libertarian historians have devoted relatively little attention to this question, for the traditional liberal and Soviet schools it has been of vital importance. For on it depends the significance to be attached to the revolution. Is the outcome of 1917 explicable in terms of a relatively backward country being caught off balance at a critical moment in its development by the contingencies of international relations? Or does it represent a model, a paradigm which, when the peculiarities of Russia's development are stripped away, reveals the direction towards which capitalism inevitably leads? Was the Empire rudely torn by the war from its 'natural' evolution towards a capitalist and constitutional order comparable to that of the West? Or did the war merely serve to hasten and precipitate a 'law-governed' (*zakonomernyi*) process that was bound to culminate in the overthrow of tsarism and capitalism alike?[1] The controversy revolves around the direction in which Russia was developing before August 1914.

The Soviet view

In the Soviet view, pre-war developments pointed unmistakably towards not just one but two revolutions.[2] The first of these would be

---

[1] In common parlance *zakonomernyi* means 'normal', 'regular' or 'natural' and is less deterministic than the formal translation 'law-governed'. In this context, however, orthodox Soviet historians have used the term to denote conformity to the Marxist–Leninist interpretation of history and in analysing the prospects of revolution before 1914 have freely used the more rigidly deterministic *neizbezhnyi* (inevitable).

[2] For the most recent, and perhaps one of the last, authoritative general statements of the orthodox Soviet view, see P. A. Golub *et al.*, eds, *Istoricheskii opyt trekh rossiiskikh revoliutsii* (3 vols, Moscow, 1985–7) I, pp. 11–119, 443–495; II, pp. 5–76.

'bourgeois-democratic'. It would complete the task set by the revolution of 1905–7. The regime had managed to crush that upheaval, and despite cosmetic concessions to bourgeois constitutionalism, had survived more or less intact. Yet semi-feudal autocracy, denying the most basic democratic liberties, was doomed. It had failed to remove any of the fundamental causes behind the revolutionary challenge. Concessions strengthened the forces arrayed against it; reaction guaranteed renewed revolutionary protest. This insoluble predicament was the source of the decay, corruption and mounting tension evident within the upper echelons of the regime. Tsarism was inherently incapable of resolving the country's problems. It was, by its very nature, committed first and foremost to the interests of the landed nobility.[3] And, in the Soviet analysis, the land owned by the nobility was the crucial issue in the first revolution on the agenda.

The Emancipation settlement (1861) had reduced the land available to the peasantry, and confirmed noble ownership of much of the best land, together with forests and meadowlands. It had thereby perpetuated the peasants' servile dependence on the nobles. Not only did they need access to the non-arable resources controlled by the nobility, but their ever-growing land shortage compelled them to work for the nobility on conditions which had much in common with those of serfdom. The payments the peasantry made for access to noble land, whether in the form of share-cropping, labour rent or money rent, constituted a massive burden upon the rural economy. As the population grew land rents soared, multiplying sixfold between Emancipation and the turn of the century, thereby enabling the nobility to cream off and fritter away a huge surplus from peasant labour. This 'semi-feudal' exploitation of their large estates, their 'latifundia', was both economically unproductive and socially oppressive. It represented the major factor retarding the development of capitalism, investment and a free labour market in the rural economy.

The prime task of the 1905 revolution had been to break up the large estates and with them the political and economic power of the nobility. But that revolution had not succeeded. True, redemption dues were abolished, and Stolypin's attack on the commune broadened the labour market and encouraged trade in land. It hastened the growth of the *kulaks*, peasant farmers hiring labour to produce a surplus for the market, and increased their productive power. But the obstacles to the free development of capitalism and of successful peasant farming remained. The Stolypin reforms, Soviet historians would maintain, had not solved the basic problem which made revolution inevitable. In so far as the reforms accelerated the growth of capitalism and differentiation between employer and employee among the peasantry,

---

[3] For Tsarist politics in the period see A. I. Avrekh, *Stolypin i Tret'ia Duma* (Moscow, 1978) and *Tsarizm i IV Duma, 1912–1914gg.* (Moscow, 1981).

they served only to intensify the misery and oppression of the poorer peasants, to advance the struggle between rich and poor peasants. Above all, they did nothing whatsoever to tackle the primary source of peasant rebelliousness: their semi-feudal exploitation. Although rural disturbances were temporarily subdued after 1907, repeated out-breaks demonstrated peasant determination to destroy the bonds which continued to weigh upon them, and to transfer the landed estates into their own hands. Such a transfer could and would only be brought about by a bourgeois-democratic revolution.[4]

Unlike the situation at a comparable juncture in western develop-ment, however, this revolution could not be carried through under the leadership of the bourgeoisie. In the last years before the war that class undeniably wielded increasing economic power, rapidly developed its own economic organizations, and demonstrated growing political maturity and unity behind its prime political mouthpiece, the Kadet party. But in Russia the bourgeoisie was fatally inhibited from chal-lenging the old order by the spectre of a second revolution, ripening alongside the first: a proletarian and socialist revolution.

Despite the archaic structure of the State and the semi-feudal character of agrarian relations, by the turn of the century Russian capitalism had entered its final stage, that of imperialism. The revol-ution of 1905 had already demonstrated the explosive contradiction implicit in imperialism: the control by a handful of monopolistic capitalist syndicates of vast industrial enterprises employing hundreds of thousands of impoverished proletarians. During the immediate pre-war years the characteristic features of imperialism rapidly inten-sified. On the one hand, production was modernized in ever larger factories and ownership was concentrated in a network of trusts, cartels and syndicates increasingly dominated by a few major banks. On the other, the ranks of the proletariat swelled and their exploitation, impoverishment and discontent became ever more acute. Both the economic and the social prerequisites for socialism matured.[5]

What ensured that inchoate proletarian protest would yield a conscious revolutionary movement was the creation of a genuine revolutionary Marxist party, Lenin's 'party of a new type'.[6] The construction of the party was an essential condition for the victory of the socialist revolution. It provided the ideological, strategic and tactical guidance, together with the organizational strength and disci-pline, that guaranteed victory. It bound together the most advanced

---

[4] See P. S. Trapeznikov, *Leninism and the Agrarian and Peasant Question* (2 vols, Moscow, 1981) I, pp. 182–219 for a standard Soviet account available in translation.
[5] On the working class in the period, see V. Ia. Laverychev *et al.*, eds, *Rabochii klass Rossii. 1907-fevral' 1917g.* (Moscow, 1982).
[6] On the party in the period, see for example B. P. Ponomarev *et al.*, eds, *Istoriia Kommunisticheskoi partii Sovetskogo Soiuza* (Moscow, 1982), pp. 109–52.

sections of the working class. It constituted the institutional embodiment of proletarian unity and class consciousness. A looser structure, a willingness to compromise the party's programme and dilute its composition, would have been fatal. It would have laid the movement open to the bourgeois and petty-bourgeois revisionism, opportunism and adventurism to which other supposedly revolutionary Marxist parties, both Russian and western, fell victim. But, under Lenin's brilliant leadership, the Bolshevik party was able to resist all such deviations. The result was that in Russia the proletariat was not side-tracked into mere trade-unionism or reformism, nor were its energies dissipated in futile and ill-coordinated protests. Instead, the party moulded the spontaneous protest of the working class into a consciously socialist revolutionary movement.

In 1905, under Bolshevik leadership, the proletariat brought the tsarist regime to its knees. The repression which followed temporarily halted the labour movement and dealt the party a heavy blow. But the increasing discipline and class consciousness of the workers was reflected in the mounting ascendancy which the Bolsheviks achieved over the Mensheviks, SRs and non-party activists. After 1910 the workers' movement regathered momentum, and from 1912 the country was hit by wave upon wave of strikes, ever more political in motivation and ever more directly under Bolshevik leadership, culminating in a general strike in St Petersburg on the very eve of the war. Brutal repression broke the strike, and mobilization for the war initially subdued the labour movement. Yet Russia's involvement in the Great War was no extraneous fluke. It was itself a direct product of her involvement in an imperialist system riven by competition for markets. And the effect of the war was only to heighten the contradictions and class conflict evident before it began.

It is the majestic rise of the working-class movement which, for Soviet historians, stands at the centre of the pre-war stage. It exerted a growing influence over the peasantry. It drove the bourgeoisie, despite their interest in political and economic reform, into closer and closer collusion with the autocracy. And it confronted the tsarist regime with a challenge it could not withstand. Forged into an irresistible revolutionary force by its vanguard party, the proletariat was destined to carry through first the bourgeois-democratic revolution and then the socialist revolution.

The liberal view: the revolution as the chance product of war

The liberal tradition rejects each facet of this picture. According to this view, despite her political and economic backwardness, early-twentieth-century Russia had embarked on the path trodden by her western neighbours. Conditions in the aftermath of the 1905 revolution were propitious for stable development in countryside and city alike.

The reforms introduced after 1905 promised a solution to the rural poverty and land hunger which had brought peasant unrest to the surface in that year. Immediate pressure on peasant living standards was relieved by the abolition of redemption dues and restraint of the tax burden. The amount of land available to peasants was substantially increased. The resources of the Peasant Bank were expanded, making funds available for peasants to purchase land from the nobility. The rapid decline in noble land-holding continued, so that by 1914 the nobility owned less than a third of what they had owned in 1861. Additional relief was provided by a sustained programme of migration from European Russia to Siberia. Above all, the Stolypin land reform, by dismantling the peasant commune, was smoothing the path for sustained growth in agricultural productivity.

Peasants were permitted, indeed encouraged, to withdraw from the commune. The potential benefits were enormous. Private enterprise and initiative would replace the stultifying effect of joint responsibility and periodic redistribution of land. Consolidated farmsteads would overcome the inefficiences of strip-farming. Modern techniques, fertilizer and crops would replace the archaic implements and the three-field system under which Russian agriculture had stagnated. While raising output, the reform also opened the way for less successful peasants to withdraw from the commune, sell their share of the land, reduce rural overpopulation, and provide the mobile labour force necessary for the development of private enterprise in both agriculture and industry. Already many of the remaining noble landowners were developing modern capitalist methods of farming their estates. Rural Russia's problems had not disappeared overnight. But the sharp decline in peasant disturbances in the pre-war years pointed to peaceful development. With each year that passed, peasant interest in and support for the status quo would increase. Given a sustained period of peace and tranquillity, tension in the countryside would gradually lessen and in the longer term, the population curve could be expected to level out.

The prospects of such a period of tranquillity were greatly increased by urban developments. Here, too, 1905 marked a decisive turning point. Despite the worst efforts of the revolutionary intelligentsia, the working class was showing signs of following in the path of reformist labour movements in central and western Europe. Raw villagers recruited into the unfamiliar discipline of industrial labour would continue to be unruly, and so long as the harsh conditions typical of early industrialization prevailed, the workers would no doubt prove highly strike-prone. But industrial growth would gradually provide the resources for improvements in wages and conditions of the kind which had taken the sting out of revolutionary ferment in the West. Differentials between sections of the labour force could be expected to grow, fostering the emergence of a 'labour aristocracy' with little interest in apocalyptic dreams of revolution. Moreover, the channels were being opened for peaceful management–employer bargaining within the framework of a private enterprise economy. There were voices, if as yet in a minority, within both industry and government favouring the establishment of free collective bargaining. A start had been made in legalizing trade unions, and in 1912 legislation to bring in accident and sickness insurance was passed. The legal basis was being created for workers to set up their own professional, cultural and leisure-time organizations through which they would become integrated with the rest of society.

The changes overcoming the peasantry and working class contributed to and complemented a rapid increase in the power and influence of social groups in favour of liberal evolution rather than violent change. In the countryside, the new class of yeoman farmers would provide a mass base for liberal democracy comparable to that in the French Third Republic, while the growing legions of the so-called 'third element' working for the zemstvos – doctors, teachers, midwives, agricultural experts, and the like – provided a natural constituency for liberal reformism. In the cities, the relative moderation of groups of workers such as the printers pointed the way to co-operation between the working class and progressive sections of 'society' in pressing for liberal reforms. At the same time, the economic and social weight of the middle classes was visibly growing. As dependence on foreign capital slowly declined, and the domestic market expanded, so the domestic banking system developed, native entrepreneurial activity increased, and new small enterprises and consumer industries came into being. Equally, the traditional gulf separating the industrial and commercial middle classes from the intelligentsia was narrowing. On the one hand, a dramatic expansion of educational facilities – primary, secondary and tertiary – was raising the cultural level and aspirations of the merchant class. On the other, with the widening of opportunities in commerce, industry, and the professions, Russia's intelligentsia was shedding its ultra-radical preoccupations and image. Like the working class, it was becoming integrated into an increasingly dynamic and self-confident civil society.

Moreover, in the aftermath of the 1905 revolution, the state order was becoming increasingly amenable to evolution along liberal-constitutional lines. The establishment of the State Duma, together with a wide range of political parties, created a national forum wherein social conflict could be peacefully resolved. Within the central bureaucracy, sympathy for reform was growing, and traditional high-handedness was giving way to a new respect for the law. Even in the army, the old stranglehold of reactionary officers was giving way to the increasing professionalism of soldiers drawn from varied social backgrounds. For all its blemishes, the judicial system was coming abreast of western practice. At the local level, rural zemstvos and urban dumas provided the institutional framework for wider public involvement in self-government and expanding educational, medical, and other services. Restrictions on the freedom of assembly were gradually being relaxed, and the massive growth and increasing boldness of the press was lending ever greater muscle to public opinion. Democratic principles would, of course, take time to percolate through a population accustomed to autocracy. But conditions were set fair for stable political and economic development.

The prospects would have been even brighter if only Russia had been blessed with a less benighted tsar. On the one hand, Nicholas could have worked positively to ease the way towards peaceful constitutional evolution. Instead, he treated the Duma with contempt, refused to throw his weight behind Stolypin's wide-ranging programme of legal and local government reforms, and jealously guarded his personal prerogatives at the expense of coherent cabinet government. On the other, he could have devoted his energies to shoring up the regime's prestige, authority and ability to maintain order. Instead, he destabilized his own government by selecting totally inadequate ministers and, deferring to his hysterical wife, allowed the depraved 'holy man' Rasputin to tarnish his own popular image and that of tsarism itself.

Nevertheless, the fortress of autocracy had been breached and liberal pressure for further reform could be expected to gather momentum. Meanwhile, the military power of the State remained sufficient to maintain order while the beneficial medicine of socio-economic development consolidated the bases for a western-style pluralist democracy.[7] 'Then, as a thunderbolt, came the terrible catastrophe of 1914, and progress changed into destruction.'[8]

The revisionist view

The controversy over the pre-war period revolves around five central questions: the likelihood of renewed rebellion by the peasantry; the dynamics of working-class protest; the prospects for the consolidation of the Empire's middle classes into a formidable social and political force; the solidity of the tsarist forces of repression; and the effect of

---

[7]For a succinct summary of the most influential liberal treatment of pre-war socio-economic trends see A. Gerschenkron, 'Agrarian policies and industrialization in Russia, 1861–1917', in M. M. Postan and H. J. Habakkuk, eds, *Cambridge Economic History of Europe* (Cambridge, 1965) vi, pt 2, pp. 706–800.

[8]G. A. Pavlovsky, *Agriculture on the Eve of the Revolution* (London, 1930), p. 321.

Russia's entry into the First World War upon socio-political conditions in the Empire. On each of these questions revisionist work has taken issue with the liberal view and demonstrated the mounting instability of pre-war Russia. Yet at the same time, it has challenged central features of the Soviet view. Pre-war trends suggest that revolution was on the cards, but they bear little resemblance to the 'law-governed' process depicted by Soviet historiography.

The peasantry

So far as the prospects of stability in the countryside are concerned, revisionist work has stressed that, whenever consulted, peasants continued after 1905 to express an unequivocal demand for the abolition of noble landownership. The fierceness with which peasant deputies in the first two Dumas pressed for all noble land to be handed over startled and frightened the government. Even after peasant representation had been abruptly cut in 1907, and the nobles had been guaranteed a virtual veto against undesirable peasant candidates, the peasant deputies elected to the Third and Fourth Dumas remained unshakeable on the land question.[9] Elections to the zemstvos, too, demonstrated the intense hostility of the peasantry towards the landed nobility. They became increasingly outspoken in denouncing noble domination of local government institutions, and the zemstvo taxes they had to pay. In the zemstvo elections of 1909–10 they used the marginally greater electoral freedom granted after 1905 to elect vigorous upholders of the peasant interest. Only when it became clear that the rules made it impossible for them to shake the landowners' grip on the zemstvos did interest decline so that the last pre-war zemstvo elections were marked by peasant apathy.[10] In only a few areas were there significant differences of political attitude between richer and poorer peasants, and these were wholly overshadowed by a common antipathy towards the landed nobility and determination to see their land transferred into peasant hands.[11]

Attention has also been drawn to the evidence of continuing peasant unrest even after the mass disturbances of 1905–7 were brought to an end. True, the global figures advanced by Soviet historians to plot the graph of peasant disorders leave much to be desired. They are based on the very unsystematic police reports about local incidents, and much depends upon the criteria used to identify politically significant disturbances of the peace. Liberal historians have been inclined to dismiss such figures altogether, scorning their use as evidence of

[9] E. D. Vinogradoff, 'The Russian Peasantry and the Elections to the Fourth State Duma', in L. H. Haimson, ed., *The Politics of Rural Russia, 1905–1914* (Bloomington, Ind., 1979), pp. 219–49.
[10] R. D. MacNaughton and R. T. Manning, 'The Crisis of the Third of June System and Political Trends in the Zemstvos, 1907–1914', in Haimson, *Rural Russia*, pp. 199–209.
[11] Vinogradoff, 'The Russian Peasantry', pp. 235, 245–9.

revolutionary sentiment among the peasantry as 'fatuous . . . street-pamphlet reasoning.'[12] Revisionist historians, while treating the figures with caution, have been somewhat less dismissive. They have pointed out that the total of 20,000 disturbances recorded between 1907 and 1914 indicates that a small proportion of peasants were involved. On the other hand, comparison with statistics on disturbances before 1905 suggests that the 'normal' level of peasant disturbances was never re-established. Moreover, after relative tranquillity between 1907 and 1910, the number of disturbances appears to have risen abruptly in the last years before the war.[13] Despite the ferocious measures of repression after 1905 (equated by one revisionist historian with American 'pacification' in Vietnam), despite the exceptional harvests of 1909–10 and 1911–13, and despite the strong recovery in grain prices in this period, peasant discontent remained intense.[14]

To conclude that the potential for peasant revolution against the status quo remained undiminished in the decade after 1905 does not, of course, dispose of the liberal contention that given a longer period of peaceful development the prospects would have changed. But here, too, recent analysis presents a bleaker picture than that of the traditional liberal view.

Revisionist analyses of socio-economic trends in the countryside fall into two distinct categories. In the first belong those economic historians whose primary concern has been to re-examine the overall economic performance of Russian agriculture. In the second belong a number of 'neo-populist' social historians whose primary concern has been to elucidate the distinctive structure and culture of the traditional peasant family farm. Their differing concerns have led the two groups to dwell upon different regions of the Empire. Whereas economic historians have been more interested in the periphery, in regions where agriculture was more dynamic and evidence of change greater, neo-populists have focused upon the Russian heartland – the provinces of the Central Black Earth region, the Mid Volga and Little Russia – where change was least evident. At their most strident, scholars in each group have claimed that the trends they have identified constitute the norm for the whole Empire. The inadequate statistical material available makes it impossible to prove either claim. If the central provinces are taken as typical, the neo-populist case is persuasive; if, on the other hand, the outlying provinces are regarded as blazing a trail which central Russia would follow, it falls to the ground. In the words of a recent review of the evidence, 'in the centre, progress was

[12] G. L. Yaney, *The Urge to Mobilize: Agrarian Reform in Russia, 1861–1930* (Urbana, Ill., 1982), pp. 186–9.
[13] D. Atkinson, *The End of the Russian Land Commune 1905–1930* (Stanford, Cal., 1983), p. 106.
[14] R. T. Manning, *The Crisis of the Old Order in Russia: Gentry and Government* (Princeton, 1982), p. 172.

peripheral, but on the periphery there was progress.'[15] Yet, provided the regional distinction is borne firmly in mind, the work of both groups may serve to illuminate the debate over the prospects of social stability in the countryside.

The most striking aspect of recent analysis by economic historians has been the relatively favourable picture they have drawn of agricultural development in the decades immediately preceding the revolution of 1905. Late-nineteenth-century Russian agriculture was not stagnant. On the contrary, it responded to opportunities both of export abroad and of an increasingly integrated internal market. As from the 1880s, it developed significantly. New land was brought into use. New crops, new seed strains and new rotations were introduced. There was greater specialization and more effective use was made of fertilizer. Modest but significant improvements were made in farming equipment. The result was a substantial rise in yields and an increase in output that outstripped the rise in population. Moreover, it was improvements in peasant husbandry that were primarily responsible for the growth. By the late nineteenth century, peasant farmers were responsible for the great bulk of farm produce, whether on allotment land belonging to the commune or on private land bought or rented from the nobility. Although progress was somewhat faster on privately-owned land than on allotment land, crop yields on the latter rose between 1861 and 1910 by almost 50 per cent.[16]

These conclusions have led revisionists to cast doubt on three of the assumptions underlying the liberal interpretation. First, they have argued that the gradual increase in peasant investment and in levels of consumption both of food and consumer goods in the countryside suggests that, abjectly poor though many were, on average peasant living standards may have been rising rather than falling in the decades immediately prior to the revolution of 1905. On the same grounds they have argued that the taxation burden borne by peasants before 1905 has been much exaggerated.[17] The implication is that peasant militancy in 1905 was not a function of overall impoverishment and that minor concessions, such as the reduction in taxes and ending of redemption dues, were unlikely to transform peasant attitudes. Second, they have stressed that many of the innovations in peasant agriculture before 1905 were undertaken in areas where the commune prevailed. Where it was advantageous to do so, the peasantry had already found ways to circumvent the formal constraints of the commune. Revisionists have therefore questioned the notion that the

[15] P. Gatrell, *The Tsarist Economy 1850–1917* (London, 1986), p. 139.
[16] *op. cit.*, pp. 98–140; P. Gregory, *Russian National Income, 1885–1913* (Cambridge, 1982), pp. 70–77.
[17] J. Y. Simms, 'The crisis in Russian agriculture at the end of the nineteenth century: a different view', *Slavic Review* 36 (1977), pp. 377–98; see the comments in Gatrell, *Tsarist Economy*, pp. 137–8.

commune in itself had been a major barrier to improvement or labour mobility and, equally, the notion that dismantling the commune would in itself provide a major stimulus to agricultural development.[18] Third, they have questioned the belief that Stolypin's 'wager on the strong', his efforts to stimulate differentiation between richer and poorer peasants, were effective in distracting the peasantry from their resentment against noble landownership. The commercialization of peasant agriculture had been fostering such differentiation long before Stolypin threw his weight behind it, yet it had done nothing to temper the ferocity of the peasants' attack upon the nobility in 1905.

In short, revisionist economic historians have played down the significance of the reforms introduced after 1905, and controverted the liberal belief that it promised to bring social stability to the countryside. The intensification in rural unrest before 1905 owed less to an overall fall in living standards than to the rising expectations and assertiveness of the peasantry. Besides the evidence that the peasantry were economically more rational and dynamic than liberal treatments have commonly allowed, revisionists have pointed to their closer contact with urban life, the improving levels of literacy, and the declining respect for the Orthodox Church and for established authority in general. They have underlined peasant demands during 1905–7 for equality of legal status, for reform of the court system, for the curbing of police power, for local democracy, and for education.[19] And these trends tended to accelerate rather than slacken after 1905. At the same time, while accepting that tension between richer and poorer peasants was growing and that Stolypin's reform created fierce friction between those who separated from the commune and those who remained within it, revisionists have stressed that it did not shake their common determination that noble land should be transferred into their hands. And the land reform bypassed this problem altogether. Certainly, the amount of land held by the nobility continued to decline after 1905, as it had been doing ever since Emancipation. But following a brief period of panic sales in the immediate aftermath of the turmoil of 1905, noble land sales slowed down markedly. Indeed, in the last years of the Empire a smaller proportion of noble land passed from their hands than at any time since Emancipation.[20] Noble landownership, the prime source of peasant resentment, was far from fading peacefully away.

The second category of revisionists, neo-populist historians concerned with peasant society, have likewise emphasized the limited

[18] Gatrell, *Tsarist Economy*, pp. 122–5, 232.
[19] On the range of peasant concerns, see L. Edmondson, 'Was there a Movement for Civil Rights in Russia in 1905?', in O. Crisp and L. Edmondson, eds, *Civil Rights in Imperial Russia* (Oxford, 1989), pp. 272–5.
[20] Manning, *Crisis of the Old Order*, pp. 364, 374.

impact of government policy after 1905 in general and of the Stolypin land reform in particular. True, in the country as a whole the reform helped to reduce the proportion of peasant households within the commune. The most convincing recent estimate records a fall in that proportion from 77 per cent in 1905 to 61 per cent in 1916. There was a comparable fall in the proportion of allotment land held by communal peasants – from some 83 per cent to about 66 per cent.[21] Yet the number of peasants applying to withdraw their holdings from the commune peaked in 1909, long before the war, and thereafter underwent a precipitate decline. Nor did dramatic economic change result from those withdrawals which took place. Much of the land withdrawn from communal tenure continued to be farmed in strips under the three-field system. Less than half of those who left the commune proceeded to consolidate their strips of land, and of these only a quarter actually moved their homesteads out of the village. As a proportion of all peasant land, the area in which scattered strips were consolidated into coherent holdings failed to reach 10 per cent.

Moreover, it was only on the periphery of the Empire – in the West, the South and the South East – that the reform made any significant headway at all. There capitalism was making some progress. There some noble estates were being adapted to farming directly for the market with hired labour; there a measure of differentiation between successful peasant farmers and their proletarianized neighbours was evident; there the traditional repartitional commune either did not exist or was decaying. And it was there that the peasant response to the Stolypin reform was most positive. But the densely populated central provinces present a very different picture. Here investment, the use of hired labour, the differentiation between richer and poorer peasants, made minimal progress. Most noble estates, rather than moving towards direct farming, continued to rely upon share-cropping and labour rent, while among the peasantry, communal tenure remained dominant. A would-be separator from the commune in these areas had little prospect of acquiring sufficient land and commanding adequate capital to establish a viable independent farmstead. For the vast majority, the option of leaving the commune held little attraction and resistance to the Stolypin reform was fierce.[22]

For neo-populists, it is the social structure in these central provinces that is crucial. The most significant feature of the rural scene here both before and after 1905 was the prevalence of peasant households which were neither *kulak* nor 'semi-proletarian'. Rural society was characterized by the overwhelming predominance of family farms which

[21] D. Atkinson, 'The Statistics on the Russian Land Commune, 1905–1917', *Slavic Review* 32 (1973), pp. 781–3.

[22] The differing regional response to Stolypin's reform is most clearly brought out in W. E. Mosse, 'Stolypin's Village', *Slavonic and East European Review* 43 (1964–5), pp. 257–74.

neither relied upon hired labour nor hired out their own labour. According to this neo-populist view, which was outlined before the revolution and developed in the 1920s but has been vigorously re-asserted in the last two decades, the spread of the market was not having the expected impact on peasant society. The 'classical' effect of the market and commercial competition, which both Marxist and liberal economists had taken for granted, namely a differentiation between successful and unsuccessful producers, between rural 'bourgeoisie' and rural 'proletariat', was not taking place.

The neo-populist view points to a variety of factors which counter-acted the tendency of commercialization to foster differentiation. The communal redistribution of land, the heavy impositions of the State, the vulnerability of even the most successful household to the vagaries of the climate – all provided major obstacles to the emergence of households sufficiently enterprising to hire labour, invest and expand. Most significant was the process by which peasants divided large households to set up new families in their own homes, and merged those which old age and death had rendered unviable. The economy of a peasant household tended to follow a biological pattern, rising as the family expanded, declining as the adults grew old and the children left home. As a result, hired labour in the rural economy remained minimal. Landownership was not becoming more concentrated. In-deed, in the pre-war years peasant households of this kind were increasing their proportion of the land, output and inventory of central Russia.[23]

In the central provinces, therefore, neither sturdy yeomen with a solid stake in the status quo, nor landless peasants were destined to emerge. The vast majority continued to be 'middle peasants' bound together in the village commune. Tensions within the village would still be wholly overshadowed by a sense of common interest, a shared way of life and outlook. Peasants were united in their hostility towards the small number of households who left their villages to set up separate homesteads under Stolypin's provisions, and, above all, towards the nobility. Thus after 1905, as before, the landowning nobility of the central provinces were confronted by a homogeneous and cohesive peasant society. Moreover, peasant land hunger grew ever more acute as the population swelled. Neither the programme of resettlement in Siberia, nor peasant purchases of noble land came close to compensating for the continued steep rise in the rural popu-lation in these regions. As soon as the opportunity presented itself, the likelihood was that they would show the same determination to seize the nobility's land that they had displayed in 1905.[24]

[23] The argument is developed in detail in T. Shanin, *The Awkward Class* (Oxford 1972); see also T. Shanin, *The Roots of Otherness: Russia's Turn of Century* (2 vols, London, 1985, 1986) I, pp. 93–102, 150–1.
[24] *op. cit.* I, pp. 172–3.

Both currents of revisionist work, then, contradict liberal optimism about the prospects of social stability in the countryside. The explanations which they offer for continuing peasant unrest, however, run counter to important aspects of the Soviet explanation. They make it difficult to equate the social tensions in the countryside with the economic processes at the heart of the Marxist interpretation. The substantial rate of progress in agriculture – and the possibility that overall rural living standards rose – suggests that 'semi-feudal' fetters on peasant enterprise were less significant than Soviet orthodoxy insists. Likewise, the rising proportion of noble farmers who had switched from 'semi-feudal' to direct, 'capitalist' farming by 1914 is difficult to reconcile with the notion that the assault upon noble landownership in 1917 constituted an economically progressive 'bourgeois-democratic' revolt against 'feudal' practices.[25] Moreover in many areas the assault upon the nobility was led by middle peasants whose family farms were anything but capitalist. Equally, hostility towards peasants who had left the commune came not from a proletarianized peasantry presaging a movement beyond capitalism to socialized large-scale farming, but from 'traditional' households who desired a redistribution of the land amassed by their more successful neighbours.[26]

Nor does revisionist work confirm Soviet insistence that the peasant movement, in 1905 as in 1917, followed in the wake of a proletarian vanguard.[27] Peasants had shown themselves fully capable of organizing resistance around their traditional village institutions, and their determination to take over the nobility's land was their own. It was sustained by rising expectations, an increasing sophistication and, in the central agricultural provinces, by the ordeal of acute land hunger shared by traditional family farmers.

The working class

Despite their differences over the long-term socio-economic trends in the countryside, all sides accept that the outcome there would be crucially affected by urban developments. The revolution of 1905 had made plain the disruptive power of the industrial labour force. Here, too, revisionist analysis has rejected the liberal interpretation and the view that, but for the war, working-class militancy would have declined. The strike record in the immediate pre-war years is difficult to reconcile with the notion that workers' protest was becoming less intense. The number of workdays lost and of workers involved rose steeply from 1912. By 1914, strike action was running at a rate

[25] According to one estimate, by 1914 two-thirds of gentry land was being farmed directly, Manning, *Crisis of the Old Order*, pp. 20–1.
[26] M. Perrie, 'The Russian Peasant Movement of 1905–1907: Its Social Composition and Revolutionary Significance', *Past and Present* 55 (1972), pp. 123–55.
[27] Shanin, *Roots of Otherness* II, pp. 138–73.

comparable to that of 1905.[28] Moreover, the section of the work-force most given to strike action showed every sign of increasing its weight both in relative and absolute terms. There was a loose correlation between large factories (1000–8000 workers) and proneness to strike, and the proportion of workers in factories of over 1000 workers was rising.[29] The most militant and politically conscious trade was that of metal workers and the government's commitment to massive military expenditure promised to sustain its rapid growth. Worse still, the epicentre of labour militancy was the capital itself. The contrast between Moscow and St Petersburg is instructive. In Moscow, where the average factory was smaller and factory workers were outnumbered by artisans in small workshops, social polarization was less extreme and labour protest less fierce. St Petersburg, on the other hand, had the highest concentration of large factories, and of metal-working factories in particular, and in 1914 the capital and its environs accounted for almost half the number of strikers in the Empire.[30] If the modernity and concentration of labour which St Petersburg epitomized were the pattern of the future, the prospects for urban stability were poor.

Nor is there much comfort for the liberal view to be drawn from the motives behind the strike wave. The statistics provided by the contemporary factory inspectorate distinguishing between 'political' and 'economic' strikes show a growing preponderance of those with political motivation. These statistics must be treated with caution, but if anything it is more likely that they underrate rather than overrate the political content. Strikes sparked off by specific incidents such as the Lena goldfields massacre of 1912, or short stoppages called to mark May Day, were manifestly political in motivation. But many of those arising over factory conditions and economic issues often included a political dimension. Indeed, the fusion between economic and political goals, the fact that workers often did not draw a sharp line between protest against their employers and protest against the government, boded ill for liberal hopes of channelling worker discontent into peaceful, non-political waters.[31]

[28] L. Haimson, 'The Problem of Social Stability in Urban Russia, 1905–1917', *Slavic Review* 23 (1964), pp. 619–42 and 24 (1965), pp. 1–22.
[29] S. A. Smith, *Red Petrograd. Revolution in the Factories 1917–1918* (Cambridge, 1983), pp. 9–12; J. H. Bater, 'St Petersburg and Moscow on the eve of revolution', in D. H. Kaiser, ed., *The Workers' Revolution in Russia, 1917. The View From Below* (Cambridge, 1987), pp. 25–7, 37–8. That Russia should so quickly have acquired the largest factories in the world was as much a product of backwardness, and the need for enterprises to be self-sufficient in a variety of secondary products, as of the introduction of the most modern plant.
[30] Smith, *Red Petrograd*, pp. 5–36; D. Koenker, *Moscow Workers and the 1917 Revolution* (Princeton, 1981), pp. 25–31.
[31] See the review article by R. Zelnik, 'Russian Workers and the Revolutionary Movement', *Journal of Social History* 6 (1972), pp. 214–36.

Of course, political protest against the autocracy is not of itself proof that the working class was aspiring to a political revolution that would go beyond the limits of liberal democracy. But the evidence suggests that the fragile though real co-operation between liberals and workers of 1905 had broken down by the pre-war years. Wherever they had the opportunity, workers solidly supported socialist parties – in elections to the Duma, to social insurance councils, to trade-union boards. Moreover, the immediate pre-war period saw clear signs that in the factional struggle among Social Democrats it was the more extreme Bolsheviks and Interdistrict faction, rather than the more moderate Mensheviks, who were gaining ground. The Bolsheviks took six of the nine labour curias in the elections to the Fourth Duma in 1912.

Liberal faith that the militancy of Russia's working class was on the wane, therefore, seems misplaced. True, workers' protest moved in close correlation with the business cycle, rising as demand for labour rose, falling with mass unemployment; and the rapid turnover of workers in the pre-war period ensured considerable ebb and flow in the movement. But it seems difficult to refute the Soviet contention that in Russia the advance of industrial capitalism, rather than fostering moderation, reformism and concern with purely economic goals, was nourishing an increasingly radical and politically conscious proletariat.

The implications to be drawn, however, are less obvious. Does the sustained militancy of the Russian working class reveal the 'law-governed' essence of capitalist development and the inevitability of its overthrow, or was the Russian case an aberration, a unique deviant from the norm represented by western Europe? What was the crucial variable which distinguished the Russian working class from its western counterparts?

At first glance the obvious explanation for Russian working-class militancy lies in the appalling conditions in which the workers lived and worked. Wages were pitiful and despite recovering somewhat in certain sectors in the last years before the war, they remained very low. Working hours, averaging almost 60 per week in 1914, were significantly longer than in the West. The rate of industrial accidents was horrific. Management was crude and brutal. Legislation to create a factory inspectorate (1885) made little impact, and the Insurance Law of 1912 provided no insurance against invalidity, occupational diseases, old age or unemployment. Urban amenities available to workers – transport, education, health and leisure facilities – were derisory and the overcrowded housing conditions of the major cities were sordid and degrading.[32] Moreover, the particularly sharp curves of the

---

[32] J. Bradley, 'Moscow: From Big Village to Metropolis', J. H. Bater, 'Between Old and New: St Petersburg in the Late Imperial Era', in M. F. Hamm, ed., *The City in Late Imperial Russia* (Bloomington, Ind., 1986), pp. 9–42, 43–78.

Russian business cycle induced intense job insecurity, and correspondingly sharp fluctuations in wage levels. Russian workers had much to protest against. The contrast between their life and that of genteel society provided endless potential for resentment. If deprivation alone were enough to provoke militancy, there would be no need to look any further.

In fact, however, international·comparisons strongly suggest that it is not the most downtrodden and deprived who provide the most militant source of protest. Rather than being closely correlated with any absolute level of poverty, unrest has generally been sparked by a decline in living standards or by the disappointment of rising expectations. Different sections of the pre-war work-force suffered from one or the other. Widespread wage reductions were imposed during the recession of 1906–9 and price inflation thereafter impeded the recovery of real wage levels. At the same time, the introduction of closer managerial supervison, piece-rates, and in some cases, more modern machinery sharply intensified the pace of work. In neither respect, however, as recent work on the western and especially the German workforce in the pre-war period demonstrates, was the experience of the Russian working class unique.[33]

A second line of argument points to the rapid influx of peasants into the Russian work-force as the key cause of its militancy. The thesis is that, on the one hand, these raw recruits were disorientated by the transition to urban life and therefore unable to accept the discipline and demands of the factory. On the other, their sense of injustice in the countryside was compounded by experience of urban conditions and bred a particularly acute sense of grievance, 'a uniquely volatile and dynamic mixed consciousness that combined a peasant resentment against the vestiges of Russian "feudalism" [i.e. serfdom] with a proletarian resentment against capitalist exploitation in the factories.'[34]

It is true that in 1914 most Russian workers still had rural ties and very often owned land. Even in St Petersburg, where the proportion of hereditary proletarians was greatest, only a narrow majority of workers had severed their ties with the countryside. There can be no doubt that newly-recruited peasants, given to short bursts of extremely militant action, added a volatile and inflammable element to working-class protest. But the notion that these raw recruits were the critical ingredient is open to doubt. The network of family, village and regional ties, the *zemlyachestva*, which 'peasant-proletarians'

[33] For a stimulating comparative analysis see D. Geary, *European Labour Protest 1848–1939* (London, 1981), pp. 90–126.
[34] Zelnik, 'Russian Workers', p. 218; for seminal contributions to this debate see Haimson, 'Problem of Social Stability' and, for the period before 1900, R. E. Johnson, *Peasant and Proletarian. The Working Class of Moscow in the Late Nineteenth Century* (Leicester, 1979).

imported into the city provided them with a social nexus which at least limited the disorientation and *anomie* imputed to them. Moreover, the fact that they had a stake in the village – a piece of land, an extended family network – on which to fall back tended to retard their involvement in urban protest: they had less motive to endure the risks of industrial action than those whose future lay exclusively in the city. Indeed, many of the distinctive characteristics of the 'peasant-proletarian' – the relatively low level of their skill, wages and education, and even their marked tendency to marry earlier than their more urbanized counterpart – appear to have weakened their commitment to sustained protest.[35]

The most important point is that the volatility of raw recruits from the countryside was not complemented by increasing moderation on the part of their more thoroughly 'proletarianized' comrades. On the contrary, it was the most urbanized workers, those with the highest levels of skill, education and wages who were at the forefront of labour protest. There was minimal evidence of a settled, reformist 'labour aristocracy' emerging.[36] The most promising candidates for such a role were the print workers. They were highly skilled, exceptionally well paid, often drawn from non-peasant and non-worker backgrounds, and by the nature of their work were exposed to liberal literature and enjoyed a relatively close relationship with liberal *intelligenty*. Yet even they remained adamantly loyal to the socialist parties, and, although generally identifying with the Mensheviks, moved markedly to the Left in the pre-war period. It is true that artisans with skilled crafts initially developed craft unions and displayed a distinctive group consciousness, a 'craft consciousness'. But this was not accompanied by deradicalization, and by contrast with many western societies, did not conflict with their sense of belonging to a wider working class. Indeed, artisans with craft skills working in small firms played a leadership role, underrated in Soviet accounts, in developing broader working-class consciousness. In the large metal-working enterprises of St Petersburg, too, the initiative for working-class organization and activism was taken by workers with artisan skills. And more generally, the relatively highly-skilled and urbanized workers in the metal-working industry displayed greater sustained militancy than did those in the textile industry who were less educated and retained closer links with the countryside.[37]

[35] Koenker, *Moscow Workers*, pp. 43–93.
[36] R. Zelnik, 'Russian Bebels: An Introduction to the Memoirs of the Russian Workers Semen Kanatchikov and Matvei Fisher', *Russian Review* 35 (1976), pp. 249, 441–4.
[37] V. E. Bonnell, *Roots of Rebellion: Workers' Politics and Organizations in St Petersburg and Moscow, 1900–1914* (Berkeley, Cal., 1983), pp. 427–38; W. G. Rosenberg, 'Workers and Workers' Control in the Russian Revolution', *History Workshop* 5 (1978), pp. 89–97; S. A. Smith, 'Craft Consciousness, Class Consciousness: Petrograd 1917', *History Workshop* 11 (1981), pp. 33–58.

This pattern is confirmed by analyses of the process underlying the development of class consciousness among workers. The most skilled and literate combined the keenest sense of grievance with the ability to articulate their aspirations. It was they who bore the brunt of efforts by employers to restructure, shift to more intensive labour, subject them to closer supervision from above, and in some cases introduce new machinery which dispensed with their skills.[38] It was the more sophisticated who developed a consciousness of human dignity which was most deeply offended by the crudity and brutality of the Russian factory order. It was they who most resented the contempt of factory management, the humiliation of public examination for venereal diseases, the lack of privacy in the lavatories, the insecurity of their jobs, the degradation of their living quarters.[39] It was for them that the vision of a transformation in political, social and economic relationships held greatest appeal. At the same time, it was those with the highest level of education who were best able to draw from particular grievances – against their own foreman or management – a more general analysis of the system which oppressed them. It was those with the highest levels of skill in whom the capacity for independent thought and initiative was most developed. It was those with the deepest roots in industry and the urban environment who developed the strongest sense of the workers as a class apart with its own distinctive interests and goals. Moreover, their ability to make sense of the workers' predicament and articulate their grievances played an important part in mobilizing less sophisticated ranks. In the words of an SR worker, 'The "self-made" agitator spoke of that which each worker had in his head but, being less developed, was unable to verbalize. After each of his words, the workers would exclaim: "That's it! That's it! That's just what I wanted to say!"'[40]

It was workers of this kind, with the level of articulacy and the modicum of leisure necessary for political involvement, who provided the hard core of labour activists. It was they who formed the trade unions when they were first legalized in 1906. It was they who maintained a skeletal union organization through the years of repression and recession even when membership promised little short-term benefit and involved considerable risk of discrimination by employers. Despite apparent sympathy with Menshevik moderation between 1908 and 1912, they never accepted the idea of winding up the underground party. In the immediate pre-war period, the Bolsheviks' *Pravda* attracted much more support than the Menshevik organ,

[38] H. Hogan, 'The Reorganization of Work Processes in the St Petersburg Metal-Working Industry, 1901–1914', *Russian Review* 42 (1983), pp. 163–90.
[39] H. Hogan, 'Labor and Management in Conflict: The St Petersburg Metal-Working Industry, 1900–1914', (Ph.D. Dissertation, University of Michigan, 1981), pp. 509ff.
[40] D. Mandel, *The Petrograd Workers and the Fall of the Old Regime*; *The Petrograd Workers and Soviet Seizure of Power* (2 vols, London, 1983–4) I, p. 16.

Luch. In the largest union, that of the St Petersburg metal workers, the Menshevik leadership of the early years was swept from office in 1913. And among the leadership cadres of almost every industry there was a clear tendency to go beyond the Menshevik call for a degree of co-operation with the liberals, to the clearer cut, class-distinctive slogans of the Bolsheviks.[41]

In the Soviet view, as we have seen, it was neither their living standards, nor the prominence of peasant workers among them which distinguished the Russian proletariat from those of the West. What made them the 'vanguard of the world revolutionary movement' was the 'party of a new type'. It was the presence of a disciplined, united and ideologically-sound Marxist party to lead the working class towards revolution and away from trade-union reformism which, ultimately, set it apart. The picture that emerges from the work of revisionists, however, casts grave doubt on this. They do not deny that Social Democrats helped to implant worker-consciousness of such international emblems of solidarity as May Day and assisted in the development of working-class organizations. Nor do they deny the growing popularity of Bolshevik rather than Menshevik slogans and strategy in the pre-war years. Where they differ is in their assessment of the nature, extent and source of Bolshevik influence. The limited resources of the party, its extremely tenuous lines of communication, the repeated depredations of the Okhrana – all severely restricted the role the party could play.[42] The fledgeling organizations – unions, social insurance councils, and workers' clubs – in which their influence was felt were much too small to play a dominant role in the great strike wave of 1912–14. As a fully-independent organization, the party only became established in 1912. Only then did party members begin to identify with one or other wing – and it was a minority of non-party workers who could differentiate at all between the Bolsheviks and the Mensheviks. For those who could do so, to subscribe to the militant slogans of *Pravda* was not the same as to accept the party line on every issue, still less that of Lenin. Even while moving to the Left, trade-union activists remained hostile to Lenin's fierce factionalism.[43] Above all, worker radicalism was not the product of furious *démarches* by Bolshevik leaders against trade unionism, liquidationism and reformism. It was the product of the experience of workers themselves. Bolshevik maximalism spoke to their needs, expressed their frustration. Bolshevik influence before the war was less a cause than a consequence of the radicalism of the Russian working class.

The unique militancy of Russia's working class, then, cannot be

[41] Bonnell, *Roots of Rebellion*, pp. 390–417.
[42] R. C. Elwood, *Russian Social Democracy in the Underground. A Study of the RSDLP in the Ukraine, 1907–1914* (Assen, 1974), pp. 237–40.
[43] G. Swain, *Russian Social Democracy and the Legal Labour Movement* (London, 1983), pp. 159–84.

adequately explained by reference to the deprivation among workers, to the prominence among them of rural migrants, or to the leadership provided by the Bolshevik party. The key factor lies elsewhere: it lies in the political environment of tsarist Russia. The policies and attitudes of the autocracy virtually ruled out the emergence of a moderate, reformist labour movement. Although in 1905–6 the government had in principle conceded the right to form trade unions and to strike (for defensive purposes only), it subsequently put a host of obstacles in the way of effective collective bargaining. Nationwide union organization remained forbidden, and unions were repeatedly closed down on technical grounds. Union activists were identified by employers and police alike as subversive and risked blacklisting and arrest. Even the most significant unions could recruit no more than a small fraction of the workers in their industry. Employers refused to recognize their right to negotiate and called freely upon the State for armed support against worker protest, as in the case of the Lena goldfields strike in 1912. As a result, despite the potentially strong bargaining hand which the pre-war boom gave to skilled labour, workers sustained an almost unbroken record of failure in strike action. Faith in collective bargaining could not take root. At every turn workers found themselves coming up against the State. It required no elaborate analysis to draw the lesson: economic grievances could only be redressed by achieving political change. The autocracy provided no space for the expression of working-class interests through reformist or apolitical organization.[44]

Nor could labour interests be effectively pursued through the ballot box. The Duma's powers, severely restricted from the start, had been curtailed further in 1907. Moreover, working-class political parties remained illegal to the end, and in the elections to the Fourth Duma in 1912, workers were represented by a mere 13 deputies out of a total of 415. There were signs that the Social Democratic deputies were displacing expatriate revolutionaries as the centre of the socialist movement, and tentative connections were established between Menshevik deputies and those of the liberals. But these delicate flowers of parliamentary politics could not blossom in the climate of autocracy. Just as the regime's handling of industrial relations precluded the emergence of a moderate trade-union movement, so its political stance precluded the emergence of a reformist party with a stake in the status quo comparable to the German Socialist party.

To stress the importance of the repressive political environment is not to imply that it is the 'natural' destiny of labour movements to become moderate and accept the basic ground rules of capitalism. That development was anything but smooth in the West. In the

[44] Bonnell, *Roots of Rebellion*, pp. 450–2; R. B. McKean, 'Government, Employers and the Labour Movement in St Petersburg on the Eve of the First World War', *Sbornik* 12 (1986), pp. 78–86.

immediate pre-war period Britain, Germany and to a lesser extent France witnessed a dramatic upsurge of labour militancy. The moderate socialist and trade-union leadership which had established itself since the late nineteenth century came under severe pressure from below. Skilled workers, subject to the same 'de-skilling' threat that their Russian counterparts were just beginning to experience, joined with previously unorganized workers in large factories to challenge the caution of the old artisan-dominated labour movement. Moreover, the sequel to the war was not the ready integration of the western working class into parliamentary democracy but revolutionary upheaval in much of central Europe and the emergence of mass Communist parties to rival the socialists in most developed countries on the continent. That this radicalism was contained may have had more to do with the strength of the State in the West, together with the size, cohesion and resilience of anti-socialist groups among the middle classes and peasantry, than with any natural tendency for the working class to become 'integrated' and its aspirations attenuated.[45]

No more than in the West, therefore, could the emergence of effective trade unions and moderate political representation for workers have been expected to reconcile the most radical sections of the working class to capitalism. But such institutions could well have exercised a restraining influence on some groups of workers. They would have provided the basis for greater parliamentary co-operation between labour representatives and liberal politicians, and a framework in which the appeal to nationalism and the efforts of Church, school and middle-class reformers might have had more effect in moderating working-class attitudes. They might have precipitated a split between moderate and radical wings of the labour movement comparable to that which proved so critical to the stabilization of the West in the aftermath of the First World War. The tsarist political system was the critical factor distinguishing the experience of the Russian working class from that of its western counterparts. The prospects of the working class embarking upon a reformist path in the pre-war years therefore depended upon the prospects for a liberalization of the political system.

The middle classes

According to the liberal interpretation, as we have seen, such liberalization was underway. The economic growth of the pre-war years was generating an increase in the strength of the middle classes whose concern was to dismantle the restrictions of the old regime. Revisionist analysis has confirmed the economic and social development of the middle classes in the period. But it has also underlined the absence of any equivalent increase in their political weight.

[45] Geary, *European Labour Protest*, pp. 107–26.

The work of revisionist economic historians credits the tsarist economy in the years before the war with impressive growth. Recent estimates place Russia among the more rapidly growing economies of the early twentieth century.[46] Moreover, in most respects the pattern of growth was not far out of line with that of early industrialization in western industrialized countries. Foreign investment continued to play a vital role in industry. Foreign capital accounted for half the new capital in industry between 1909 and 1913, and on the eve of the war 47 per cent of the joint-stock capital in Russian industry was foreign owned.[47] Government expenditure, concentrated now on armaments rather than railways as in the late nineteenth century, also remained a major stimulant. But domestic capital investment grew markedly and the banking and credit system became increasingly sophisticated. Moreover, under the shadow of the great metallurgical and textile factories, small-scale enterprise and handicraft production grew at a pace comparable to that of heavy industry.[48] The domestic market, wholesale trade and retail trade developed rapidly.

Russia's middle classes expanded in line with this economic development. Not only did the number of wealthy native industrialists, merchants, bankers and insurance dealers swell, but so too did the ranks of humble businessmen, small-scale manufacturers, self-employed artisans, petty traders and shopkeepers. There was a rapid rise in the number of white-collar workers, clerks and technical specialists employed in commerce, industry and the service sector, as well as in the number engaged in the free professions – lawyers, doctors, journalists, teachers.

Equally, the period saw swift development in the range and size of organizations, associations and congresses representing industrialists, merchants, engineers and professionals of various kinds.[49] Culturally, too, conditions in the cities were becoming more propitious for the independence, individualism and involvement in public affairs of which liberals dreamed. The government, which had long spent a disproportionate amount on higher and secondary as opposed to primary education, began to implement a programme to establish universal primary education.[50] Popular literature appealing to the semi-educated proliferated, reflecting the growth of a reading public

---

[46] Gregory, *Russian National Income*, pp. 192–4, *passim*; Gatrell, *Tsarist Economy*, pp. 231–2, chaps 5, 6.

[47] J. P. McKay, *Pioneers for Profit. Foreign Entrepreneurship and Russian Industrialization 1885–1913* (Chicago, 1970), p. 28.

[48] O. Crisp, *Studies in the Russian Economy before 1914* (London, 1976), pp. 34–52.

[49] For discussion of the legal congresses which took place in the period, see Swain, *Legal Labour Movement*, chaps 1, 3, 4.

[50] J. Brooks, *When Russia Learned to Read. Literacy and Popular Literature, 1861–1917* (Princeton, N.J., 1985), pp. 35–46; J. C. McClelland, *Autocrats and Academics. Education, Culture and Society in Tsarist Russia* (Chicago, 1979), pp. 49–55.

not unlike that of the contemporary West.[51] Even before 1905, a solidly-based mass press had come into being, and in the last decade of the Empire there was an explosion in the publication of newspapers, while the number of books appearing more than trebled in the first decade and a half of the century. Moreover, after 1905 the press was increasingly adept at escaping censorship, and it became more assertive.[52] The unprecedented freedom of expression facilitated a 'semi-decadent' cultural revival which saw the flowering of avant-garde experiment in art, music, theatre and literature. The increase in the size, wealth, sophistication and security of the educated public was reflected in a more diversified and self-confident public life.

It would be a mistake to assume that the various strata of middle-class 'society' would naturally press for liberal reform. After all, socialist thought had exercised a powerful attraction before 1905, and comparison with Imperial Germany underlines the potential appeal of conservative and anti-liberal ideas among major industrialists and large sections of the lower middle class.[53] Yet after 1905 the predomi-nant mood undoubtedly was liberal in spirit. On the one hand, while socialist sympathies remained strong among university students, graduates were now readily absorbed into the economy and the proportion engaging in radical politics declined sharply. The most famous symbol of the tendency for the educated élite to move from radicalism towards liberalism was the publication of *Vekhi*, a thor-oughgoing rejection of the revolutionary heritage by leading members of the intelligentsia.[54] On the other, different strata among the middle classes found much to object to in the status quo. Industrialists were exasperated by the obstacles to creating joint-stock companies, the morass of red tape, bureaucratic sloth and corruption.[55] In those few cities (Moscow is the most striking case) where the business and social élites entertained ambitious plans for social reform, expansion of municipal services and widening of the local government franchise, they found their efforts resisted by the tsarist State.[56] Among the professional middle classes, the lack of guaranteed civil rights – underlined by repeated interference with university autonomy, the inconveniences of residual censorship, the manifestly inequitable franchise for zemstvos and urban dumas alike – bred criticism and

[51] Brooks, *When Russia Learned to Read*, pp. 61, 112.
[52] C. Ferenzi, 'Freedom of the Press under the Old Regime, 1905–1914', in Crisp and Edmondson, *Civil Rights*, pp. 191–214.
[53] D. Blackburn and G. Eley, *The Peculiarities of German History: Bourgeois Society and Politics in Nineteenth-Century Germany* (Oxford, 1985), pp. 75–90.
[54] C. Read, *Religion, Revolution and the Russian Intelligentsia 1900–1912* (London, 1979), pp. 97–140.
[55] R. A. Roosa, 'Russian Industrialists and "State Socialism", 1906–17', *Soviet Studies* 23 (1972), pp. 395–417.
[56] See R. W. Thurston, *Liberal City, Conservative State: Moscow and Russia's Urban Crisis, 1906–1914* (Oxford, 1987).

discontent. The 'third element' were frustrated by the restrictions on zemstvo initiative imposed by both government and by gentry deputies.[57] Among the lower middle class, the feebleness of efforts by municipal councils to improve services for all but the most privileged quarters was a constant irritant. In each of the four elections to the Duma, the bulk of the non-working-class vote in the major cities voted for liberal parties.[58] Pre-war Russia was possessed of a middle class deeply critical of autocracy.

The growth of the potential constituency for liberalism, then, is undeniable. Yet the prospects of this constituency making a major political impact and extracting liberal reforms from the regime appear poor. Indeed, paradoxical as it may seem, revisionist analysis suggests that the leverage of the liberal parties was actually declining in the years following 1906.

That year had appeared full of promise. The creation of the Duma, for all the limitations on its powers, had planted the notion of parliamentary government at the centre of political life, provided a forum for the assertion and propagation of the liberal cause, and elevated liberal leaders to a position of national prominence. The Kadets had won the largest block of deputies to the First Duma; they had enjoyed the spectacle of leading figures in the government sounding them out on the terms on which they would enter the cabinet; power seemed almost within their grasp. Yet the moment passed. The Tsar wavered briefly and then, urged by Stolypin and others to stand firm, he rejected any step which might lead to parliamentary government and dissolved the First Duma.[59]

Thereafter, the government's refusal to heed criticism in the press and in the Duma became increasingly intransigent. Whereas in the immediate aftermath of the Manifesto, the landed nobility and conservative interests generally had been disorientated and ill-organized, during 1906 their influence over the government was rapidly consolidated. Alarmed by the scale of peasant unrest unleashed during 1905, and appalled at the composition and radicalism of the First Duma, the landed nobility moved to assert their interests. Kadet sympathizers were swept from office in the zemstvo elections of 1906, and even the more moderate Octobrist party, dedicated to cautious co-operation with the government on the basis of the Fundamental Laws, found growing difficulty in resisting the rightward shift of rank-and-file

[57] See J. Brooks, 'The zemstvo and the education of the people'; S. C. Ramer, 'The zemstvo and public health'; N. M. Frieden, 'The politics of zemstvo medicine', in T. Emmons and W. S. Vucinich, eds, *The Zemstvo in Russia* (Cambridge, 1982), pp. 243–78; 279–314; 315–42.
[58] T. Emmons, *The Formation of Political Parties and the First National Elections in Russia* (Cambridge, Mass., 1983), pp. 277–9, 365–71.
[59] Manning, *Crisis of the Old Order*, pp. 205–59. For a particularly lively Soviet reconstruction of these negotiations see V. I. Startsev, *Russkaia burzhuaziia i samoderzhavie v 1905–1917 gg.* (Leningrad, 1977), pp. 8–130.

noblemen.[60] The formation in 1906 of the United Nobility created a powerful pressure group of major landowners which included strategically-placed members of government and legislature and could rely upon direct access to the Tsar himself.[61] The landed nobility showed no inclination to build bridges with urban property-owners, let alone workers and peasants. Liberal attempts to find a middle way between radical demands for outright confiscation of noble land and conservative rejection of land reform failed to save the Second Duma. The franchise reform of June 1907 ensured a preponderance of landowners in the Third and Fourth Dumas. And throughout they dominated the State Council, the upper house endowed with effective veto powers over Duma proposals.

Just how formidable a barrier these noble-dominated strongholds presented to evolution in a liberal-constitutionalist direction was fully revealed during the premiership of Stolypin. Stolypin was no liberal. During his period in office restrictions on working-class organization were sharply tightened. The reforms which he proposed – including measures to increase religious toleration, reduce legal disabilities of Jews, extend primary education, discipline local officials, strengthen respect for the law among rulers as well as ruled, extend peasant representation in the zemstvos and establish a new lower-level tier of zemstvos elected on an all-class franchise – touched only the outer fringes of noble privilege and executive power. Yet his proposals were denounced in the provinces, delayed in the Duma and rejected outright in the State Council. Even this moderate package, advanced by the man appointed by the Tsar to head the government, was blocked by the entrenched power of the Right.[62] The Octobrist party, whose leaders attempted to provide him with a base of support within the Duma, found themselves coming under increasing criticism, and the party fell apart. Even before his death in 1911 Stolypin's position had become untenable, and thereafter the government moved further to the Right, and ministers treated the Duma with ever greater contempt.

In the face of this intransigence, the liberals proved helpless. Revisionist work has highlighted two main factors to explain this helplessness. In the first place, it has confirmed the Soviet charge that the liberals were both unable and unwilling to appeal for mass protest to break the government's resolution. Their influence over the masses

[60] See R. T. Manning, 'Zemstvo and Revolution: The Onset of the Gentry Reaction, 1905–1907' and MacNaughton and Manning, 'Political Trends in the Zemstvos' in Haimson, *Rural Russia*, pp. 43–52, 194–9.

[61] G. A. Hosking and R. T. Manning, 'What Was the United Nobility?', in Haimson, *Rural Russia*, pp. 142–83.

[62] G. A. Hosking, *The Russian Constitutional Experiment: Government and Duma, 1907–1914* (Cambridge, 1973), pp. 244–6; on the influence of the Orthodox Church see P. Waldron, 'Religious Toleration in Late Imperial Russia' in Crisp and Edmondson, *Civil Rights*, pp. 103–19.

had been tenuous even at the height of their prestige in 1905. The electoral success of the Kadets in the First Duma owed little to their largely unsuccessful attempts to attract the support of peasants and workers. It owed more to the boycott of the elections by the socialist parties and to the Kadets' skilful use of the indirect electoral system which enabled them to win a disproportionate number of seats.[63] In the Second Duma, although their urban vote held up, they fared much less well at the hands of more politically-conscious peasants, they failed dismally to attract working-class support, and their representation fell by half. The early dismissal of the Second Duma, the drastic curtailment of the franchise, and the naked exposure of the Duma's limitations made matters even worse. Having no foothold on power, they could offer no inducements to moderate reformism; they were unable to hold out the prospect of even limited concessions to peasants and workers. In these conditions, to encourage mass protest over which they would have no control appeared sheer lunacy. The intensity of the rebellion by workers and peasants from 1905 to 1907, and the radicalism of the proposals from left-wing representatives in the first two Dumas, presented the liberals with an alarming spectre: a violent upheaval which would sweep away not merely tsar and nobility but the entire social order and all hope of peaceful liberal reform.

From as early as 1906, therefore, they showed greater concern to restrain than to encourage mass protest against the high-handed actions of the autocracy. Whereas in 1905 the emergent Kadets had endorsed political strikes and been slow to condemn revolutionary violence and peasant protest, by the following year their attitude had changed dramatically. Convinced in the summer of 1906 that the government's contemptuous dismissal of the First Duma might ignite renewed revolutionary action, they did their best in the Vyborg Manifesto to channel any such protest into passive resistance.[64] Despite their indignation at the equally abrupt dismissal of the Second Duma, and at Stolypin's *coup d'état* in June 1907, they resolved to offer principled yet constructive opposition in the Third and Fourth Dumas. Nor does the evidence of a renewed upsurge of potentially revolutionary protest from below in the immediate pre-war years suggest that this source of their inhibition would fade with time.

Whereas for Soviet historians this fear of revolution is in itself a sufficient explanation for liberal weakness, revisionist work has stressed, in addition, the deep divisions that beset Russia's middle classes. They failed to close ranks and mobilize effectively in defence of their common interests. The cautious line of the Kadet leadership was bitterly criticized by more radical spirits, and by 1914 the party was

---

[63] Emmons, *Political Parties*, pp. 297ff.
[64] W. G. Rosenberg, 'Kadets and the Politics of Ambivalence', in C. E. Timberlake, ed., *Essays on Russian Liberalism* (Columbia, Miss., 1972), pp. 144–8.

perilously close to schism. The leaders of the new Progressive party, founded in 1912 and dedicated to bridging the gap between the professional middle classes and businessmen, proved much more adventurous and vigorous than the Kadets in exploring – without success – the possibility of co-operation with parties to the Left. Moreover, both parties found it impossible to sustain widespread interest in political organization. The Progressives barely existed outside the Duma itself, while the Kadets, the major liberal party, failed to make any significant inroads into the business community. Kadet party membership, estimated at 100,000 in 1906, dwindled drastically, few of those who remained paid their dues, and outside a handful of major cities, local branches of the party virtually disappeared except in the immediate run-up to elections.[65] The government's refusal to broaden the franchise for municipal councils – in most cities less than 1 per cent of the population had the vote – deprived liberals of an alternative forum for mass political activity.[66] No way was found to rally or organize the urban lower middle classes.

In part this failure of the middle classes to present a unified political front arose from the very intransigence of the regime. Firmly distanced from the levers of power, the liberal parties were unable to carry conviction among their potential constituents. But the failure reflected, too, the host of divisions – economic, regional, ethnic and cultural – that fractured the middle classes. Heavy industry was largely concentrated in a handful of favoured regions, dominated by a small number of major and in part foreign-owned firms, and closely dependent upon the government for subsidies and contracts. Light industry, on the other hand, was more widely dispersed geographically and in terms of ownership, foreign capital played little part, and even the largest firms were relatively independent of government favour. The distinction was epitomized by the contrast between St Petersburg and Moscow. It created a wide divergence of attitude over a range of policy issues, generated acute mutual suspicion, and prevented either capital from providing a core around which the nation's business community could coalesce.[67] As each major region developed its own distinctive manufacturing interests and trading patterns, marked differences arose over tariff, labour and transport policy. Further divisions arose from the growing tension between Great Russian merchants concentrated in the centre of the Empire and those from ethnic minorities – Poles, Jews, Germans, Armenians, Greeks and Tartars – on the periphery.

Moreover, although sophisticated and assertive entrepreneurial

[65] Emmons, *Political Parties*, pp. 375–6.
[66] For the politics of urban local government, see the essays in Hamm, *The City*.
[67] Even within St Petersburg, industrialists proved unable to unite behind a common policy in reacting to labour unrest in the immediate pre-war period. See McKean, 'Government, Employers and the Labour Movement', pp. 65–78.

groups emerged in all the major industrial areas, their dynamism stood out in sharp contrast to the conservatism and traditionalism prevalent among petty merchants and manufacturers. The cautious, inward-looking merchant ethos, encouraged by the legal distinctions of the merchant estate, was reinforced in the late nineteenth century by the influx of culturally conservative peasants. At the same time, even the most highly-educated 'modern' entrepreneurs were acutely resentful of what they regarded as the disdain for business prevalent among the professional intelligentsia and 'enlightened public opinion'. In any case, few of them could share the enthusiasm of liberal politicians for such reforms as the establishment of free trade unions. For the most part, leading industrialists preferred to press their case through narrow professional associations while humbler businessmen remained resistant to appeals to engage more openly in public life.[68]

Such fissures were by no means peculiar to the middle classes of the Russian Empire: analogous divisions can be found throughout Europe. But nowhere were they more pronounced, and rather than fading as the economy developed they appear to have been becoming deeper in the immediate pre-war years.[69] Their effect was to compound the difficulty the liberal leadership had in bringing pressure for reform to bear upon the regime.

At the time and ever since, the liberal leadership was criticized for ineptitude, naïvety and lack of courage. The complaints of radical Kadets that Miliukov and his colleagues were going too far towards compromise with the regime were matched by the regret of right-wing Kadets such as Maklakov and Struve at the party's failure to grasp the offers made by Witte and Stolypin of representation in the cabinet. Certainly the chosen strategy of Miliukov and his colleagues failed. Given the miserable legislative record of the Duma and its manifest inability to impose its will on the government, the policy of clinging to the Duma in the hope that popular respect for the Russian parliament would grow proved vain. Yet in the light of revisionist work, the liberal predicament appears insoluble. The intransigence of the Right, the radicalism of peasants and workers, and the profound divisions within their own potential constituency suggests that liberal leaders were stymied. Move to the Right, accept Witte's or Stolypin's terms for a few posts in the cabinet, and they risked becoming hostages in a regime over which they would exercise no control. Move to the Left, encourage mass protest, and they risked being marginalized in a revolutionary confrontation.

The role of Nicholas II
Even if the structural, social roots of liberal weakness are conceded,

---

[68] The fissures within the business classes are explored in detail in A. J. Rieber, *Merchants and Entrepreneurs in Imperial Russia* (Chapel Hill, N.C., 1982).
[69] *op. cit.*, pp. 415–26.

the traditional liberal interpretation can take refuge in its emphasis on the crucial role played by the key political figure, the Tsar. Nicholas II, so the argument runs, was personally responsible for failing to exercise either of two options open to the regime. A more dynamic and far-sighted monarch than Nicholas could have taken the initiative himself, drawn upon generations of loyalty to God's annointed, forced through reforms to avert revolution, and opened the way to liberal evolution. Alternatively, a more resolute and impressive personality on the throne could have upheld the status quo. But for his weakness and vacillation, peasant unrest and working-class militancy could have been kept in check by efficient and unwavering repression.

In the light of revisionist work it is difficult to treat Nicholas's resistance to liberal reform as a matter of chance or historical accident. In the first place, the fact that his value system was centred upon the principle of autocracy was hardly fortuitous. Every word from his father, every lesson from his tutor, Pobedonostsev, every symbol he saw, every ceremony he performed was designed to inculcate in the young Tsar a sense of his God-given duty to uphold his supreme office. In the second, the constitutional reforms demanded – be it cabinet responsibility to the Duma, legislative control of the budget, or even effective prime-ministerial control of a unified cabinet – threatened his autocratic power. And major social reforms – the establishment of free trade unions or the redistribution of noble land – would have had the same effect. Zubatov's experiments before 1905 had already exposed the impossibility of creating workers' organizations without affecting the political order. Trade unions implied a host of civil rights, beginning with freedom of association, which were incompatible with autocracy.[70] Equally, to sanction an attack upon noble landownership would have been to alienate and undermine the prime basis of support for autocracy. Above all, whoever occupied the throne would have been subject to the powerful pressure that Nicholas experienced from the United Nobility, the Orthodox Church and reactionary leaders of the Right. Nicholas's personal judgement may well have been crucial in blocking negotiations with the Kadets in the fluid situation that prevailed in the first half of 1906. But as conservative influence became mobilized and entrenched, the pressure upon him to resist reform mounted rapidly. If liberal Russia's hopes depended on an autocrat determined to phase out autocracy in the teeth of conservative opposition, those hopes were bleak indeed.

Little more persuasive is the argument that under another tsar the regime could have withstood revolutionary pressure indefinitely. Certainly, Nicholas's personal deficiencies were in part responsible for the speed with which the regime's authority was undermined. In the

---

[70] This is brought out in J. Schneiderman, *Sergei Zubatov and Revolutionary Marxism. The Struggle for the Working Class in Tsarist Russia* (Ithaca, 1970), pp. 367, although the treatment of working-class attitudes predates revisionist work.

pre-war years, his lack of charisma and poor judgement of men contributed significantly to tension within the establishment. The royal couple were unpopular at court, inspired little personal loyalty even among those whose respect for the throne was greatest, and their mounting preoccupation with the haemophiliac Tsarevich – and devotion to Rasputin – cut them off from all but a minute family circle.[71] Nicholas's isolation and willingness, after Stolypin's death, to appoint a series of inadequate ministers clearly helped to destabilize the regime.

Yet revisionist work underlines the enormous difficulties that would have confronted even the most gifted of tsars in shoring up a rigidly conservative regime. It was the attempt to do so which had provoked the upheaval of 1905–6. Thereafter, the Duma could not be abolished altogether – not least for fear of undermining the confidence of Russia's foreign creditors – yet even the drastic franchise reform of 1907 failed to produce a stable far-Right majority. Moreover, it was precisely his determination to uphold the status quo which had led the Tsar to frustrate Stolypin, undermine the authority of the premiership and dismantle collective cabinet responsibility. The result was lack of co-ordination between different departments. The last pre-war years saw counter-productive oscillations over such questions as the legal rights to be granted to trade unions, repeated clashes between the Ministry of Finance and that of the Interior, sharp conflict between civilian and military leaders, massive ill-judged increases in naval expenditure at the expense of the army, and the disruption of an ever more complex administrative structure.[72]

More fundamentally, the view that pressure for change could have been indefinitely held in check by resolute repression overrates the resources available to unrepentant autocracy. The upheaval of 1905 and repression which followed had dealt a body-blow to the popular, paternal image of the Tsar. The ideological and cultural support of the Orthodox Church, whose moral authority was also in steep decline, was a wasting asset. The landed nobility provided tsarism with a perilously narrow social base. By 1914 there were no more than 20,000 noble landowners fully enfranchised to vote in the landowners' curias of the Duma and the zemstvos, as well as in the provincial assemblies of the nobility. They had increasing difficulty in providing even tolerably competent candidates for the array of provincial posts reserved for them.[73]

---

[71] The best recent treatment is A. de Jonge, *The Life and Times of Grigorii Rasputin* (London, 1982).

[72] McKean, 'Government, Employers and Labour Movement', pp. 78–86; W. C. Fuller, *Civil–Military Conflict in Imperial Russia, 1881–1914* (Princeton, N.J., 1986); D. Geyer, *Russian Imperialism: The Interactions of Domestic and Foreign Policy, 1860–1914* (Leamington Spa, 1987), pp. 277ff.

[73] Manning, *Crisis of the Old Order*, pp. 366–7.

Above all, the coercive force at the disposal of the Tsar fell far short of its imposing image. The police force inherited by Nicholas was small, corrupt and ill-trained.[74] It had proved hopelessly inadequate during the revolution of 1905–6. Among the Cossacks, traditionally the epitome of loyalty to the throne, there was evidence that accumulating financial grievances and resentment over inadequate land grants were fuelling disenchantment with the regime.[75] Worse still, the reliability of the main body of the army as an instrument of social control, as the ultimate bastion of autocracy, was being undermined.

Military reforms initiated in the 1870s, which reduced the standing army, introduced universal conscription, and built a large reserve of trained men on the western model, had made it more and more difficult to insulate soldiers from civilian life and inculcate unquestioning obedience. The shorter the period of service – cut to three years before the war – the more closely opinion in the army was affected by the stresses of civilian society.[76] Moreover, both the War Ministry and a growing number of officers were increasingly conscious and resentful of the damage to morale and efficiency caused by use of the army for internal 'policing' duties. As the officer corps became more professionalized, it became more determined that the army should not be used again to quell civilian protest as in 1905–6.[77] Most ominous of all were the implications of the mutinies of 1905 and 1906. Revisionist research has underlined the major scale of those mutinies, and the abruptness with which soldiers refused to implement orders to crush disturbances and began instead to press their own grievances. The peasant rank and file had demonstrated how deeply they were alienated from their masters and how readily they would seize upon civil disorder and weakening of the regime's authority to rebel against the serf-like conditions of service.[78] The writing was on the wall even before the war broke out. Tsarism was 'a deadlocked political system, drifting helplessly toward destruction.'[79]

War and revolution

In any case, revisionist analysis suggests that liberal treatment of the war as a 'bolt from the blue', unconnected to Russia's domestic condition and distorting its natural development, is artificial. True, recent work on the general origins of the conflict has lent little support

[74] N. Weissman, 'Regular Police in Tsarist Russia, 1900–1914', *Russian Review* 44 (1985), pp. 45–68.
[75] R. McNeal, *Tsar and Cossack, 1855–1914* (New York, 1987), pp. 154–222.
[76] A. K. Wildman, *The End of the Russian Imperial Army* (2 vols, Princeton, N.J., 1980, 1987) I, chaps. 1, 2.
[77] Fuller, *Civil–Military Conflict*, pp. 259–62.
[78] See J. Bushnell, *Mutiny amid Repression. Russian Soldiers in the Revolution of 1905–1906* (Bloomington, Ind., 1985), chaps. 1, 4, 7.
[79] Manning, *Crisis of the Old Order*, p. 356.

to the Soviet view that it was the inevitable product of rivalry between Europe's capitalist powers in the age of imperialism. The economic causes of the war constituted but one dimension of a process which can only be grasped by a multi-causal approach.[80] But attention has been drawn to the close interaction between the socio-political structure of the major protagonists and the foreign policies they pursued. In the case of Russia, revisionist research has underlined the manner in which the specific nature of the tsarist regime conditioned the decision to take on the Central Powers.

In 1914 the Russian government had good cause to avoid war. Major naval, military and railway construction programmes scheduled to come to fruition in 1917–18 argued strongly for delay. Only a decade earlier the war with Japan had proved the trigger for a revolutionary storm which the regime had barely survived. Moreover, in 1914 the Empire had no urgent territorial claims and there was no direct threat to her territorial integrity. The case for reaching a *modus vivendi* with Germany was indeed cogently argued by a faction within the Foreign Ministry. 'The Slav idea, indirect Austrian control over Serbia or even German domination of the Straits do not, in the light of cold reason,' concludes a recent review of Russia's options, 'seem to have justified the appalling risks Russia faced in entering a European war.'[81] Russia's response to the crisis of 1914 can only be understood in terms of the nature of the tsarist regime and of the pressures upon it.

For one thing, the Tsar's personal prerogative in foreign affairs handicapped the conduct of Russian diplomacy. It encouraged the tendency for uncoordinated initiatives to be taken at different levels of the diplomatic hierarchy and contradictory signals to be sent out to foreign powers. It obstructed coherent cabinet consideration of the issues, and full consultation between civilian and military leaders. It was characteristic that only after ordering partial mobilization, against Austria but not Germany, did the Tsar learn from the High Command that this was logistically unfeasible.

More fundamentally, the humiliation of the defeat by Japan in 1905, exacerbated from 1908 by a series of diplomatic reversals in the Balkans, built up a widespread sense of frustration over foreign affairs. In the Duma and in the press loyalists were loudest in their demands that Russian interests be vigorously defended, that the massive expenditure on armaments be put to good use. The government found itself derided for its failure to stand up for Serbia, assert Russian interests in the Straits – the focal point of nationalist aspiration – and face the confrontation between Slav and Teuton which was widely thought to be inevitable. Only a government commanding enormous

---

[80] For a succinct synthesis of recent work see J. Joll, *The Origins of the First World War* (London, 1984).
[81] D. C. B. Lieven, *Russia and the Origins of the First World War* (London, 1983), p. 101.

confidence and authority could have accepted the blow to its prestige entailed in acquiescing in the Austrian assault upon Serbia. Yet the cumulative effect of the revolution of 1905, mounting social tension and the clamour of public criticism had been precisely to undermine government confidence and authority.[82] In any case, the majority of senior officials, as well as the Tsar himself, had imbibed from childhood a sense of personal and national honour inextricably bound up with Russia's military might and international status. They were intensely sensitive to criticism for diplomatic and military weakness and could not contemplate accepting the role of 'second fiddle on the world stage.' A regime whose 'raison d'être, prestige and pride rested on its claim to defend Russia's standing in the world' was singularly ill-equipped to back down or even postpone a reckoning with the Central Powers.[83]

Conclusion

In the light of recent research, then, the traditional liberal view of the revolution as the fortuitous product of war is unacceptable. Before 1914, neither peasant land hunger nor working-class militancy were abating. Middle-class pressure for liberal reforms was ineffectual. At the same time the gradual erosion of the regime's social base and its repressive power pointed firmly towards a revolutionary upheaval likely to be fatal to tsarism and liberalism alike. And the confrontation with Germany and Austria-Hungary, which triggered the upheaval, cannot be treated as a purely extraneous catastrophe unrelated to Russia's social, economic and political development. On the other hand, revisionist analysis contradicts central features of the Soviet view of the revolution as the product of a 'law-governed' process. The structure of agriculture makes it difficult to treat the peasant drive for noble land as the harbinger of rural capitalism. The crucial ingredient behind the militancy of Russia's working class was the political environment rather than Bolshevik leadership. The political weakness of the liberals reflected not only their fear of the threat from below but also the profound divisions within the middle classes. And the war, rather than being the product of imperialism, arose from an infinitely complex interaction between European and indeed world developments. Yet its timing, duration, scale and outcome were to have a profound effect upon the form that the revolution took.

[82] Geyer, *Russian Imperialism*, pp. 293–317.
[83] Lieven, *Origins*, pp. 6, 83.

4 THE REVOLUTIONARY INTELLIGENTSIA

Nowhere are the issues at stake in the dispute between the three traditional schools of thought thrown into clearer relief than in their respective treatments of the revolutionary intelligentsia. While Soviet, liberal and libertarian accounts each attribute a role of enormous importance to the *intelligenty*, they differ profoundly over the significance of that role.

The Soviet view

The point of departure for Soviet historians is their belief that all political and ideological struggle is at root a manifestation of class struggle. Political movements and ideological divisions are to be understood in terms of the conflict between the major classes at a given stage of social development. The intelligentsia – which is defined as those engaged in 'intellectual labour' – do not themselves form a distinct class. They are a necessary product of every social formation based on the division of labour, and the advance of capitalism involves a major expansion in their numbers. Those who become involved in cultural and political activity serve, as it were, as the mouthpiece for the classes into which society is divided. 'The intelligentsia', in Lenin's much-quoted words, 'is called the intelligentsia because it most consciously, most decisively and most precisely expresses the development of the class interests and political groupings in society as a whole.'[1] It is in these terms that the ideas and activity of the revolutionary wing of the intelligentsia have to be understood. Just as reactionary and liberal politicians, journalists and thinkers gave voice to the interests of nobility and bourgeoisie respectively, so the revolutionary intelligentsia gave expression to the interests of the exploited masses.

During the period from the 1860s to the 1890s, the revolutionary intelligentsia represented the peasantry. There was nothing mysterious about the process by which a small but significant segment of the intelligentsia came to espouse the cause of a class to which they did not belong. It directly reflected Russia's social development. As capitalism advanced, the need for qualified personnel inevitably grew. From the middle of the century, there was a marked change in the

[1] Lenin, 'The Tasks of Revolutionary Youth', 1903, *Polnoe sobranie sochinenii* (55 vols, Moscow, 1958–65) VII, p. 343.

social composition of the student body. Earlier it had been drawn overwhelmingly from the privileged strata, the sons of the landed nobility and higher ranks of the civil service, and only a few outstanding figures had emerged as pioneers in the 'gentry stage' of the revolutionary movement. But now it included a growing number of *raznochintsy*, men of different ranks, the children of humbler officials, the clergy, the lower urban estates. Their closer ties with the masses, their unprivileged background and often grinding poverty, made them more acutely conscious of the oppressive conditions of Imperial Russia. Not only did their desire for greater freedom at university lead them into conflict with the authorities, but at the same time they responded to issues of much wider social significance raised by the 'revolutionary situation' of 1859–61, the massacre of peasants protesting against the terms of Emancipation, the repression of radical journalists such as Chernyshevsky. The most progressive, self-sacrificing and heroic among them were receptive to the advanced ideas drawn from the West or propagated by Herzen and other leading democrats. The institutions of higher education became a sounding board for class conflict, and decade by decade a minority became committed to the cause of the masses. They rightly identified the link between the reactionary, repressive nature of the regime and the plight of the peasantry. Moved by a profound commitment to social justice, they did their utmost to understand the sources of exploitation and to discover the means, and build the organization necessary to free the peasants.

The 'populist' ideology they developed was, in the Soviet view, utopian. It rested on the myth that the peasantry were instinctively socialist and that it was possible for Russia to bypass capitalism, moving directly from semi-feudalism to socialism based on the peasant commune. In reality, the peasantry had no interest in socialism. Their aspirations were petty bourgeois. They sought not the abolition of hired labour, private enterprise and the commodity market but the abolition of the many semi-feudal bonds which survived the Edict of 1861; and they sought the transfer of noble land into their own hands. Nevertheless, the 'socialist' intelligentsia expressed the interests of the non-socialist peasantry. The explanation for this apparent paradox is provided by the distinction between the *subjective* and the *objective* role of historical figures. The subjective role of the intelligentsia describes their self-perception, their hopes, their dreams, their motives. Their hatred of exploitation and their knowledge of western capitalism and the socialist movement it had brought into being led them to utopian socialist illusions. This reflects no discredit on them. Given the predominance of feudal relations in Russia it was impossible for the men of the 1860s and 70s to see that capitalism was already spreading and inevitably must do so. In fact though, as Lenin said, populism had not a grain of socialism in it. Indeed, had the populist programme been realized, the effect would not have been direct transition to socialism at all, but the more rapid development of capitalism. 'Without knowing it, the populists acted as the expression of the bourgeois-democratic aspirations of the peasantry.'[2] Yet this does not detract from their objective role, which is the impact made upon the developing class struggle. In this case, the significant element in the revolutionaries' programme was the demand for the distribution of noble land to the peasantry and the destruction of all feudal fetters. This expressed precisely the interests of the peasantry.

The strategy developed by the revolutionary populists reflected the same mixture of heroic struggle for the peasantry's cause and utopian illusions. The early 1860s saw the first of a whole series of underground organizations designed to spread populist propaganda and prepare for revolutionary action against the regime. Their efforts were marred by weaknesses of both theory and organization. They tended to exaggerate grossly the role which the intelligentsia could play regardless of socio-economic developments. For a long time they treated the question of political power as wholly subordinate to the social struggle. The movement 'to the people' in 1874, when they tried to live and work in the villages of Russia to spread the word and arouse revolution, was heroic but quixotic. Their efforts were swiftly dealt with by the police and in the late 1870s, unable to mobilize peasant revolt, they became increasingly conscious that class struggle could not be divorced from political struggle. The People's Will, their most effective organization, drew the conclusion that the supreme goal must be to shake the regime by assassinating the tsar. But having grasped the importance of the political sphere, they tended to pay inadequate attention to the need for a mass movement to bring about revolution. Nevertheless, for all their errors and illusions, the driving force of the movement was profoundly democratic and progressive. The great majority of revolutionary populists resolutely rejected the deception and unprincipled adventurism of a few untypical deviants like Nechaev.[3] They did all they could to encourage peasant resistance, to enlighten the masses and to expose the myth of the Tsar as a caring 'little father'. On the basis of their experience, they developed some of the essentials of an effective revolutionary organization, concentrating on firm discipline and full commitment. Despite their pitifully limited numbers they threw down an inspiring challenge to the might of the autocratic regime. They bequeathed an invaluable legacy of moral integrity, revolutionary thought and political organization on which their Bolshevik heirs were to draw.

[2] R. V. Filippov, *Iz istorii narodnicheskogo dvizheniia na pervom etape 'khozhdeniia v narod'. 1863–1874* (Petrozavodsk, 1967), p. 47.

[3] A. I. Volodin, Iu. F. Nariakin and E. G. Plimak, *Chernyshevskii ili Nechaev?: o podlinnoi i mnimoi revoliutsionnosti v osvoboditel'nom dvizhenii Rossii 50–60-kh XIX veka* (Moscow, 1976), chaps. 1, 7.

During the 1880s, some of the leading populist activists emigrated and began to deduce the lessons to be learnt from the populist failure. Their search for a new revolutionary perspective led them to Marxism and over the next decade Plekhanov, Axelrod and their 'Emancipation of Labour group' established in Switzerland a centre for the dissemination of Marxist ideas among Russian revolutionaries. At first their success was limited, but capitalism had by now taken an unmistakeable hold in industry and agriculture alike. In the cities a nascent proletariat was beginning to flex its muscles, forming short-lived illegal organizations of its own and staging its first major strikes. The further capitalism developed the more compelling the Marxist analysis became. It laid bare the dynamics of the transformation overcoming the Empire. Capitalist development was generating a factory proletariat bearing all the characteristics Marx had depicted. It was brutally exploited, profoundly alienated, capable of striking heavy blows against employers and government alike, and infinitely more receptive to socialist ideas than the peasantry had been.

In the early 1890s a growing proportion of revolutionaries were converted to Marxism. At first they devoted much of their energy to bringing the fruits of 'scientific socialism' to a limited number of hand-picked workers. By the mid nineties the most advanced Marxist circles ventured beyond 'propaganda' to mass agitation. The culmination of this breakthrough was the formation of the 'Union of Struggle for the Emancipation of the Working Class' (1895), under Lenin's leadership. The revolutionary Marxist ideology adopted by the intelligentsia began to merge with the working-class movement. The firm establishment of the Social Democratic party early in the new century completed the fusion. The consistently revolutionary wing of Social Democracy, the Bolsheviks, became the authentic vanguard of the proletariat. Following the schism at the Second Party Congress (1903), Lenin built his 'party of a new kind'.

The party was 'called to life by the whole course of the Russian and international workers' movement', confronted as the movement was by the enormous political, military, economic and ideological power at the disposal of the tsarist regime and the ruling classes in the age of imperialism.[4] But the contribution that the intelligentsia made to its development represented their supreme service to the revolution. For in the Soviet view, as we have seen, the construction of the party with its distinctive democratic-centralist structure was an essential condition for the victory of the socialist revolution. It made possible both Lenin's defeat of revisionism and the adventurism of hot-headed figures such as Bogdanov, and the dissemination among advanced workers of the scientific understanding of the laws of history dis-

[4] P. N. Pospelov *et al.*, eds, *Istoriia kommunisticheskoi partii sovetskogo soiuza* (Moscow, 1967), I, p. xi.

covered by Marx and developed by Lenin. The revolution of 1905 saw Social Democracy become a truly mass movement, and Bolshevik influence rose rapidly. The reaction which followed hit the Bolsheviks particularly hard, but a network of local party organizations survived, regrouped and exerted ever greater influence as working-class protest resumed in the years immediately before the war.[5]

With the establishment of the party, the distinction between workers and orthodox Marxist members of the intelligentsia was effectively erased. A very real distinction remained between the vanguard of the class (i.e. party members) on the one hand, and, on the other, rank-and-file workers who had not yet become conscious of their real interests or understood revolutionary Marxism. But this distinction had nothing whatever to do with the difference between intelligentsia and workers within the party. Guided as they were by scientific socialism and the objective interests of the proletariat, the social origin and educational background of party cadres became irrelevant.[6] And the genuine fusion of Marxism with the working-class movement was reflected in the changing social composition of the party.[7] From the turn of the century worker-revolutionaries began to outnumber those from the intelligentsia. They made up two-thirds of the membership during the period of rapid growth between 1905 and 1907, and during the reaction of 1907–10 workers came to the fore in local party organizations across the country.[8] Even among those best versed in Marxist theory, workers came to predominate as the party's 'underground university' turned out hundreds of 'worker-*intelligenty*'.

By no means all members of the revolutionary intelligentsia came over to – or, as Lenin put it, were 'taken by' – the proletariat. Many, unable or unwilling to see that by the 1890s the emergence of the proletariat had redefined the terms of the class struggle, failed to cut themselves adrift from their bourgeois and petty-bourgeois roots. As a result, despite their ostensible commitment to revolution, they played an ambivalent and ultimately counter-revolutionary role. Some continued to labour under the illusions of the populists. They rejected the main tenets of revolutionary Marxism, denied the central role of the proletariat, and dreamed of a peasant-based socialism. Even their claims to represent the interests of the peasantry as a whole became increasingly empty. Differentiation between petty rural capitalists and poor or landless rural labourers was drawing a minority of peasants to the side of the bourgeoisie, while the interests of the majority

[5] I. E. Gorelov, *Bol'sheviki v period reaktsii (1907–1910gg.)* (Moscow, 1975), pp. 80–1.

[6] S. A. Fediukin, *Partiia i intelligentsiia* (Moscow, 1982), pp. 20–1.

[7] For the most recent summary of information on the social base of the party, see N. A. Ivanova, *Struktura rabochego klassa Rossii 1910–1914* (Moscow, 1987), pp. 201–11.

[8] M. S. Volin, 'K voprosy ob izuchenii sostava bol'shevistskoi partii nakanune i v period revoliutsii', in *Revoliutsiia 1905–1907 godov v Rossii i ee vsemirno-istoricheskoe znachenie* (Moscow, 1976), pp. 175–8; Gorelov, *Bolsheviki v period reaktsii*, p. 44.

objectively coincided with those of the proletariat. True, all peasants still shared a common interest in the overthrow of the remaining traces of feudalism – including the tsarist regime itself – and the SR Party founded in 1901 came to express this common ground. But the SRs were riven by the divisions, indiscipline and illusions typical of their petty-bourgeois nature. They resorted to terror and adventurism, for which there was no justification now that a powerful Social Democratic movement had taken shape, and they failed to acknowledge the leadership that must be exercised by the proletariat over the peasantry and the democratic movement as a whole.

Other sections of the revolutionary intelligentsia proclaimed their loyalty to Marxism but tended in fact towards mere reformism. In the late 1890s the so-called 'Economists' encouraged the workers to settle for piecemeal improvement in their economic conditions, for mere trade unionism, rather than revolutionary struggle against capitalism. At the Second Congress of the RSDWP those who opposed Lenin – the Mensheviks – sought to dilute the revolutionary purity of the party and weaken its discipline. Their vision of the party pointed towards a loosely-organized entity open to the revisionism from which western Marxist parties were suffering. Moreover, in their anxiety to forge an alliance with the bourgeoisie and their blindness to the revolutionary potential of the peasantry, they were willing for the proletariat to accept a position of subordination to liberal bourgeois leadership. Following the revolution of 1905 some of them even recommended liquidating the revolutionary organization altogether. They served, in effect, as the agents of the bourgeoisie and petty bourgeoisie, seeking to soften the revolutionary commitment of the proletariat. Both the SRs and the Mensheviks attracted a measure of support among the more backward, less class-conscious workers. But as the full measure of SR and Menshevik subordination to the bourgeoisie was revealed, the overwhelming majority of workers recognized that the Bolsheviks were the true spokesmen of their interests.[9]

The liberal view

The traditional liberal interpretation casts the revolutionary intelligentsia in a role of even greater importance that does the Soviet version. 'No class in Russian history', to quote a leading liberal historian, 'has had a more momentous impact on the destinies of that nation or indeed of the modern world.'[10] But far from accepting that

[9] For a recent general treatment which broadly adheres to the orthodox Soviet version but has an air of freshness imported by *glasnost*, see V. Khoros, I. Pantin and Ye. Plimak, *The Russian Revolutionary Tradition* (Moscow, 1988).
[10] M. Malia, 'What is the Intelligentsia?', in R. Pipes, ed., *The Russian Intelligentsia* (New York, 1961), p. 4.

they gave expression to some all-important class struggle, liberal historians regard the ideas of the revolutionary intelligentsia as the product of their own psychological needs. Their revolutionary strategies and organizations reflected not their leadership of popular protest but a near-total isolation which led them to resort to conspiracy and manipulation. Their attitude towards the masses was condescending, high-handed and ultimately dictatorial. They established a tradition 'of terroristic conspiracy by dedicated and disciplined intellectuals who would seize power in the name of the masses.'[11] Throughout they were distinguished by their 'extremism, intolerance, maximalism, irreconcilability with the existing order, doctrinaire faith in theory, idealization of violence, dedication to revolution [and] indifference to the means used.'[12]

There are various ingredients in the liberal explanation for the emergence of the revolutionary intelligentsia. From the late eighteenth and early nineteenth centuries, the educated élite became exposed to a heady concoction of western romantic, Idealist, and socialist ideas. This fuelled dissatisfaction with the repressive structures of tsarism. The contrast between Russian reality and the ideal vistas opened out by western doctrines could not have been more stark. Most members of the élite accepted the contrast or worked for gradual reform. But a handful became captivated by the vision of an all-cleansing revolution. Deprived of a tradition of open and rational intellectual debate, let alone a political forum, they uncritically swallowed whole the most fantastic dreams and schemes.

In the liberal view the attraction exerted over them by extremist doctrines had little or nothing to do with the social composition of the radicals. Certainly, many were recruited from higher education, and from the 1860s there was a gradual if uneven increase in the number drawn from the less privileged social backgrounds. The increase in the 1870s in the number of students drawn from the seminaries, moulded by the doctrinal rigidity of Russian Orthodoxy, left its mark. But the notion that the *raznochintsy*'s 'closer ties with the people' explain the upsurge of radicalism is rejected.

The key to the protest of the revolutionary intelligentsia lies in their psychology. For some liberal historians, it is the idealism of the young rebels, their commitment to liberty or even an altruistic wish to atone for their own privileges by improving the lot of the wretched peasants and workers, which lies at the heart of the matter. More often, their fanaticism is explained in term of some kind of personal deficiency. The revolutionaries tended to be drawn from those who could not cope with normal life, with a regular profession, with human relationships. They embraced the myth of revolution to compensate for

[11] R. V. Daniels, *Red October* (London, 1967), p. 7.
[12] T. Szamuely, *The Russian Tradition* (London, 1972), pp. 178–9.

their own inadequacy, as a substitute for love, friendship, human affection.

The pattern was set by the first fanatics, destined to become the heroes of later generations. Men like the radical literary critic of the 1840s, V. G. Belinsky, or Chernyshevsky and his colleague N. A. Dobroliubov, were cold and embittered men. They could not form healthy friendships with either women or men, and 'identified with abstract collectivities to compensate for their failure and/or inability to relate to individual human beings.'[13] It was their personal frustration which led them to indulge in wild self-deception, to embrace with fanatical conviction the most extreme and fanciful ideologies. It became the mark of the true revolutionary that he should allow no personal feeling, no moral scruple to soften his commitment to revolutionary ideology. The incarnation of the 'ideological mentality' was Lenin. He 'carried ideology to the point of perfection, [was] incapable of perceiving the world as it is, [and was] totally dominated by an unreal vision of things.' In Lenin 'the self did not exist . . . the doctrinal framework had completely replaced it.'[14]

That they took on the importance they did was in part the fault of the government. Tsarist higher-education policy was ill-judged. On the one hand, its emphasis on western-style academic rather than practical subjects created 'hothouse' institutions conducive to abstract theorizing rather than down-to-earth realism. On the other, the government mishandled student protest, wildly overreacting to an essentially ephemeral product of youthful idealism. In 1861 student disorders at several universities, encouraged by the reforming initiatives undertaken by the government following the Crimean War, were treated as a mortal threat to the social order. There were widespread arrests, popular professors were silenced, and St Petersburg University was closed for almost two years. The pattern was repeated again and again in the following decades, thereby creating an atmosphere of confrontation which encouraged a few incorrigible spirits to make a lifelong commitment to war against authority. When the government began to adopt more sensible policies after 1905, the supply of fanatics dried up. Student protests continued, but the apocalyptic ethos of the revolutionaries gave way to a more mature, responsible support for liberal reform. As modernization proceeded, the overwhelming majority of graduates became healthily integrated within existing society. By 1914 obscurantist maximalists like Lenin had become an anachronism.[15]

Even at their height, the number of these 'misfits', many of whom

[13] V. Nahirny, *The Russian Intelligentsia: From Torment to Silence* (New Brunswick, N.J., 1983), p. 120.
[14] A. Besançon, *The Intellectual Origins of Leninism* (Oxford, 1981), pp. 191, 197.
[15] Malia, 'Intelligentsia', p. 16; H. Seton-Watson, 'The Russian Intellectuals', *Encounter* (September 1955), pp. 49–50.

'could not have found a profession under any circumstances',[16] was very limited. But there were enough to constitute an underground community, a clandestine network of social outcasts and émigrés. And it is in terms of the rarefied atmosphere of the underground that the ideologies and organizations developed by the radicals are to be understood. The coterie of would-be revolutionaries commanded no widespread support. In Russia's stratified society they lacked social and economic leverage of any kind; their inflammatory proclamations and resort to violence and terrorism alienated even the progressive wing of educated society. Their very weakness, their distance from practical affairs, and their isolation made them ever more extreme. They occupied a surreal world in which those whose commitment, whose ruthlessness, whose fanaticism was greatest commanded most respect; in which the real concerns of ordinary men and women, of people of flesh and blood, were reduced to abstractions; in which complex social relations were interpreted in terms of black and white, good and bad, friend and foe. The imperial regime was cast as the epitome of evil and the revolutionaries as the champions of freedom, justice and the people. The revolutionary intelligentsia became fanatically convinced of its own exclusive moral and intellectual superiority. There were, of course, countervailing currents: Herzen in the 1850s, P. L. Lavrov in the 1870s, the Mensheviks and more responsible SRs in the twentieth century represented less arrogant trends. But they were scarcely more realistic than their more unscrupulous rivals, and within the revolutionary milieu the odds were against them. From the 1890's 'the component of social idealism among . . . [the revolutionaries] was very weak.'[17] The lofty and democratic values with which some of the intelligentsia began became overlaid by a ruthless devotion to 'revolution for revolution's sake'.[18]

Accordingly, the ideologies they adopted were divorced from reality. They persuaded themselves that their visions of revolution and the total reconstruction of society were somehow in accordance with historical development. During the 1860s and 70s the populists attributed to the primitive peasant commune all the characteristics of a latent socialist order. Longing for revolution, they convinced themselves that the peasantry were on the point of a mighty revolt. They dreamed of a great alliance with the masses which would destroy the society they detested and create a utopia of peasant socialism. Russia would avoid the torments of western capitalist industrialization and become an egalitarian, decentralized and harmonious Arcadia based on the village commune. Noble these ideas may have been. But in their 'almost unbelievable' hostility to industrial development, they were

[16] A. Ulam, *In the Name of the People* (New York, 1977), p. 144.
[17] A Gleason, *Young Russia. The Genesis of Russian Radicalism in the 1860s* (New York, 1980), p. 26.
[18] R. E. Pipes, *Struve. Liberal on the Left, 1870–1905* (Cambridge, Mass., 1970), p. 236.

utterly divorced from the real world.[19] Their portrayal of peasant life represented 'an intellectually sterile attempt to capture an imaginary, romantic past'.[20] That their ideas were absurd, that they had but the dimmest understanding of what the masses wanted, was amply demonstrated by the reception they received from the peasantry. The 'mad summer' of 1874, when they went 'to the people' in their hundreds, was a dismal failure. The peasantry were at best apathetic, at worst downright hostile. They believed in the Tsar; socialism meant nothing to them; in some cases they actually handed the 'troublemakers' over to the police. With undisguised relish a leading liberal historian embellishes the account left by one populist of what the peasants did with the revolutionary pamphlets distributed: ' "They tore them up to roll cigarettes – paper was so scarce, they explained" – and one may assume they used them for less delicate purposes as well.'[21] The revolutionaries might as well have come from another planet for all the relevance their schemes had to the real concerns of the peasantry.

The revolutionaries' reaction to this disillusioning experience was revealing. Instead of rethinking their programme, they redoubled their efforts to implement it. They knew the interests of the peasants better than the peasants themselves. If the masses were too preoccupied by prosaic day-to-day concerns, the revolutionaries would take matters into their own hands. The populists resorted to conspiracy, terror and regicide. From the start there had been a strong streak of élitism in their outlook. The immorality and authoritarianism of Nechaev, who organized the murder of one of his fellow conspirators to buttress his own authority (1869), was no unfortunate perversion of the revolutionary ethic, it was integral to it. The members of the People's Will convinced themselves that in hounding the Tsar they acted in the name of the people, but their 'subconscious ideal', never fully achieved, 'was of a militant authoritarian party imposing its will on the masses.'[22]

Unable to mobilize peasant support, the revolutionaries cast around for alternative strategies. While some clung to the fading dream of direct transition to socialism based on the peasantry, others became intoxicated by Marxism. Here was a recipe perfectly designed for them: dogmatic, all-embracing, pseudo-scientific, and promising ultimate victory. It pandered to their inflated notion of their own importance; and the restiveness of the working class during this early phase of

[19] A. Gerschenkron, 'The Problem of Economic Development in Russian Intellectual History of the Nineteenth Century', in E. J. Simmons, ed., *Continuity and Change in Russian and Soviet Thought* (Cambridge, Mass., 1955), p. 32.
[20] W. McClennan, *Revolutionary Exiles: The Russians in the First International and the Paris Commune* (London, 1979), p. 232.
[21] Ulam, *In the Name of the People*, p. 227.
[22] *op. cit.*, p. 252.

Russian industrialization gave them renewed hope that they had at last found a willing instrument for their revolutionary dreams.

The apparent contrast between Russian populism and Russian Marxism masked the essential continuity between the two. The attitude of the Social Democrats towards the proletariat was little different from that of the populists towards the peasantry. 'Psychologically the Marxists represented little more than rejuvenated populists.'[23] There was constant friction between them and the workers they sought to dominate. Workers valued the education that the *intelligenty* could give them. They protested vigorously when in the mid nineties the revolutionaries abandoned the thorough education of a few hand-picked pupils and turned to mass agitation and manipulation. There were fierce disputes over the intelligentsia's determination to exclude all but a token worker or two from their policy-making committees and to assert their own control over workers' mutual support funds and the content of newspapers written for the workers.[24] Above all, they were divided over whether the emphasis should be placed upon political or economic issues. In the late nineties when workers showed excessive interest in bread-and-butter issues, the revolutionaries denounced their petty-bourgeois, trade-unionist mentality. They were determined to turn the workers' essentially economic goals into political goals. They would unite with the workers over their struggle for economic improvements only so that 'by smuggling in the Marxian doctrine, [they could] transform it into the ideological struggle of classes.'[25]

The epitome of all that was most dogmatic, authoritarian and amoral in the tradition was Lenin. His 'deepest motive was the drive for personal power', and he worked tirelessly to concentrate control of the party into his own hands.[26] To achieve this end, he readily subjected the Social Democrats to ceaseless strife. Time and again he split the party, castigating one group of opponents after another – the 'Economists', the Mensheviks, the Bogdanovites. Utterly ruthless in the methods he used, he created a highly-centralized, tightly-knit organization of professional revolutionaries obedient to his will. He drew an unbridgeable line between this élite and rank-and-file workers. Only those workers who fully accepted the intelligentsia's theories and guidance, he insisted, should be admitted to the party. The rest would be urged, steered and if necessary forced onto the path laid down by the dogma of their self-appointed leaders. The 'spontaneous' strivings of the working class were treated with distrust bordering on disdain. Working-class organizations which exhibited

[23] Nahirny, *Russian Intelligentsia*, p. 136.
[24] This theme is developed in detail in R. E. Pipes, *Social Democracy and the St Petersburg Labour Movement* (Cambridge, Mass., 1963).
[25] Nahirny, *Russian Intelligentsia*, p. 140.
[26] Daniels, *Red October*, p. 20.

independent initiative – be it soviets or trade unions – were regarded with acute suspicion unless and until they were firmly under party tutelage. 'The essence of Bolshevism was a rigid authoritarian mistrust of mass movements and a sectarian revulsion for co-operative ventures.'[27]

Moreover, although the Marxists had more success than the populists in creating links with their chosen constituency, those links remained extremely tenuous. During the sharp decline in strike activity which accompanied the industrial downturn of 1899–1901, worker-intelligentsia contact withered as the revolutionaries became absorbed in internal party bickering. The socialist parties played a peripheral role in the revolution of 1905. During the period of industrial calm which followed 1906, SRs and Social Democrats alike were reduced to a rump, party membership of the latter falling from the probably inflated figure of 150,000 to some 10,000. The fact that 2000 of these, including Lenin and many of the leading figures, were in exile abroad reinforced the division between the intelligentsia and the workers. The revolutionary intelligentsia seemed doomed to doctrinaire squabbles over increasingly irrelevant issues. It was only the turmoil unleashed by Russia's involvement in the First World War, the breakdown of imperial authority, of the army, and of the economy, which gave them their chance. 'The meeting of two causal series, the real series of the war and the imaginary series of Bolshevik politics, lent Bolshevism the reality it had always lacked.'[28]

The libertarian view

The libertarian interpretation rejects the notion that the revolutionaries represented no more than the extravagant daydreams of isolated malcontents. But equally it rejects the Soviet claim that the revolutionaries were spokesmen for the masses. According to this view, instead of representing workers or peasants, they spoke for a new class spawned by advancing capitalism, the class from which they themselves sprang – the intelligentsia.

The members of this new class did not own the means of production, but they were set apart from the proletariat by possession of a distinct form of capital – intellectual capital. What gave rise to the protest of the intelligentsia, and what lay behind the revolutionary protest of its extreme wing, was the lack of opportunity afforded them by tsarist society. From the mid nineteenth century, their number grew consistently faster than the number of suitable openings the backward

[27] P. Pomper, *The Russian Revolutionary Intelligentsia* (Arlington Heights, Ill., 1970), p. 187.
[28] Besançon, *Intellectual Origins*, pp. 257–8.

economy could provide.[29] Their skills, their art, their knowledge commanded scant respect and a pitiful price in the market. Many were forced to choose between cringing service in what seemed an irrational bureaucracy or relegation to an impotent periphery of writers and artists. Either way they were led to find fault both with the traditional tsarist regime and with the spreading market system. They criticized a political order run on semi-feudal lines where economic development and social welfare were left to chance. They criticized a social order based on private property and commerce, where those who could afford to buy showed so little taste and discrimination. Most came to terms with the constraints of the existing order but a radical wing refused to do so and dreamed of a society run on rational lines laid down by acknowledged experts (themselves) – a society they dubbed 'socialist'.

Since they commanded no capital, the members of this new class did not become entrepreneurs, they did not develop a 'mercantile mentality'. But their education and employment, whether in the bureaucracy or the tertiary sector, gave them a distinctive 'technocratic, managerial outlook'.[30] And this was faithfully reproduced in the ideas of the revolutionaries. With each decade the revolutionaries became more and more concerned with efficiency. While early generations of the class's radical wing had concentrated on problems of distribution, questions of production and organization came to preoccupy their successors in the 1870s and 80s. The intelligentsia came to feel responsible for the Russian economy. They yearned for a society where the surplus product of labour would be at the disposal not of idle capitalists or degenerate gentry but of expert administrators.

Lacking any tangible levers of their own with which to bring about change, the revolutionary wing of the intelligentsia sought to mobilize the masses. They addressed themselves first to the peasantry. They painted an enticing portrait of the bliss that lay ahead if only the peasantry would heed their call and rise up against the established order. The Tsar and nobility would be swept away and a new society based on the social justice and decentralized self-government of the peasant commune would emerge. But populist rhetoric was deceptive. Far from being content with the prospect of a society based on primitive agriculture they were becoming ever more deeply committed to economic development and efficiency. And however attracted they were to direct democracy and peasant self-government, they were increasingly concerned to take power into their own hands. This was reflected in their strategy. At first their efforts were disorganized and

---

[29] G. Konrad and I. Szelenyi, *The Intellectuals on the Road to Class Power* (Brighton, 1979), pp. 118–19.
[30] R. Gombin, *The Radical Tradition. A Study in Modern Revolutionary Thought* (London, 1978), p. 56.

almost anarchist in inspiration: the movement 'to the people' in 1874 virtually ignored the political sphere. By the late 1870s, however, they had developed a truly Jacobin approach. The People's Will revealed their mounting impatience to seize state power and use it to reconstruct peasant society on rational lines from above. That section of the intelligentsia which continued right up to 1917 to lay primary emphasis on the peasantry rather than the proletariat remained permeated by statist assumptions. If the SRs had achieved power, 'their actions would have been exactly like those of the Bolshevik Party.'[31]

The conversion of the bulk of the revolutionary intelligentsia from populism to Marxism was fully in line with this trend. Marxism's vision of socialism was much more congenial to the intelligentsia than that of a peasant-based utopia. It endorsed their growing concern with economic development. Backward, peasant Russia would be transformed into a dynamic, modern, industrial society in which their talents and expertise would find full scope. Moreover, the version of Marxism they imbibed – dominant throughout European Social Democracy by the late nineteenth century – placed 'the theory of productive forces' and the question of property relations at its centre.[32] On the one hand, large-scale machine industry was seen as the necessary prerequisite for socialism. Unless and until it had been created, socialism was unrealizable. On the other, the pith and core of socialism was seen as the abolition of private property and the nationalization of the means of production. The key lay not in the direct transfer of power into the hands of workers on the factory floor but the administration of industry by a 'workers' state' in their interests. Such administration would be truly scientific: it would do away with all the irrationalities, the waste, the inefficiency of private enterprise. The very essence of Lenin's version of Marxism lay in 'presenting socialism as the acceleration of history in terms of production and productivity. The professional revolutionaries who [came] to power in October 1917 were concerned to develop Russia's capitalist potential to the utmost, to carry the country farther and faster along the road than the feeble bourgeoisie.'[33]

The intelligentsia may not have been insincere, they may have believed their own rhetoric. But that rhetoric, the proletarian and liberating ideology of Marxism, concealed the profound clash of interest between intelligentsia and workers, between those who sought to maximize the state budget at their disposal for investment and redistribution, and those who wished to realize the full value of, and exercise real control over, their own labour. The intellectuals' temporary false-consciousness' 'served the power interests of the rising

[31] Voline, *The Unknown Revolution 1917–1921* (Montreal, 1974), p. 257.
[32] P. Corrigan, H. Ramsay and D. Sayer, *Socialist Construction and Marxist Theory* (London, 1978), pp. 40–7.
[33] Gombin, *Radical Tradition*, p. 27.

intellectual class. By deceiving themselves they were better able to deceive others.'[34]

The Social Democrats found a much more responsive audience than their populist predecessors. Their ambition to replace the capitalist order with one created in their own image ran parallel to a mounting roar of revolt from below. The more moderate and orthodox Marxists – the Mensheviks – struggled to channel this protest in accordance with their own strategy. They had drawn the conventional conclusion that socialist revolution in Russia must await the full-scale development by capitalism of the necessary industrial infrastructure. The political corollary was that the masses should accept the social and political premises of capitalism and the establishment of bourgeois rule. But in Russia the masses refused to do so, refused to resign themselves to an indefinite period of subjection to capitalist exploitation. Popular support for the Mensheviks shrivelled accordingly. Matters were more complex where the Bolsheviks were concerned. What distinguished Lenin and his party was that they saw that in Russia liberal rule could be overthrown while capitalism was still in its infancy. Lenin was acutely aware of the ferment from below and the potential for an alliance of all democratic elements in Russian society, spearheaded by the proletariat, which would destroy traditional authority. He developed a strategy skilfully designed to establish intelligentsia leadership over this revolt.

The heart of Lenin's strategy lay in the creation of a party of professional revolutionaries. The party was portrayed as the vanguard of the proletariat. In fact, however, its function 'was not to represent the workers' interests, but to prepare for the seizure of power and to serve as the organizational prototype of a new form of state power.'[35] The party was organized along strictly hierarchical lines. Theory and tactics were to be laid down from the centre. And leadership was deliberately concentrated in the hands of non-workers. True, Lenin was anxious to take the most 'advanced' members of the proletariat into the party. But what this meant in reality was recruiting a thin stratum of educated and loyal workers and removing them from the factory floor. As a result, in the course of their rise through the party hierarchy, even Bolsheviks of working-class origin became intellectuals. The party represented the most effective political organization of the new class of intelligentsia.

The revisionist view

Revisionist research has credited the revolutionary intelligentsia with a somewhat more modest role than does each of the three traditional

[34] D. H. Lasswell and D. Lerner, eds, *Worlds Revolutionary Elites* (Cambridge, Mass., 1965), p. 86.
[35] Konrad and Szelenyi, *Intellectuals*, p. 140.

schools of thought. The focus of this research has reflected growing
awareness that preoccupation with a handful of leading figures may
create a distorted picture; that Chernyshevsky, Plekhanov and Lenin
may not be typical in terms of social background, personality or
motivation; that both their own ideological development and that of
the rank and file must be more firmly located in its social context; that
the schemes and blueprints drawn up by leaders – and the criticisms
hurled by their rivals – may be a poor guide to how the revolutionary
parties actually functioned. More attention, therefore, has been paid
to the process by which rank-and-file *intelligenty* were recruited into
the underground; the interaction between their ideological development and the popular pressure for change welling up from below; the
social composition and structure of the revolutionary organizations
they created; and the impact which those organizations had upon
the masses they sought to represent. The effect has been to highlight
weaknesses in each of the traditional interpretations and to
demythologize the revolutionary intelligentsia.

The source of radicalism among the intelligentsia

So far as the genesis of the revolutionary intelligentsia is concerned,
revisionist work suggests that none of the traditional explanations is
entirely satisfactory. Liberal emphasis on the psychological problems
of the radicals appears misplaced. True, the formation of each revolutionary was a deeply personal process. Biographies written in the
liberal tradition come much closer to recreating the mentality of their
subjects than formalistic, hagiographic Soviet equivalents. But the
scale of recruitment to the revolutionary underground suggests that it
cannot be explained in terms of individual maladjustment.

There is still no adequate head count of the revolutionary intelligentsia. For one thing, it is difficult to arrive at consistent criteria by
which to identify the species. Activists with a sustained commitment to
the underground were revolutionaries in a very different sense from
those who had no more than fleeting involvement. Moreover, the
sources available are patchy and uneven. A combination of a bio-
graphical dictionary of activists begun in the 1920s (which was cut short
by Stalin after completion of only the volumes covering the 1860s, 70s
and a small proportion of the activists of 1880–1904) and the meticulous records of the Police and Justice Departments on political arrests
have made possible rough estimates of the number who actually fell
foul of the authorities. They suggest that the number of political
offenders from the intelligentsia rose from about 1000 in the 1860s to
between 3000 and 4000 in each of the following three decades, before
increasing very sharply in the period of the revolution of 1905.[36] With

[36] V. R. Leikina-Svirskaia, *Intelligentsiia v Rossii vo vtoroi polovine XIX veka* (Moscow, 1971), pp. 308–19; R. Leikina-Svirskaia, *Russkaia intelligentsiia v 1900–1917 gg.*
(Moscow, 1981), pp. 249–54.

the firm establishment of the Social Democratic and SR parties early in the new century, membership in one or other of them offers an alternative guide. Before 1905 each of the two parties attracted between 3000 and 4000 *intelligenty* members.[37] During the upheaval of 1905–7 overall membership leaped upwards, the Social Democrats claiming as many as 150,000 members. To become a member during that brief period demanded a lower level of commitment than in the more repressive years which preceded and followed it, and *intelligenty* members were now heavily outnumbered. Nevertheless, it was not until the last pre-war years that recruitment from the intelligentsia declined. Around the core that these estimates seek to identify was a much large penumbra of sympathizers willing to assist the revolutionaries, be it with money or temporary lodgings. What is clear is that the total over six decades ran into tens of thousands. A social phenomenon of this magnitude suggests that more was at work than either the inadequacies or the moral heroism of a few individuals.

Scarcely more satisfactory is the Soviet view that the emergence of a significant minority of committed radicals among the intelligentsia reflected the changing social origins of the student body. The upsurge in student activism in the late 1860s did coincide with a rise in the proportion of *raznochintsy* in higher education, many of the new-comers being sons of priests.[38] But detailed analysis of a sample of St Petersburg radicals of the 1860s and 70s has shown that, in these decades at least, lower-born students were no more – if anything, less – likely to become radical than their noble counterparts.[39] Thereafter the proportion of radicals coming from noble backgrounds decreased, but the correlation between political allegiance and social origins was still very weak in the period before 1914.[40]

Libertarian emphasis on the radicalizing effect of restricted employment opportunities, too, appears exaggerated. Certainly, the occupations which in the West absorbed the products of higher education – the free professions, medicine, law, teaching, journalism, publishing, finance, commerce, industry and the civil service – were more restricted in Russia and subject to greater political interference. For certain groups of students there clearly was a correlation between radicalism and frustration over employment prospects. Official and

[37] D. Lane, *The Roots of Russian Communism. A Social and Historical Study of Russian Social-Democracy 1898–1907* (Assen, 1969), pp. 12–15, 46–51; M. Perrie, 'The social composition and structure of the Socialist-Revolutionary Party before 1917', *Soviet Studies* XXIV (1973), pp. 223–50.

[38] M. Pushkin, '*Raznochintsy* in the University: Government Policy and Social Change in Nineteenth-Century Russia', *International Review of Social History* XXVI (1981), pp. 33–44.

[39] D. R. Brower, *Training the Nihilists. Education and radicalism in Tsarist Russia* (Cornell, 1975), pp. 41–68, 110–18.

[40] D. R. Brower, 'Student Political Attitudes and Social Origins: The Technological Institute of St Petersburg', *Journal of Social History* 6 (1972–3), pp. 202–13.

unofficial anti-Semitism ensured that educated Jews faced the greatest obstacles to entering a satisfying career. This was one reason why, even when the State successfully cut back Jewish access to higher education, they furnished a wholly disproportionate number of radicals.[41] But there is little evidence of an overall graduate unemployment problem except in the late 1870s and early 80s.[42] For most students education in the universities and professional and technical colleges promised access to a relatively privileged position in society. And yet decade after decade thousands of students were drawn into radical activity.

To account for this process revisionist work has focused attention on the experience of students in higher education. They were deliberately nurtured by the regime as an élite destined to man the upper reaches of the military and bureaucratic apparatus of the State. Yet far from ensuring loyalty to the status quo, their elevated position developed in them a sense of their own importance and dignity which gave them the confidence to question the conventions of tsarist society. Young, ebullient and articulate, the student world became highly conducive to the free flow of new ideas and encouraged a disregard for differences in social origin, an egalitarian sense of solidarity quite unlike the stratified society outside. It was this which fuelled their increasingly vigorous reaction to the restrictions which a nervous government imposed on student activity and university autonomy. From the late 1850s to the revolution, controversy over student fees, police brutality, or interference by the authorities – be it with the freedom of speech of progressive professors, the content of the curriculum, or the right of students to form their own organizations – sparked recurrent outbursts of student protest.[43] The punishment of an entire college tended only to strengthen student *esprit de corps*: 'The formula, simply put, was dignity plus student solidarity equals resistance.'[44]

The student movement formed a distinct current of protest, responding primarily to the students' own experience.[45] Most students resisted being drawn beyond protest over specifically student issues to broader political involvement. But in the highly-charged political atmosphere of late tsarist Russia, it was a short step from dispute with the authorities over issues of higher education to more general criticism of the socio-political structure. Radical ideas and literature circulated within student assemblies, cafeterias, libraries, voluntary schools and communes. A semi-institutionalized 'school of dissent'

[41] R. Brym, *The Jewish Intelligentsia and Russian Marxism* (London, 1978), pp. 49–56.
[42] Pushkin, '*Raznochintsy*', p. 49.
[43] For the period to the 1880s see Brower, *Training the Nihilists*; for the last two decades before the revolution, see S. D. Kassow, *Students, Professors, and the State in Tsarist Russia* (Berkeley, Cal., 1989).
[44] Brower, *Training the Nihilists*, p. 139.
[45] Kassow, *Students, Professors and the State*, pp. 398–9.

took root. It introduced successive generations of students to an emergent radical subculture, and it provided a transmission belt through which a small minority became involved in illegal political activity. It was the steady flow of student and ex-student recruits which brought into being and helped to sustain the radical circles, organizations and nation-wide parties of the revolutionary underground.

The development of revolutionary ideology

In analysing the ideology of the underground, recent work has underlined the extent to which it reflected social change and popular pressure within Russia. The charge made by liberal historians, that the revolutionary ideologies and programmes were the hothouse creation of intellectuals isolated from the masses they claimed to represent, does not stand up to close scrutiny.

The intellectuals were much less ignorant of the concerns of peasants and workers than this view implies. In the 1860s and 70s, many of the populists gained firsthand knowledge of conditions in the village and of acute peasant discontent with the terms of Emancipation. Even so eccentric a character as D. V. Karakozov, who attempted to assassinate Alexander II in 1866, had gained direct experience while serving as an assistant to one of the peace arbiters appointed to work out the details of the Emancipation settlement. From the 1880s thousands of activists began to establish direct contact with workers on the factory floor and acquired detailed knowledge of workers' conditions and grievances. Similarly, the rank-and-file intelligentsia of the SR party were teachers and medical personnel whose working lives were spent in the villages.

The revolutionary intelligentsia did draw extensively upon socialist currents of thought imported from the West and much of the factional in-fighting and abstruse philosophical controversy among émigrés bore little relation to developments within Russia. But it was only because much, too, bore very directly upon the most urgent domestic questions that it made an impact at home. Rather than passively absorbing the latest word from abroad, the *intelligenty* selected those ideas which helped them to address their own problems. Although they tended in the early decades to entertain an idealized image of the peasantry, their subsequent reappraisals could hardly have been more thorough. The economic ideas of the populists and SRs may have been unsophisticated. But far from being hostile to industrialization they showed increasing concern with economies of scale, technological innovation and economic growth.[46]

Moreover, the revolutionaries were anchored to Russia by sheer

---

[46] E. Acton, 'The Russian Revolutionary Intelligentsia and Industrialization', in R. Bartlett, ed., *Russian Thought and Society 1800–1917* (Keele, 1984), pp. 92–113.

necessity. Even before the abject failure of the People's Will conspiracy, many radicals were aware that on their own they could not overthrow the existing order. By the late 1880s it was clear that their only hope lay in mass revolt. They were therefore under the most powerful compulsion to adapt their ideas and tailor their programmes to ensure that they had mass appeal. Thus, dependence on and interaction with this wider constituency encouraged the intelligentsia to harmonize their visionary programmes with the aspirations of the masses. Their ideological development should be viewed as much in terms of this harmonization as in terms of the abstract thought of isolated intellectuals. The switch of allegiance from populism to Marxism, for example, was less the product of intellectual fashion, the 'pseudo-scientific' attractions of the new creed, or the persuasiveness of Plekhanov's advocacy, than of the direct experience during the 1880s of activists on the ground.[47] The emergent working class exhibited an eagerness and aptitude for organized protest, and an interest in socialist ideas, that the peasantry at the time lacked. Equally, there was more behind the successful launching of the SR party at the beginning of the new century than nostalgia for the romantic populism of a bygone age. It cannot be understood without reference to the growing land hunger and militancy of millions of peasants.[48] It was above all in response to this mounting agitation over the land, not least among workers whose rural ties were still significant, that the Bolsheviks devoted more and more attention to the land question.[49]

The influence of the intelligentsia

By the same token, revisionist work has tended to play down the extent to which the intelligentsia set the goals and moulded the aspirations of peasants and workers. It has questioned how far they were in a position to 'smuggle in' alien dogmas and indoctrinate the masses, and how far they were responsible for the development of class consciousness among workers. They helped to propagate a language through which the working class could articulate their frustrations; they provided radical literature, leaflets and newspapers; they furnished agitators with greater financial means and mobility than those drawn from the working class; and they took a lead in establishing underground organizations able to build links between workers in different factories and cities and to survive recurrent police assaults. But the notion that

[47] N. Naimark, *Terrorists and Social Democrats. The Russian Revolutionary Movement under Alexander III* (Cambridge, Mass., 1983), pp. 239–42.
[48] M. Perrie, *The Agrarian Policy of the Russian Socialist-Revolutionary Party from its Origins through the Revolution of 1905–1907* (Cambridge, 1976), pp. 1–69.
[49] Brym, *Jewish Intelligentsia*, pp. 104–5. For a stimulating general discussion of the relationship between *intelligenty* and workers, see R. Brym, *Intellectuals and Politics* (London, 1980), esp. pp. 42–8.

they diverted the workers – let alone the peasants – from their 'spontaneous' tendencies is open to question.

The most significant impact on popular attitudes attributed to the intelligentsia by traditional liberal – and Soviet – historians concerns the increasingly political nature of working-class protest. The intelligentsia are blamed – or praised – for instilling in the working class the conviction that the solution to their problems lay not in economic reform but political revolution. In the late 1890s, the argument runs, Lenin took alarm that the working class might drift in the direction of mere trade-unionism. Earlier in the decade 'propaganda' among a few chosen workers had been rejected in favour of mass agitation as revolutionaries found they could articulate the detailed grievances of workers in specific factories and print them in agitational leaflets. After initially welcoming this movement, Plekhanov, Lenin and other 'orthodox' Social Democrats became afraid that concentration on immediate economic goals might lead the emergent labour movement to become preoccupied with merely economic rather than political goals. They furiously denounced a so-called 'Economist' heresy among Social Democrats for fostering such a switch in priorities and insisted on the primacy of the political task. By the turn of the century, the 'Economist' trend had died away and under the tutelage of the intelligentsia workers became progressively more politically conscious.

As we have seen, however, trade-unionism failed to take root less because of intelligentsia influence than because of the constraints placed upon it by the tsarist State.[50] Moreover, revisionist work on the underground has demonstrated that the supposed conflict between politically-orientated *intelligenty* and economically-motivated workers has been much exaggerated. At times workers displayed suspicion of the pretensions and relatively privileged way of life of their educated allies, but for the most part the discord between the two was slight. The intelligentsia found their services positively welcomed by both discontented workers and, from the turn of the century, peasants. Detailed analysis of the early period of social-democratic activity, during the late 1880s and early 90s, has found that 'the relationship between worker and intelligentsia leaders was characterized for the most part by trust, co-operation and mutual respect.'[51] During the later 90s, too, the relationship was marked by 'its comradely and democratic spirit'.[52] By 1901 worker activists were overwhelmingly committed to the need for political revolution.[53] The more closely the dynamics behind mass unrest are examined, the clearer it becomes that mass political

[50] See above, chapter 3 pp. 68–70.
[51] Naimark, *Terrorists and Social Democrats*, p. 186.
[52] A. K. Wildman, *The Making of a Workers' Revolution. Russian Social Democracy, 1891–1903* (Chicago, 1967), p. 250.
[53] *op. cit.*, pp. 149–51.

militancy was generated from below rather than whipped up from above, and that 'intelligentsia initiative was successful only when it reflected . . . basic popular impulse.'[54]

The intelligentsia, the masses, and the revolutionary parties

Revisionist analysis of the internal structure and composition of the revolutionary parties has demonstrated that to treat the underground as synonymous with the revolutionary intelligentsia is profoundly misleading. Contrary to the view projected by traditional liberal and libertarian accounts, neither the RSDWP nor the SR party was made up predominantly of *intelligenty*. Even before 1905 a large minority and probably even a majority of their members were drawn from the lower classes.[55] The explosive growth in membership of 1905–7 was drawn overwhelmingly from workers and peasants. After the onset of reaction, activists from the working class heavily outnumbered *intelligenty*; and as membership began to recover in the years before 1914, their preponderance grew further.[56] In 1917 itself the intelligentsia were swamped by members from the lower classes.

Nor were plebeian members mere foot-soldiers at the disposal of *intelligenty* party officials. Certainly, the establishment of an organized party involved a division of labour. The task of smuggling and distributing illegal literature and co-ordinating local cells and committees was carried out by a network of itinerant activists. With the help of access to party funds and forged papers they were able to move rapidly from one centre to another, and evade the intervention of the Okhrana. At the same time, continuity and efficiency demanded the appointment in each local committee of officials with specialized tasks – a secretary, a treasurer, and in the more substantial branches, a variety of other officials including a publications officer and chief propagandist.[57] Before 1905 the intelligentsia supplied the great majority of these 'cadres'. For a brief period, between 1901 and 1905 this proved a source of resentment among worker activists keen to assert themselves and conscious that they were often in the best position to decide such questions as the timing of strikes.[58] After 1905, however, a growing proportion of party cadres were drawn from the working class. In some cases workers spent their evenings and spare

[54] L. Engelstein, *Moscow 1905. Working-Class Organization and Political Conflict* (Stanford, Cal. 1982), p. 14.
[55] Lane, *Roots of Russian Communism*, pp. 20–7.
[56] R. C. Elwood, *Russian Social Democracy* (Assen, 1974), pp. 60–70; M. Perrie, 'The Russian Peasant Movement of 1905–1907: Its Social Composition and Revolutionary Significance', *Past and Present* 55 (1972), pp. 223–50; for the SRs see also C. Rice, *Russian Workers and the Socialist-Revolutionary Party through the Revolution of 1905–7* (London, 1988), where the prominence of workers is stressed, and for the period up to 1914, Ivanova, *Struktura rabochego klassa*, pp. 211–13.
[57] Elwood, *Russian Social Democracy*, pp. 90–106.
[58] Wildman, *Making of a Workers' Revolution*, pp. 90–103.

time on party tasks. Where personnel and funds permitted, worker cadres became full-time officials supported by membership dues, gifts to the party, income from newspaper sales, legal fund-raising activities – and robberies. Among the Social Democrats the dwindling of *intelligenty* cadres was underlined in a questionnaire organized by Trotsky in 1910 which found all local officials to be workers. Of local delegates to the Bolsheviks' Prague Conference of 1912 almost two-thirds were workers.[59]

The highest reaches of the Menshevik, Bolshevik and SR parties, it is true, continued to be dominated by members of the intelligentsia throughout. *Intelligenty* monopolized the Central Committee of each and provided the leading figures on the national stage in 1917. They ran the most influential party journals, drew up the agenda for party conferences and congresses, and spearheaded the internecine struggle in which the parties were involved. But the authority exercised by the leaders within each party in the period before the revolution should not be exaggerated.

Even in the case of the Bolsheviks, the image of a highly-disciplined and centralized organization run by Lenin has been modified significantly. Between 1903 and 1912 local activists prevented the outright split in the party to which émigré divisions were leading, Lenin himself faced powerful challenges from within the Bolshevik faction, notably from Bogdanov, and he came close to losing control altogether. Even after establishing a separate party, his authority was anything but absolute. When *Pravda* became the Bolsheviks' legal mouthpiece in St Petersburg in 1912, he suffered the frustration of having many of the articles he submitted for publication rejected by the editors in Russia; communication between the Central Committee and local party organs was much too tenuous to admit of close supervision; and, as we shall see, during the war and the revolution itself, Lenin's word was by no means accepted as holy writ.[60]

Certainly Lenin was a singularly astute and ruthless political operator: the Prague Conference of 1912, at which he established an effectively autonomous Bolshevik Central Committee, was staged in flagrant disregard of democratic nicety and procedural precedent.[61] In the period before 1914 his vitriolic polemics against supposed threats to 'orthodoxy' often distorted the views of his victims. But his skill at political in-fighting and his doctrinal tussles with Mensheviks and renegade Bolsheviks only took on the importance they did because

[59] Elwood, *Russian Social Democracy*, pp. 64–6.
[60] R. C. Elwood, 'Lenin and *Pravda* 1912–1914', *Slavic Review* 31 (1972), pp. 355–80; R. Service, *Lenin: A Political Life. 1. The Strengths of Contradiction* (London, 1985), pp. 187–90; Swain, *Legal Labour Movement*, pt II; R. C. Williams, *The Other Bolsheviks. Lenin and his Critics, 1904–1914* (Blooming, Ind., 1986), *passim*.
[61] R. C. Elwood, ed., *Vserossiiskaia Konferentsiia Ros. Sots.-Dem. Rab. Partii 1912 goda* (New York, 1982), pp. ix-xxxvi.

they led his party to positions which found a response within the wider revolutionary movement. Until after the revolution, his power and influence depended above all on his success in articulating the aspirations of a substantial plebeian constituency in Russia.

The same point may be made about the revolutionary intelligentsia in general. The political significance the radicals assumed from the 1890s was first and foremost a measure of the close correspondence between their programmes and mass aspirations. As soon as the authorities were in no position to prevent the lower classes expressing their wishes – in 1905, in the elections to the workers' curias for the Duma elections of 1906, 1907 and 1912, and in 1917 itself – their demands in large measure coincided with those of the major revolutionary parties. Liberal parties were able to make minimal impact on peasant and working-class constituents. The peasantry wanted noble land without paying compensation; they wanted to see taxation and conscription done away with. The working class wanted a drastic improvement in their wages and conditions; a transformation in their relationship with management; and firm entrenchment of their civil rights. In 1917 the socialist parties, created but no longer dominated by the revolutionary intelligentsia, commanded the support of the vast majority of both workers and peasants.

Conclusion

In the light of revisionist work, then, the revolutionary intelligentsia emerge neither as superhuman heroes nor as demons. Their recruitment into the underground was facilitated by a regularized 'school of dissent' within the institutions of higher education. For all the creativity and fury of their ideological disputes, their impact upon mass goals was decidedly limited. Although they founded the major revolutionary parties of the twentieth century, they were soon outnumbered within them. And the importance these parties assumed reflected less the intervention of thousands of *intelligenty* than the support provided by millions of workers and peasants.

5 THE FEBRUARY REVOLUTION

Russia's involvement in the First World War, it is agreed by all sides in the controversy over the revolution, intensified unrest and discontent with the tsarist government. So much is common ground. But beyond that, liberal and Soviet historians are deeply divided over the nature of the causal link between the war and the revolution which broke out in February 1917. The positions taken by the two schools on this issue complement those we have seen them adopt in the controversy over the pre-war period.

The liberal view

Liberal historians have traditionally emphasized the novelty of the situation created by the outbreak of the war.[1] In their view, it abruptly reversed the stabilizing trends of the pre-war period and totally transformed the political, social and economic situation. In the first place, the war placed a qualitatively new burden of responsibility on the Tsar. It invested with fateful significance his personal inadequacy and susceptibility to his wife's constant urging that he 'be a man' and assert himself. His decision in 1915, in defiance of almost universal advice to the contrary, that he would himself take on the supreme command at the front was disastrous. It identified him personally with military reversals and greatly increased the damage they did to the authority and prestige of the Crown. By stubbornly refusing to reach any *modus vivendi* with the Progressive Bloc in the Duma, he frustrated every effort to establish a competent government which could galvanize the country behind the war effort. Instead, under the guidance of the Tsarina and Rasputin, he appointed a rapid succession of nonentities to run the country. Thus Nicholas undermined the loyalty of even those closest to the throne, opened an unbridgeable breach between himself and public opinion, and disrupted civil and military administration alike. 'From the summer of 1916 the whole system of government began to disintegrate', and the essential cause

---

[1] Liberal treatments of the war's impact have drawn extensively upon a major series of monographs on the subject which was published between 1929 and 1931 under the aegis of the Carnegie Endowment for International Peace. See in particular the general treatment by M. T. Florinsky, *The End of the Russian Empire* (Yale, 1931).

of the February revolution itself was 'the mere decomposition and collapse of the Tsar's government.'[2]

The effect of the autocracy's abysmal record at a time of national emergency was to provoke a storm of opposition which transcended class barriers and embraced the whole of society. Through the zemstvos, urban dumas and WICs, nobility, industrialists, members of the third element and even many workers joined forces to harry the government into more effective action and to take responsibility upon themselves for key aspects of the war effort. They denounced the regime for proving wholly incapable of marshalling the country's resources against the Germans, for being guided by 'dark forces' behind the throne, and for forfeiting the nation's confidence. The Duma leaders tore into the tottering government and in his famous 'Is this stupidity or treason?' speech of November 1916 the Kadet leader Miliukov spoke for the whole country. Prominent public figures, including the Octobrist leader Guchkov, reached the conclusion that a *coup d'état* to replace Nicholas with a more acceptable monarch had become essential. Nicholas lost the confidence even of members of the imperial family, and it was right-wing monarchists who murdered Rasputin in December 1916. At the end of February, while workers in the capital went on strike and the garrison mutinied, the Duma leaders and the generals delivered the *coup de grace* and forced the Tsar to abdicate.

For liberal historians, the mass disturbances were also a direct product of the war. The outburst of popular frustration owed virtually nothing to the efforts of the revolutionary underground. Such limited influence as the revolutionaries had exerted before the war was lost as hundreds of thousands of new workers fresh from the countryside swamped the pre-war work-force. Moreover, the war threw the revolutionary parties into disarray. Their organizations were smashed by the government, they were deeply demoralized by the divisions between 'defencists' and 'internationalists' which the war provoked, and Lenin and other leaders in exile virtually lost contact with the few activists at large in Russia. Social Democrats and SRs alike were reduced to impotence. The influence of the Bolsheviks in Petrograd, for example, was no more than 'limited and sporadic'. It could not compare with that of the moderate Labour group elected to the Central WIC.[3] Lenin himself, isolated in his Swiss exile, was driven in January 1917 to tell an audience of students that his generation might not live to see the revolution.

What re-ignited industrial unrest after the first year of the war was sheer material deprivation. The workers' motivation was essentially

[2] R. Charques, *The Twilight of Imperial Russia* (London, 1958), pp. 230, 241.
[3] J. L. H. Keep, *The Russian Revolution. A Study in Mass Mobilization* (London, 1976), p. 56.

economic: even by 1916 the number of working days lost through economic strikes outnumbered those lost through political strikes by almost six to one.[4] In February, with the masses 'driven by elemental passion, by hatred of the war, by feelings of rancour and revenge which could no longer be endured passively', spontaneous disturbances, rioting and looting broke out in the capital.[5] The streets were overrun by a 'revolt of the urban poor', an 'anarchical mob . . . with no thought but destruction.'[6] And the garrison, which dreaded nothing so much as being sent to the front and now saw a chance of avoiding that fate, refused to fire on the crowds and mutinied. One resolute officer with a few hundred reliable troops might have crushed the chaotic, unorganized protests. But so far advanced was the regime's inner decomposition, so confused and incompetent were its efforts to maintain order, that it simply crumbled.

The regime's disappearance was greeted by universal joy. Expressions of support for the Provisional Government established by the liberal leaders of the Duma poured in from every section of society. The only development to mar the prospect of all classes rallying behind the new government was the re-emergence of the revolutionary intelligentsia. At the same time as the Duma members were moving to take control of the situation, a group of predominantly Menshevik intellectuals seized the opportunity to set up a Soviet of workers' and soldiers' deputies in the capital. And, instead of buttressing the government with this new institution, they weakened it. On the one hand, guided by a doctrinaire belief that in accordance with the Marxist timetable this was to be a bourgeois revolution, they would not participate in the government let alone form one of their own. On the other, they were prepared to give only the most grudging and conditional support to the liberal Provisional Government and 'did everything in their power to restrict the activity of the liberal politicians.'[7] They thereby implanted a fatal division of power and authority at the very outset of the new era.

The Soviet view

Soviet historians, by contrast, have emphasized the essential continuity between developments before and after the outbreak of war. First and foremost they have insisted upon the continuity in the growth of the revolutionary movement. Under the leadership of the most politically-conscious stratum of the proletariat, it mounted an increasingly organized and sophisticated challenge to the regime. In the

---

[4] op. cit., pp. 48–9.
[5] Charques, Twilight of Imperial Russia, p. 237.
[6] Keep, Mobilization, p. 60; L. Schapiro, 1917. The Russian Revolutions and the Origins of Present-Day Communism (Hounslow, 1984), p. 43.
[7] J. D. Basil, The Mensheviks in the Revolution of 1917 (Columbus, Ohio, 1983), p. 19.

Soviet view, despite the inevitable component of spontaneous protest provoked by material deprivation, the February revolution was above all a conscious assault upon tsarism, spearheaded by the proletariat which mobilized behind itself both the peasantry (as represented in the army), and the other 'democratic' strata of the urban population – artisans, servants, clerks, students and progressive members of the intelligentsia.

The organic development and increasing maturity of the workers' movement is central to the Soviet interpretation of February. Accordingly, they have fiercely rejected the liberal notion that the vortex of war had in effect replaced the pre-war proletariat with a new generation whose level of literacy, organizational experience and political consciousness was drastically lower. Instead, they have stressed the presence of hundreds of thousands of workers who had been through the schools of 1905–7 and 1912–14 and preserved the traditions and lessons of the pre-war era. In Petrograd, where the number of industrial workers rose from 250,000 to about 400,000 during the war, just over half those of 1917 are regarded as pre-war cadres.[8] They broadened their organizational experience by maintaining at least a skeletal trade-union structure and by energetic involvement in such legal organizations as were permitted, notably the social insurance councils.

It was this core of cadre workers who provided the muscle behind the rapid resumption of strikes and protests from the first half of 1915. They saw through the efforts of liberal Duma leaders and moderate labour leaders to rally them behind the war effort. When workers were invited to elect representatives to join the WICs, they succeeded in securing a boycott in most cities. At the first meeting of electors for the Central WIC, held in Petrograd in September 1915, a majority supported a Bolshevik resolution rejecting participation in these organs of class collaboration. And after Menshevik and SR defencists had secured the election of a Labour group at a second, illegitimate meeting, support for them was steadily eroded by the growing influence of the vanguard of the proletariat.[9] Less skilled and less experienced workers tended at first to protest over immediate economic grievances, but the cadre workers instilled growing political awareness into the movement. The response to calls for political demonstrations became ever more vigorous. By 1916 workers involved in economic strikes outnumbered those in political strikes by less than two to one, and in the last four months running up to the revolution, those involved in political strikes were in a majority of

[8] I. P. Leiberov, *Na shturm samoderzhaviia. Petrogradskii proletariat v gody pervoi mirovoi voiny i Fevral'skoi revoliutsii (iul' 1914–-mart 1917g.)* (Moscow, 1979), p. 19.
[9] P. A. Golub *et al.*, *Istoricheskii opyt trekh rossiiskikh revoliutsii* (3 vols, Moscow, 1985–7) II, pp. 135–7.

more than three to two.[10] In the final assault upon the regime in February 1917, it was the skilled, literate, politically conscious workers who were at the forefront.

Moreover, the proletariat established 'hegemony' over the revolutionary movement as a whole. Their example exerted a decisive influence over other classes, and especially over the army. For one thing, among the predominantly peasant rank and file were a significant leaven of workers, drafted as often as not for their 'seditious' behaviour. More important, soldiers stationed near focal points of worker militancy felt the reverberations of proletarian strikes as well as receiving direct political propaganda. The fact that mass mutiny broke out first in the capital owed less to the soldiers' supposed fear of being sent to the front, than to their proximity to the epicentre of worker activism. The revolution, then, was neither a spontaneous outburst against wartime conditions, nor an all-class national movement. Rather, it was the product of acute class struggle by the proletariat, the fruit of the accumulated strength, discipline and political consciousness of the Russian revolutionary movement.

An absolutely critical factor in the continuity across 1914, and in the galvanization of the revolutionary movement, according to the Soviet view, was the sustained impact of the Bolshevik party. The influence on the proletariat exerted by the party is seen at once as the prime cause and the surest measure of the workers' growing political consciousness. Soviet historians have gone to immense lengths to trace Bolshevik activity during the war. Evidence has been found of Bolshevik organization in 200 towns, of widespread activity in garrisons, at the front and in the fleet, of 18 illegal party periodicals appearing at one time or another, and of almost 2 million copies of over 700 leaflets.[11] Party membership by February 1917 was about 24,000 – and that despite constant arrests which saw the Moscow organization, for example, broken no less than 25 times. The ranks were continually refilled in the capital and elsewhere, and by early 1917 there were some 3000 members in Petrograd and 115 cells. Moreover, for all the wartime disruption and the heavy blows dealt by the police, the party remained homogeneous and followed a firm revolutionary strategy. The contacts which linked one cell to another, the local committees to the Russian Bureau of the Central Committee and the Petersburg Committee, and the party in Russia to Lenin and the Foreign Bureau were maintained.

Lenin's direct contact with and leadership of the party in Russia is a vital feature of the homogeneity and ideological consistency that

[10] Leiberov, *Na shturm samoderzhaviia*, p. 114.
[11] I. M. Dazhina, *Bol'shevistskie listovki v Rossii perioda pervoi mirovoi voiny i Fevral'-skoi revoliutsii* (Moscow, 1981), pp. 7, 162.

Soviet historians attribute to the party.[12] They have found some 40 Russian addresses in the Foreign Bureau's address book, stressed the lively correspondence Lenin conducted with party activists, and underlined the role of the party's central organ, *Social Democrat*, which appeared on average once a month carrying Lenin's word to Russia. Far from being isolated and cut off, Lenin was in almost constant touch and fully confident of the outcome of the gathering revolutionary crisis. His remark of January 1917, beloved of liberal historians, that his generation might not live to see the revolution, not only ran counter to the whole tenor of his wartime corpus but referred in fact to European rather than Russian prospects.[13] He provided the unified tactical and strategic leadership which guided the party through the war. His brilliant analysis of the war as the bitter fruit of imperialism provided the Bolsheviks with a crystal-clear and consistent policy: commitment to turning the international strife into civil strife and revolution.

The contrast with the Mensheviks and SRs could not have been sharper. Their organization collapsed, their membership was derisory, and both parties were hopelessly split over the war, attitudes ranging from downright 'social chauvinism' to unstable internationalism. The bulk of both parties followed the quisling line of the Menshevik and Trudovik leadership in the Duma and of the Labour group on the Central WIC. Scattered groups of lower-level radical SRs, Internationalist Mensheviks and Interdistrict Social Democrats did play a part in revolutionary agitation. But figures showing the party affiliation of political offenders in 1915 and 1916 demonstrate the clear preponderance of Social Democrat activists over SRs, and Bolsheviks over Mensheviks.[14] The efforts of the other socialist parties were disjointed and dwarfed by the unified and disciplined activity of the Bolshevik party.

The evidence of the party's enormous influence and leadership role is, in Soviet eyes, rich and varied. As before the war, it was the proletariat that provided the great majority of party members: two-thirds of the Petersburg Committee, and 2500 out of 3000 members in

---

[12] E. N. Burdzhalov provoked a storm of protest from more orthodox historians when in 1956 in a celebrated article he challenged this picture of Bolshevik unity under Lenin's guidance during the early stages of the revolution. E. N. Burdzhalov, 'O taktike bolshevikov v marte-aprele 1917', *Voprosy istorii* (1956) 4, pp. 38–56. Nevertheless, he was eventually able to publish two major volumes on the February revolution, in 1967 and 1971. The first volume, and a central chapter of the second, are available in English, E. N. Burdzhalov, *Russia's Second Revolution. The February Uprising in Petrograd* (Bloomington, 1987), pp. 10–100, and 'Revolution in Moscow', *Soviet Studies in History* 26 (1987 –8), pp. 10–100.
[13] G. Z. Ioffe, *Fevral'skaia revoliutsiia 1917g. v anglo-amerikanskoi burzhuaznoi istoriografii* (Moscow, 1970), pp. 190–5; Lenin, *Sob. soch.* 30, p. 328.
[14] Leikina-Svirskaia, *Russkaia intelligentsiia v 1900–1917 gg.* (Moscow, 1981), pp. 252–3.

the capital in February 1917 were workers. Elections to the Petrograd social insurance councils in January 1916 saw ten Bolsheviks returned and only one Menshevik, while Bolshevik-inclined workers dominated those illegal trade unions that managed to survive. Despite all the legal advantages of the moderate labour leaders, the platforms given them by the Duma (whose Bolshevik members had been arrested), the WICs and the co-operatives, their influence was repeatedly shown to be weaker than that of the Bolsheviks. The Bolshevik call for a political strike on 9 January 1917 to mark the anniversary of Bloody Sunday evoked a massive response as 150,000 workers downed tools and held mass meetings.[15] The events of 14 February provided the clearest illustration of the respective influence of the two groups. Moderate labour leaders had called for a strike and for demonstrations outside the Tauride Palace in support of the Duma which reassembled there that day. The Bolsheviks urged workers to ignore the bourgeois Duma and demonstrate on the Nevsky Prospect in the centre of the city instead. And whereas a pitiful 500 workers showed up at the Duma, great columns of workers made for the Nevsky.

When the time was ripe for full-scale revolution, it was the party which 'gave the signal for action to begin'.[16] The Bolsheviks did not call for the initial strikes and demonstrations of 23 February, but local party cells quickly established a leading role in the movement. From that day onwards the most powerful, disciplined and politically conscious contribution was made by workers from the Vyborg district, the Petrograd suburb with the strongest Bolshevik committee where the party enjoyed the greatest influence. Leadership was provided by the overlapping and closely interwoven membership of the Russian Bureau, the Petersburg Committee and the Vyborg Committee. They called for a general strike on 25 February, orchestrated a campaign to win over the garrison, took up rank-and-file calls for the election of a workers' soviet, and on 27–28 February issued two leaflets, the second explicitly calling for the establishment of a Provisional Revolutionary Government based not on the Duma but on the Soviet.[17] By that evening the Tsar's government had been overthrown. The party had inspired the masses with its ideas and slogans, placed itself at their head, and guided them to victory.

As before the war, the rising tide of revolution conditioned the policies pursued by both government and liberal opposition. Tsarism was driven into a corner. It is true that Nicholas was incompetent, Rasputin was degenerate, and in the last months before the revolution the regime was gripped by internal crisis. But this 'crisis of the élites' was not a matter of chance. 'The essence of the matter lay not in the

[15] Golub, *Istoricheskii opyt* II, p. 165.
[16] *op. cit* II, p. 169.
[17] Leiberov, *Na shturm samoderzhaviia*, p. 241.

separate errors and personal weakness of those who ruled the country, but in the social paralysis of the ruling class.'[18] Even if the autocracy had made reforms it would have found, as in the pre-war period, that the result would be to provide greater scope for the spread of political consciousness and the development of revolutionary organization. In any case, since tsarism's 'chief strategic aim' remained the maintenance of 'the interests of the noble landowning class, its power, its social and political privileges', the regime's ability to make concessions was extremely limited.[19] And as the revolutionary threat mounted, Nicholas's room for manoeuvre narrowed to vanishing point – to that point where, in panic, even the grand dukes and great landowners urged Nicholas to try reform again.

Not that the regime simply collapsed or bowed out voluntarily. Elaborate plans to crush disturbances were drawn up; the Tsar ordered the officer in charge of the capital, General Khabalov, to restore order by force; on Sunday 26 February the proletariat were confronted by a massive show of armed strength and the number of deaths and casualties during the revolution approached 2000.[20] When the situation in the capital became desperate, the Tsar despatched General Ivanov with the express purpose of co-ordinating a major military action against the insurgents. But the revolution was too powerful. Railway workers blocked Ivanov's movement and troops sent to join him crossed over to the side of the workers. Only then, in despair, did the High Command seek political means of stemming the revolution, persuading the Tsar first to grant a ministry responsible to the Duma and when this was evidently inadequate, compelling him to abdicate.

The growing revolutionary threat had an equally decisive impact upon the liberals. Far from seeking revolution, they were terrified of it. As a result they could not bring themselves to mount any forceful challenge to the autocracy. During the war the Kadet leaders of the Progressive Bloc did not even request a ministry responsible to the Duma but merely a 'ministry of confidence', hoping to make their programme acceptable not only to right-wing deputies but to government ministers and indeed to the Tsar himself.[21] Miliukov and the other leaders explicitly stated that the Progressive Bloc was to serve as a barrier against revolution, a route by which the regime could escape revolution from below. The same could be said of the half-hearted plots by Guchkov and others to remove Nicholas from the scene. Their purpose was not revolution but its prevention, and the peaceful transfer of power to the bourgeoisie. In the face of the Tsar's intransi-

---

[18] Golub, *Istoricheskii opyt* II, p. 155.
[19] *op. cit.* II, p. 201.
[20] Burdzhalov, *Russia's Second Revolution*, pp. 337–8.
[21] N. G. Dumova, *Kadetskaia partiia v period pervoi mirovoi voiny i Fevral'skoi revoliutsii* (Moscow, 1988), pp. 60–1.

gence, it is true, a few more radical spirits criticized Miliukov's tactical caution. Leaders of the Progressive party proposed bolder statements of opposition, and there were disparate demands by radical liberals for efforts to build links with the socialist parties and with workers and peasants. But nothing came of this because no liberal programme could answer the needs of workers, soldiers, and peasants. In any case, these Left liberals were neither united nor numerically significant. It was the Kadet party that was emerging more and more clearly as the mouthpiece for bourgeois interests. The party's links with the public organizations, with the zemstvos, the WICs, and especially the urban dumas, were being steadily consolidated. The bourgeoisie as a whole was closing ranks behind its parliamentary leadership. And efforts within the Kadet party to give a more radical tinge to the policies of that leadership invariably failed.

The tension between the bourgeoisie and the autocracy did intensify the 'crisis of the élites', and *objectively* liberal criticism of the regime added to the revolutionary ferment. In the inflamed political atmosphere of November 1916, Miliukov's famous speech made an impact.[22] But the liberals made no autonomous or voluntary contribution to the revolution. Their *intentions* were hostile to the revolution throughout. As the mass movement reached its climax in the last days of February, the Duma leaders dithered. Even as late as 27 February, when the Tsar's government ordered the Duma prorogued, they hesitated to disobey. There would be no Russian equivalent of the French Third Estate's 'Tennis Court Oath' in 1789. Instead they assembled a 'private' meeting of members of the Duma and issued a statement which deliberately kept open the option of coming to terms with the Tsar should he regain control of the situation. Only when the victory of the revolution was beyond doubt did they move to form a Provisional Government, spurred to action by the establishment of the Petrograd Soviet and the danger that they would be bypassed altogether. Even the pressure that they, along with the generals, mounted for the Tsar's abdication was merely in response to the mass movement from below. And Miliukov's passionate entreaty to Grand Duke Michael to accept his brother's crown and decamp to Moscow to re-establish authority showed just how anxious he was to preserve the monarchy.[23]

The behaviour of the Mensheviks and SRs was but a petty-bourgeois variation on the bourgeois theme. Their leaders were cut off from the popular ferment, helpless bystanders. Instead of active intervention on the streets they wrung their hands in the salons of educated *intelligenty*. It was only as the revolutionary upsurge gained momentum that Chkeidze and Kerensky, the Menshevik and Trudovik

---

[22] Golub, *Istoricheskii opyt* II, p. 149.
[23] E. D. Chermenskii, *IV Gosudarstvennaia duma i sverzhenie tsarizma v Rossii* (Moscow, 1976), pp. 100, 281–91, *passim*.

leaders in the Duma, became outspoken in their criticisms of bourgeois cowardice. Likewise, it was only when it was at last borne in upon the Labour group on the Central WIC that their moderate attitude inspired no confidence among the masses that they moved Left, called for a strike on 14 February, and were promptly arrested. The moderate socialists were dragged along by events and their contribution to the revolution was modest indeed.

The prominence they rapidly achieved after the fall of the tsarist regime was not, therefore, based upon their record in the underground. They gained it by deft opportunism. On being released from prison, the Labour group found the revolution sweeping all before it. Together with the Duma socialists and other non-party *intelligenty*, they frantically sought a way of gaining a footing within it. While the Bolsheviks were busy on the streets securing the victory of the revolution, the petty-bourgeois leaders hurriedly set up a Provisional Executive Committee (EC) of the Soviet. The Bolsheviks had already called for the re-establishment of the Soviet. To ensure its autonomy and independence from the bourgeoisie they had proposed that it assemble at the Finland Station in the solidly proletarian Vyborg district. The petty-bourgeois leaders, on the other hand, with characteristic subservience to the bourgeoisie, established their Provisional EC in the Tauride Palace, alongside and under the shadow of the Duma. It was their good fortune that the politically immature soldiers gravitated towards the Tauride Palace, carrying the less conscious elements of the proletariat with them. As a result the Bolsheviks and the most class-conscious workers had to abandon the idea of using the Finland Station, follow the road to the Tauride Palace, and accept that temporarily at least the EC was dominated by the petty-bourgeois parties.

As soon as the Petrograd Soviet had emerged, workers and soldiers enthusiastically rallied behind it. So great was the popular support for it that 'it had every opportunity, by a peaceful route, without the slightest resistance from any side, to become the fully powerful organ of the revolutionary dictatorship of the workers and peasants.'[24] But the moderate socialists deliberately passed up the opportunity. They were terrified by the revolutionary zeal of the masses and strove to restrict the role of the Soviet and prevent it from developing its potential to create a truly revolutionary government. They meekly accepted the Duma Committee's assertion of control over the Soviet's Military Commission. They tried to submerge the newly-created workers' militia within the parallel militia being set up by the bourgeoisie. Only under direct pressure from soldier activists did they issue the Soviet's famous Order No. 1, which ensured the soldiers'

[24] Golub, *Istoricheskii opyt* II, p. 278.

prime loyalty was to the Soviet rather than to the emergent Provisional Government. Their anxiety to hand power to the bourgeoisie was so great that even Miliukov was astonished how readily they agreed to offer support to the liberal programme that he and his colleagues drew up. And even though every step taken by the new government demonstrated its total dependence on the Soviet, especially as soviets springing up across the country pronounced their allegiance to the Petrograd Soviet rather than the Provisional Government, the Mensheviks and SRs remained determined to smooth the path for bourgeois rule. On the pretext that it was essential to wean the bourgeoisie from a possible alliance with counter-revolution, they duped the delegates of less conscious workers and politically undeveloped soldiers into accepting bourgeois government.

The result was dual power. The Provisional Government took office, but since the Soviet retained the allegiance of the masses, much power remained with it. A similar uneasy balance, with regional variations, emerged across the country. Betrayal by the Mensheviks and SRs had temporarily stemmed the tide of revolution. It would be eight months before the masses, led by the Bolsheviks, were in a position to establish full soviet power.

Revisionist work and February

The continuity of the revolutionary movement
How, then, does the controversy over the February revolution appear in the light of revisionist work? Several features of the Soviet account are, with qualification, borne out. The massive wave of protest which overwhelmed the regime in February 1917 was deeply rooted in the experience and traditions of the Petrograd working class. A substantial proportion of the rebels of 1917 evidently were 'veterans' of pre-war campaigns: revisionist scrutiny of figures assembled by Soviet scholars puts the number of 'cadre' workers in Petrograd at between 40 per cent and 50 per cent.[25] Though exacerbated by wartime conditions, their grievances were very similar to those which had provoked them before 1914. Skilled and literate workers sought not only higher wages and a shorter working week, but an end to crude and degrading treatment by foremen and administrators. Their concern to assert their human dignity and gain control over their lives in the work place was demonstrated by the immediate steps they took to purge factories of offensive

---

[25] Smith, *Red Petrograd. Revolution in the Factories 1917–1918* (Cambridge, 1983), p. 23; T. Hasegawa, *The February Revolution: Petrograd 1917* (Seattle, 1981), p. 80; R. A. Wade, *Red Guards and Workers' Militias in the Russian Revolution* (Stanford, Cal., 1984), pp. 19–20.

bosses and to set up factory committees to reshape the factory order.[26]

It is clear, too, both that there was a close correlation between the presence of these cadre workers and the level of industrial and especially political protest, and that the ratio of political to economic strikes rose markedly during the war.[27] Since so many political strikes were expressly called for one day only, Soviet historians seem justified in concentrating on the number of strikers rather than the number of working days lost to gauge the ratio between the two. The inference that cadre workers exerted a growing influence over their initially less politicized fellow-workers seems thoroughly plausible.

The February days saw a convergence between the two groups of workers. The action of 23 February was initiated by women workers protesting specifically about the shortage of bread. But before the day was over, the most politically militant metal workers in the Vyborg district had joined the protest. The way in which workers sustained and spread the strike over the following days, and converged again and again on the centre of the city to demonstrate for the overthrow of the regime; the way they outfaced the police; and the deliberation with which they won over the garrison – all bear witness to their determination to see the political struggle through. The action of 23 February and its sequel were accompanied by more violence and robbery than Soviet accounts suggest, and were 'spontaneous' as opposed to carefully pre-planned. But if this traditional liberal label for the revolution is taken to mean that the Petrograd workers had not considered and were barely aware of the political implications of what they were doing, it is no longer acceptable. The revolution was not centrally organized but it was consciously willed.

The role of the Bolsheviks
Where the Soviet account carries much less conviction is in the claims made for the leadership role of the Bolsheviks. In the first place, it is difficult to determine how great a contribution political activists of all underground parties made to worker militancy. For Hasegawa, author of the major revisionist monograph on February, this 'sub-élite' of activists, amounting to no more than 2 per cent of the work-force, played an important role because they 'channelled the amorphous grievances aired by the masses into definite political actions.'[28] The

[26] H. Hogan, 'Conciliation Boards in Revolutionary Petrograd: Aspects of the Crisis of Labor-Management Relations in 1917', *Russian History* 9 (1982), pp. 49–66; D. Mandel, *The Petrograd Workers and the Fall of the Old Regime; The Petrograd Workers and Soviet Seizure of Power* (2 vols, London, 1983–4) I, pp. 95–100.
[27] Smith, *Red Petrograd*, pp. 48–53.
[28] T. Hasegawa, 'The Problem of Power in the February Revolution of 1917 in Russia', *Canadian Slavonic Papers* XIV (1972), p. 616.

extreme radicalism of the social insurance councils;[29] the support for the boycott of the WICs; the response to strike-calls of an unmistakably political character, such as those to mark the anniversary of Bloody Sunday – all bear the imprint at least in part of the efforts of party activists. However, the problem is that while the written evidence (party publications, memoirs and police documents) is eloquent about the claims of party activists, about the purpose of their propaganda, and about the belief of the police that they were to blame for mass disaffection, it cannot demonstrate the extent of this influence. Activists affiliated to one party or another were certainly responsible for the bulk of the underground literature produced, yet their numbers may well have been matched by activists with no party affiliation. Even if the assumption is granted that party membership betokened the highest level of political consciousness and activity, there were many gradations between that and apoliticism. The fact that protesting crowds adopted the slogans favoured by party men – 'Down with Autocracy! Down with the War!' – does not prove that ordinary men and women had not thought of these goals for themselves.

Moreover, the Soviet view appears to underrate the influence of the legal Labour group. The group's popularity increased when they moved to the Left in the winter of 1916 and even more when they were arrested, and they joined in the call for the great strike of 9 January 1917. Likewise, the events of 14 February appear in a rather different light when it is observed that it was the Labour group who originally called for the strike (in which almost a quarter of the work-force joined), that the Bolsheviks had tried but failed to pre-empt it with a strike a day or two earlier, and that one reason for the derisory turn-out at the Tauride Palace that day was that the authorities mounted a heavy guard around it.[30]

Even if the point is granted that the underground played a significant role, it is not easy to disentangle Bolshevik influence from that of activists affiliated to other parties. Popular action which Soviet historians claim was inspired by Bolshevik propaganda often turns out on closer examination to have been urged by their rivals as well. Both the Menshevik Initiative group and the Interdistrict group joined in the call for the 9 January strike and, like the Bolsheviks, denounced the call by the Labour group for demonstrations on 14 February to converge on the Tauride Palace. The activity of the Interdistrict group within the Petrograd garrison may well have exceeded that of the Bolsheviks. And radical SRs, both in the capital and at the front, sustained a vigorous if poorly co-ordinated campaign during the war.

[29] S. Milligan, 'The Petrograd Bolsheviks and Social Insurance, 1914–1917', *Soviet Studies* 20 (1968–9), pp. 369–74.
[30] See Hasegawa, *February Revolution*, pp. 204–10, and the discussion in D. A. Longley, 'The *Mezhraionka*, the Bolsheviks and International Women's Day', *Soviet Studies* XLI (1989), pp. 625–45.

They had as many as 500–600 activists in Petrograd factories by the beginning of 1916, they had a significant presence in the largest metal-working plants in the Vyborg district, and they were for the most part as intransigent as the Bolsheviks in their attitude to the war, the WICs, and the need for early revolution. Soviet computation of Bolshevik literary output is rendered dubious by the widespread cross-party co-operation in the underground and the fact that many leaflets credited to the Bolsheviks were put out jointly with other parties. Equally, since many Social Democratic committees retained joint Bolshevik–Menshevik membership until after February, Soviet head counts of Bolshevik membership and carefully plotted maps depicting the spread of Bolshevik local committees and groups suggest a degree of precision, as well as of Bolshevik predominance, that the sources do not warrant.[31] In the era of *glasnost*, Soviet scholars have themselves suggested that the traditional estimate of 24,000 members in February is exaggerated and that a figure of 10,000 is nearer the mark.[32] Similarly, the Soviet estimate that by February Bolshevik membership in the capital outnumbered the combined total of all other parties by 3000 to 1000 must be treated with scepticism. The archival evidence and the memoir literature that lead to this conclusion are badly skewed in the Bolsheviks' favour, and the incentive for Soviet historians to uncover sources pointing in the other direction has long been poor.[33] Revisionist access to the relevant archives has been very limited, but the skilled assembling of scattered evidence, to be found in various Soviet publications, about the activity of the non-Bolshevik underground has cast grave doubt on Bolshevik domination.[34]

Moreover, Soviet emphasis on the party's unity and organizational coherence during the war and the revolution does not bear close scrutiny. At the outbreak of hostilities the party was badly split. By some accounts, as many as half the members of the Central Committee itself initially supported the Allied cause. Even when activists began

[31] See for example R. G. Suny, *The Baku Commune 1917–1918. Class and Nationality in the Russian Revolution* (Princeton, N.J., 1972), pp. 89–91; D. J. Raleigh, 'Revolutionary Politics in Provincial Russia: The Tsaritsyn "Republic" in 1917', *Slavic Review* 40 (1981), pp. 194–209.

[32] V. I. Miller, 'K voprosy o sravnitel'noi chislennosti partii bol'shevikov i men'shevikov v 1917g.', *Voprosy istorii KPSS* (1988) 12, pp. 109–18.

[33] It was only at the end of the 1920s that Soviet historiography began to lay heavy emphasis on the role of the Bolsheviks in the February revolution. For discussion of the impact of the changing party line on the relevant sources, see J. D. White, 'The February Revolution and the Bolshevik Vyborg District Committee', *Soviet Studies* XLI (1989), pp. 602–24, a response to M. Melancon, 'Who Wrote What and When?: Proclamations of the February Revolution in Petrograd, 23 February–1 March 1917', *Soviet Studies* XL (1988), pp. 479–500.

[34] For the best treatment of the non-Bolshevik underground during the war, and of the SRs in particular, see M. S. Melancon, 'The Socialist Revolutionaries from 1902 to February 1917. A Party of Workers, Peasants and Soldiers', (Ph.D. Dissertation, Indiana University, 1984), chaps. 3–9.

to regroup, they never took their opposition to the war as far as Lenin's outright defeatism. And whatever the influence credited to the Bolshevik 'sub-élite' in the capital, the élite itself was in no position to provide overall leadership. Time and again during the war, and during the February days themselves, the Petersburg Committee was devastated by arrests; during the crucial period from 23–27 February the party in the capital did not even have a printing press at its disposal; and the blurring of authority between the Russian Bureau of the Central Committee, the Petersburg Committee, and the Vyborg Committee points less to homogeneity than to the fragility of the first two and to a (thoroughly understandable) muddle.[35] Bolshevik ascendancy over other parties in terms of size and coherence was less clear-cut, their internal divisions greater, Lenin's authority weaker, and their overall influence slighter than Soviet historiography claims.

The immediate sequel to the overthrow of the tsarist government bears witness to the limitations of Bolshevik unity and leadership. For one thing, significant differences of policy immediately emerged. The Vyborg Committee issued a fiery call for a Provisional Government based on the Soviet; the Russian Bureau was more cautious, and when it became clear that other socialist leaders had no wish to form such a government, appears to have accepted that the Duma leaders should take office; the Petersburg Committee endorsed the Soviet's conditional support for the liberal Provisional Government; and the group who took control of *Pravda* early in March took a similar line, and went so far as to give conditional support to the war.[36] Moreover, in the country at large, even according to Soviet figures, Bolsheviks initially gained control of a mere 27 out of 242 workers' soviets formed by the end of March.[37] In the Petrograd Soviet itself, which represented the country's most militant workers, Bolshevik deputies were in a very small minority, with only some 40 out of 600 deputies at the beginning of March. Even with sympathetic radical SRs and Interdistrict deputies, the far Left could initially muster no more than 10 per cent of the delegates.[38]

Soviet historians have wrestled long and hard with this conundrum: the failure of the masses to support the party which had led them. They have stressed the overrepresentation within the Soviet of the 'petty-bourgeois' soldiery, whose deputies came to exceed those of workers deputies by 2.3 to 1; the higher public profile which legal status had lent the WIC Labour group and Menshevik Duma leaders before the revolution; the fact that most deputies declared no party allegiance

[35] T. Hasegawa, 'The Bolsheviks and the Formation of the Petrograd Soviet in the February Revolution', *Soviet Studies* 29 (1977), pp. 86–107.

[36] D. A. Longley, 'The Divisions in the Bolshevik Party in March 1917', *Soviet Studies* 24 (1972), pp. 61–76.

[37] I. I. Mints, *Istoriia Velikogo Oktiabria* (3 vols, Moscow 1977–79, 2nd edn) I, p. 682.

[38] Hasegawa, *February Revolution*. p. 380.

and many electors failed to distinguish between the parties; the price the Bolsheviks paid for concentrating on securing the victory of the revolution in the streets rather than on the organization of power.[39] But the centrepiece of their explanation is that the early distribution of delegates among workers as well as soldiers reflected the great wave of petty-bourgeois elements suddenly drawn into the revolution. Even if the underlying equation were accepted (proletarian consciousness = Bolshevik; petty-bourgeois illusions = non-Bolshevik) the explanation would fail to reconcile the party's electoral insignificance with the notion that it led the revolution.

Proletarian 'hegemony'

It is not only Soviet claims on behalf of the Bolshevik party that seem excessive. So too does their insistence on 'proletarian hegemony' in the revolution. 'Hegemony' is a difficult concept to grapple with from outside the realm of Leninist lexicography: it is at once so assertive and so vague. Certainly the workers of Petrograd were the prime movers in the revolution. It was their protest which launched the revolution and overpowered the police, and their pleading with the troops not to shoot helped to trigger the mutiny in the garrison. It is true, too, that workers (and underground activists) exerted some direct influence on the mood of the soldiers; that barracks situated close to militant factories may have been particularly affected by the spectacle of strike action; and that communication between workers and soldiers was facilitated by the drafting of militant workers into the army as well as the employment of soldiers in the civilian economy. Yet the notion that workers therefore exercised 'hegemonic' leadership over the soldiers is difficult to sustain. The breakdown of military discipline was essentially the product of the soldiers' own experience. It reflected the profound social gulf imported into the army from a polarized rural society, exacerbated by the horror and deprivations of war.[40] Nor is the proletariat's supposed leadership of the soldiers adequate evidence that they exercised 'hegemony' over the peasantry in the countryside. Like the peasants in the army, peasants in the villages immediately saw the fall of the Tsar opening the way to drastic land reform.[41] In both cases they were moved by age-old and autonomous aspirations to which the proletariat had contributed little.

Here, too, the immediate sequel to the fall of the government casts doubt on Soviet claims. In so far as proletarian hegemony is equated with other classes falling into line with the most radical elements

---

[39] Iu. S. Tokarev, *Petrogradskii Sovet rabochikh i soldatskikh deputatov v marte–aprele 1917 g.* (Leningrad, 1976), pp. 120ff. V. P. Naumov, *Sovetskaia istoriografiia Fevral'skoi burzhuazno-demokraticheskoi revoliutsii* (Moscow 1979), pp. 130ff.

[40] A. K. Wildman, *The End of the Russian Imperial Army* (2 vols, Princeton, N.J., 1980, 1987) I, chap. 3 and p. 374.

[41] G. Gill, *Peasants and Government in the Russian Revolution* (London, 1979), pp. 21–3.

among the proletariat, it is belied by the events surrounding the establishment of the Soviet and the Provisional Government. Instead of heeding the Bolshevik call to set up the Soviet at the Finland Station in the Vyborg district, soldiers responded to the moderate socialists and converged on the Tauride Palace. They backed the EC's policy of conditional support for the Provisional Government, and in the early days of the new regime the army as a whole, while wanting peace, reacted angrily against any evidence that workers were reluctant to uphold the front. Similarly, if the proletariat exercised 'hegemony' over the wider strata of the democratic population, it is mystifying that students, clerks, the third element of the zemstvos and others should so rapidly have rallied behind the Provisional Government, lent support to the formation of a middle-class-led militia, and distanced themselves from the Soviet.

The notion of Bolshevik leadership and proletarian hegemony, then, cannot be sustained. Members of the party helped to articulate the aspirations of workers, and the actions of the workers precipitated the mutiny of soldiers and raised the hopes of peasants. But the motivation of the masses was very much their own: a determination deeply rooted in the social antagonisms of Imperial Russia to effect a fundamental shift in power away from managers, officers and land-owners towards workers, soldiers and peasants. It was this determination which brought about the February revolution and conditioned its sequel.

The tsarist regime and February

Revisionist work on the internal crisis of the tsarist regime accords more closely with the Soviet than the liberal account. It places relatively little emphasis upon the importance of Nicholas's personal shortcomings, the anachronistic advice of Alexandra, and the malign influence of Rasputin. Even Nicholas's much-criticized decision to assume supreme command in the summer of 1915 was less foolish and ill-considered than has generally been claimed. No doubt it reflected in part his personal understanding of his duty and his romantic yearning to place himself at the head of his troops in the nation's hour of need. But it reflected, too, his anxiety that the current incumbent, the Grand Duke Nikolai Nikolaevich, be replaced. For one thing, the Grand Duke's nerves had been shattered by the first, disastrous year of the war. Worse still, he had allowed himself to be drawn into intimate contact with Duma critics of the government and had become some-thing of a symbol of opposition. This, in turn, was one product of a debilitating conflict of authority between the civilian government and the High Command, a conflict which grew ever worse as Russia's army retreated and the capital itself fell within the war zone. By himself replacing the Grand Duke, and thereby combining civil and military authority in his own person, Nicholas sought to solve all these problems. His decision may have done little to improve matters but it was no mere whim.[42]

Nor was Nicholas's refusal to compromise with the Duma or grant constitutional reforms the product of his own stupidity. His intransigence was fully in line with the very nature of tsarism and was warmly supported by its traditional supporters. It was energetically encouraged by the United Nobility; it suited well the major industrialists in the capital; it corresponded closely to the outlook of the High Command; and it was matched by the determination of the traditional leadership of zemstvos and municipal dumas to resist pressure from the third element for democratization of local government.[43] The activities of the voluntary organizations, of the WICs, the Union of Zemstvos and the Union of Towns, and the more radical of the demands issuing for the Duma, challenged not only the authority of the Tsar but the traditional prerogatives and prevailing ethos of the bureaucracy and landed nobility alike. The tsarist system, in short, was 'structurally and ideologically' incapable of co-operating with and accommodating the increasingly vigorous role sought by the middle classes.[44]

Moreover, unlike liberal accounts, revisionist work rejects the notion that the regime's inability to survive in February was the result of incompetence, that greater resolution on the part of the authorities could have saved the autocracy. Khabalov, the general responsible for security in the capital, was indeed grossly inadequate. But the strength of the challenge from the working class and the depth of disaffection in the garrison would have left the most able of officers helpless. The actions of the High Command at the front, too, are to be understood primarily in terms of the upheaval from below. An attempt at armed intervention entailed such high risks, not only of disrupting supplies to the army, spreading mutiny to the front, and unleashing full-scale civil war, but of outright failure, that the generals preferred to reach a compromise. As soon as they heard that the Duma leaders rather than anti-war socialists were forming a new government they drew back from confrontation. And it was because they learned that the insurgents would not countenance Nicholas remaining on the throne that they sacrificed him. Nor had they misjudged the odds. So powerful was the revolutionary upsurge that attempts at repression would have been futile: 'a much more violent upheaval would have

[42] D. R. Jones, 'Nicholas II and the Supreme Command: An investigation of motives', *Sbornik* 11 (1985), pp. 47–83.

[43] W. Gleason, 'The All-Russian Union of Zemstvos and World War I', in T. Emmons and W. S. Vucinich, eds, *The Zemstvo in Russia* (Cambridge, Mass., 1983), pp. 365–82; W. Gleason, 'The All-Russian Union of Towns and the Politics of Urban Reform in Tsarist Russia', *Russian Review* xxxv (1976), pp. 290-303.

[44] L. H. Siegelbaum, *The Politics of Industrial Mobilization in Russia, 1914–1917. A Study of the War-Industry Committees* (London, 1983), p. 212.

been the only prospect, and the partisans of authority could not possibly have prevailed.'[45]

The liberals

At first glance, recent analysis of middle-class and liberal behaviour during the war is also close to the Soviet interpretation. The opposition which the moderate leadership in the Duma offered to the government was feeble and half-hearted. Soviet accounts may underrate their concern not to rock the boat in wartime, not to provoke the Tsar into dissolving the Duma, and not to alienate the right wing of the Progressive Bloc. But a vital source of their inhibition was fear of revolution. Throughout, this 'recurrent nightmare' cast a sickly pall over the strategy they adopted. No action followed Miliukov's fiery speech in November 1916, and even during the February days the Duma liberals proved extremely reluctant to throw in their lot with the revolution. The most detailed revisionist study of government–Duma relations during the war concludes that 'From 1914 to 1917, the moderates were campaigning not for revolution, not even for fundamental reform, but for the maintenance of the political and constitutional status quo.'[46]

If it is assumed that the Kadet leadership in the Duma, and Miliukov in particular, were representative of the middle classes as a whole, the Soviet charge that the 'bourgeoisie' were hostile to the revolution is difficult to refute. Yet closer examination of the 'bourgeoisie' demonstrates that the assumption is false. The ethnic, regional, cultural and professional divisions, the hostility between the large banks and syndicates centred on Petrograd and the smaller firms in Moscow, and the differences in wealth and social status which fractured the Empire's middle classes were not suddenly overcome after 1914.[47] And during the war they found political expression. The Moscow-based leadership of the WICs showed much greater stomach for a fight with the government than did the Duma Kadets. Equally, while the oligarchic leadership of the Union of Towns and the Union of Zemstvos were hostile to political reform, rank-and-file employees of both – doctors, statisticians, teachers, lawyers – became increasingly radical during the war and furiously criticized their own leadership.[48] Within the Duma itself, the Progressive party strove consistently to prod the Kadets to more forceful opposition, to go beyond the limits of the law, defy the Tsar, convoke the Duma illegally, and make common cause

[45] Wildman, *Russian Imperial Army* I, pp. 374–6.
[46] R. Pearson, *The Russian Moderates and the Crisis of Tsarism, 1914–1917* (London, 1977), p. 176.
[47] A. J. Rieber, *Merchants and Entrepreneurs in Imperial Russia* (Chapel Hill, N.C., 1982), pp. 372–404.
[48] Gleason, 'Union of Towns', *passim*; Gleason, 'Union of Zemstvos', *passim*.

with the socialist parties. They campaigned for legalization of trade unions, seeing collective bargaining as the best way to counter labour militancy.[49] It is true that practical efforts to build bridges with workers, notably the incorporation of worker representatives into the WICs, rapidly alienated industrialists.[50] The polarization between workers and employers, and between the peasants-in-grey and their officers, may well have ruled out the possibility that even the most radical liberals could have gained the allegiance of the masses. But Miliukov's horror of revolution and devotion to monarchy were not typical: wide sections of the middle classes were genuinely delighted when the Tsar was overthrown.

The moderate socialists

Revisionist work has cast the role played in February by the Menshevik and SR leadership of the Petrograd Soviet in a relatively sympathetic light. They emerge as less dogmatic, more sincere and more realistic than in either liberal or Soviet accounts. The primary explanation for their determination that the Duma leaders rather than the Soviet should form the new government does not lie in Menshevik commitment to the idea that the revolution must inaugurate a long period of capitalist development and that bourgeois politicians must take power. Some, it is true, were predisposed towards a period of co-operation with the bourgeoisie by their experience during the war of co-operation with Left liberals, the third element, and even a few progressive industrialists.[51] But the initiative on the Soviet EC was seized at first not by moderate Mensheviks and SRs but by radical internationalist Mensheviks. A significant number of them, including N. N. Sukhanov who played a leading role in negotiations with Miliukov and his colleagues over the formation of a liberal government, were by no means resigned to prolonged bourgeois domination. On the contrary, they were confident of approaching western revolution and expected this to make possible a much more radical transition in Russia. They therefore envisaged the working class taking every advantage of the revolution to develop its organization and political influence. They had no intention of emasculating the Soviet. Before reaching an agreement with the Duma leaders they reiterated their call for the election of soldiers' deputies to the Soviet (and renamed it the Soviet of Workers' and Soldiers' Deputies)

---

[49] A detailed analysis of the Progressists is provided by W. L. Duggan, 'The Progressists and Russian Politics, 1914–1917', (Ph.D. Dissertation, Columbia University, 1984).
[50] Siegelbaum, *Industrial Mobilization*, pp. 176–7, 211.
[51] Z. Galili y Garcia, 'The Menshevik Revolutionary Defencists and the Workers in the Russian Revolution of 1917', (Ph.D. Dissertation, Columbia University, 1980), pp. 27–36.

in order to buttress its position by establishing links with the garrison.[52]

What they feared, however, was the danger of immediate intervention from the front. It was vital, therefore, that the liberal leaders and their followers – including middle-class officers and bureaucrats – be bound to the side of the revolution. Their aim was to commit the bourgeoisie by encouraging Miliukov and his colleagues to take office while carefully circumscribing their freedom of action.[53] This policy cannot be dismissed as a product of lack of self-confidence, inexperience and disunity. It was not contradictory, still less were they feigning anxiety or deliberately misleading the masses as Soviet accounts imply. And, as the almost unanimous vote in the Soviet plenum endorsing conditional support for the Provisional Government demonstrated, the fear of counter-revolution was shared by workers in the capital including a good many Bolsheviks.[54]

Moreover, the fear was not unfounded. It was because they were persuaded that the Duma was taking control that the High Command called off plans to march on Petrograd. Had a Soviet government been proclaimed it is very likely that they would have persisted in their plans.[55] As we have seen, given the depth of disaffection in the army it is more than doubtful whether counter-revolution could have prevailed. But it does not follow, as Soviet historians charge, that the EC threw away the opportunity 'peacefully' and 'without resistance' to establish effective national government based on the Soviet. Although the Soviet was certainly strong enough to exercise a veto over the activities of the Provisional Government, its own powers were limited. Its Military Commission discovered at once that junior officers in the capital looked to the Duma. Experts on the Food Commission showed the same loyalties.[56] Nor would it have been easy, without at the very least severe disruption, to wrest control of the railway and telegraph networks from the Duma appointees whose orders were being obeyed.

Equally, the notion that the EC was in a position to form an effective government exaggerates its authority over its own popular constituency. Both workers and soldiers in the capital made clear that their allegiance was to the EC rather than the Duma. But though workers would take orders from no one else, the fierce autonomy asserted by their militia and emergent factory committees showed that they would be highly selective about which Soviet instructions to obey. The

[52] Wildman, *Russian Imperial Army* I, pp. 180–1. This point is glossed over in most but not all Soviet accounts: compare the presentation of the EC's attitude in Golub, *Istoricheskii opyt* II, pp. 256–7, with that in the pathbreaking Soviet account of February, Burdzhalov, *Russia's Second Revolution*, p. 248.

[53] Galili y Garcia, 'Menshevik Revolutionary Defencists', pp. 39–45, 68ff.

[54] Mandel, *Petrograd Workers* I, pp. 66–84.

[55] Hasegawa, *February Revolution*, pp. 473–86.

[56] Galili y Garcia, 'Menshevik Revolutionary Defencists', pp. 51–5, 72–4.

soldiers' readiness to follow any lead from above could be relied upon
even less. Their attitude to the war, on which so much else depended,
was far from clear. The prevailing mood, certainly at the front,
combined a longing for peace and deep reluctance to attempt fresh
offensives with readiness to hold the line until peace came.[57] The 'dual
power' established in February was less between the Provisional
Government and the EC than between the Provisional Government
and the insurgent masses.[58] And it is only in the light of the power
seized from below, the autonomous intervention of millions of
workers, soldiers and peasants, that the political drama of the
following months can be understood.

[57] Wildman, *Russian Imperial Army* I, pp. 219–45.
[58] Hasegawa, *February Revolution*, p. 408.

6 THE FAILURE OF THE PROVISIONAL GOVERNMENT

Why did the Provisional Government fail? This is the classic question set before generations of undergraduates studying the revolution. It is the central question addressed by the memoirs of members and close observers of the Provisional Government – by Miliukov and Sukhanov, by Tsereteli and Chernov and, with relentless perseverance, by Kerensky. At first glance, Russia's new rulers seemed to have so much running in their favour. The first cabinet was led by nationally-known liberal politicians, it was inundated with expressions of support from towns, army units and remote villages across the country, was accepted by the High Command, landowners and industrialists, and quickly secured recognition from the Allied powers. Its social base, admittedly, was narrow, but the formation of a coalition with moderate socialist leaders on 5 May seemed to place the government on firm popular foundations. The Mensheviks and SRs dominated the EC not only of the Petrograd Soviet, but of the great majority of the hundreds of worker, soldier and peasant soviets which sprang up, and of the All-Russian Congress of Soviets. Elections to the newly-democratized urban dumas during the summer confirmed the popularity of the coalition partners. And yet, after a mere eight months, the Provisional Government proved unable to rally any significant resistance to a Bolshevik-led uprising and was swept from power.

At one level, the explanations offered for this débâcle by traditional liberal and Soviet historians coincide. The Provisional Government failed to solve the major problems confronting the country and thereby forfeited much of the support it had initially enjoyed. Equally, it failed either to contain by force the popular unrest which gathered momentum during the year, or to crush the Bolshevik party which ultimately organized its overthrow. This much is agreed. But in accounting for these failures, the two lines of interpretation sharply diverge. Revisionist work, both by analysing the formation of government policy and viewing developments from below, casts light on each of the main points of contention.

The liberal view

In the traditional liberal view, the primary problem lay in the political inadequacy of the members of the Provisional Government. In the first place, they were imbued with the benign idealism characteristic of

129

moderate sections of the Russian intelligentsia. They were only really comfortable in the role to which they had become accustomed, that of criticizing the government. They had no taste for power. They were loath to use force, to ape in any way the Tsar's repressive regime. Instead, they placed their faith in the innate virtue and good sense of the much-wronged people, and relied upon persuasion, emotional appeals for support, and high-flown rhetoric. Revolutionary Russia was 'launched and would continue to be swayed by powerful gusts of hot air'.[1] Moreover, although some members of the cabinet had spent several years debating in the Duma, they had little understanding of the workings of government, of the importance of administrative order and clear lines of authority. And in their purist concern to introduce democracy of the most perfect and advanced form, they let precious time slip by while they agonized over the niceties of the new institutions they set up. To make matters worse, they were hopelessly indecisive. A serious flaw in any government, this was disastrous in the critical situation they faced. Their procrastination and lack of resolution reflected both their strong awareness that their authority was no more than provisional and their 'sense of grave responsibility which called for meticulous preparations for what were seen as momentous events in the history of Russia.'[2] It reflected, too, the bitter divisions within the cabinet. Liberal members were drawn from several different parties, and even the Kadets, the major liberal party, were themselves divided. This situation was greatly aggravated first by the external pressure which the Petrograd Soviet exerted, and then by the incorporation of socialists into the government.

The Mensheviks and SRs, in the traditional liberal view, pursued policies that were inherently contradictory, and their supposed support for and participation in the Provisional Government were at best half-hearted and at worst treacherous. While claiming to stand for the defence of the country, they helped to undermine military discipline; while paying lip service to the maintenance of government authority, they emasculated its ability to compel obedience; while preaching conciliation in industry, they incited workers against employers; while officially accepting that the problem of the land and that of minority demands for national autonomy must await resolution by the Constituent Assembly, they took pre-emptive steps on both. Instead of closing ranks with the liberals behind a clear, agreed programme, the socialists pulled in several directions at once and bitterly resisted their partners over a wide range of issues. Twice the coalition collapsed altogether, and it was only with the greatest difficulty that it was

[1] A. Ulam, *Russia's Failed Revolutions* (London, 1981), p. 302.
[2] L. Schapiro, *1917. The Russian Revolutions and the Origins of Present-Day Communism* (Hounslow, 1984), p. 217.

reformed. Starry-eyed, incompetent, indecisive and divided, the Provisional Government made a series of errors and misjudgements which led it to its doom.

The Soviet view

For Soviet historians, each facet of this description is either invalid or irrelevant. Lvov, Prime Minister in the first two cabinets, may have been a mild individual; Kerensky, his successor, was doubtless a poseur and a windbag. But the 'problem' of the Provisional Government lay a thousand versts deeper: it lay in the class interests which the government represented. Throughout, it upheld the interests of the bourgeoisie and landowners and sought to suppress the demands of workers, soldiers and peasants. The dominant influence on all four cabinets, despite their holding a minority of posts in each, was that of the Kadet party. The party had become the effective spokesman of the bourgeoisie before February and after the revolution, with the collapse of all parties to the Right of it, the nobility and those industrialists who had held aloof closed ranks behind it, while it also became the vehicle for British and French imperialist pressure.

As for the petty-bourgeois 'socialist' parties, they posed as the champions of the masses but in fact they threw in their lot with the bourgeoisie. After betraying the masses in February by handing power to the liberals, the Mensheviks and SRs proceeded in May to form a coalition in order to prop them up. While waxing eloquent on their desire for peace, they took no effective steps to bring it about and fully supported the June offensive; while preaching liberty and democracy, they joined in vigorous repression of the Bolsheviks; while promising a long list of labour reforms, they caved in to the inevitable veto by their coalition partners; and while protesting their commitment to land reform and freedom for the national minorities, they used all their influence to postpone any resolution of either problem. Their feeble gestures of independence designed to retain mass support could not disguise their anxiety to keep the bourgeoisie in power and in essence they simply followed the Kadet line. Far from being a cause of the Provisional Government's demise, they gave it an undeserved lease of life. Such divisions as there were within the coalition were tactical rather than strategic and reflected the desperate search for a way out of an impasse from which liberal-bourgeois policies offered none. The Provisional Government pursued its doomed course not because of mistakes, miscalculations and woolly idealism but because it represented a bourgeoisie under mortal challenge from the Bolshevik-led revolutionary movement.

Legal and administrative reform

In liberal eyes, the Provisional Government's lamentable lack of realism was demonstrated from its first days in office by the legal and administrative reforms it undertook. A flurry of well-meaning but ill-advised proclamations saw the end of the death penalty, flogging and exile to Siberia; a full amnesty for political prisoners; the removal of legal discrimination on grounds of religion and nationality; the replacement of the police by a thoroughly decentralized and feeble militia system; the establishment of full freedom of the press and of association. 'None of its members seems to have considered the possibility that to remove at a stroke all constraints from a people accustomed for centuries to strict rule and a minimum of freedom might be a certain recipe for anarchy.'[3] Typical of the cabinet's slender grasp of political and administrative reality was Lvov's telegram, despatched three days after the government's inception, in which he dismissed from office the chief agents of central power in the localities, the provincial governors and vice-governors. The chairmen of local zemstvo boards whom he chose as 'commissars' in their place lacked both the administrative experience and the authority of their predecessors. The government thus compounded its rash legal reforms by undermining its own control over local affairs. It followed this up by launching a complete overhaul of local government, refounding the urban dumas and the zemstvos on the basis of equal suffrage, and creating a new lower tier of zemstvos at the level of the *volost'* (rural district). It was entirely characteristic that it failed to complete arrangements for elections to the zemstvos until August, by when it was too late: a jumble of rival bodies – soviets, soldiers' committees, peasant committees and organs of the national minorities – had usurped authority and the peasants hardly bothered to vote for zemstvo candidates. Had they deliberately set out to destroy their own authority, the ministers could hardly have done more.

In Soviet eyes, the government had no option but to enact these reforms. For the most part it was merely registering liberties that the masses had seized for themselves. In most towns, for example, political prisoners had been released by popular action before the amnesty was proclaimed. Lvov's telegram dismissing provincial governors is another case in point: it was quite clear that these officials were too closely associated with the hated tsarist regime to have any chance of commanding obedience, and many of them had been driven out before instructions arrived from Petrograd. Equally, since the tsarist police had fled with the triumph of the revolution, the Provisional Government was simply making the best of things by turning to the citizens' militia created on local initiative, hoping thereby to re-establish central control by regulating them and subordinating them to the new

[3] *op. cit.*, p. 61.

commissars. Nor could there be any question of backtracking on long-held liberal commitment to freedom of the press and of association, both of which were being exercised without leave from the new government. To have granted anything short of universal suffrage to the dumas and zemstvos would have removed whatever slim chance they had of attracting mass allegiance away from the supremely democratic soviets. From the start, the Provisional Government did what it could to stem the revolutionary tide. Its true colours were revealed by the retention of as many tsarist officials as possible. Deprived of real power, compelled to give way to mass pressure (hard though the Mensheviks and SRs tried to smother this pressure), the bourgeoisie and their government had no choice but to rely on 'hot air' – or rather a barrage of bogus democratic propaganda designed to deceive the masses.[4]

Revisionist work portrays the early Provisional Government in rather more favourable colours than do either traditional liberal or Soviet accounts. Its programme was inspired by classical liberal concern for the rule of law, the guarantee of civil rights, representative democracy and the security of private property.[5] Certainly it suffered from the administrative confusion inherent in the situation, from the inadequate flow of information from the provinces, and from the enormous budget deficit inherited from the Tsar. But Lvov's energetic steps to introduce a strong contingent of new liberal officials to run the cabinet secretariat and the Ministry of Internal Affairs suggests an approach that was neither covertly sympathetic to tsarism and reaction nor ineffectual.[6] Equally, Lvov and his colleagues were alive to the dangers of breaking administrative continuity. The dismissal of the provincial governors was unavoidable; the appointment of zemstvo chairmen in their place was deeply unpopular among the peasantry, but reflected the government's firm wish to postpone further administrative changes until local government had been democratically reformed;[7] and they did all they could to prevent the local Committees of Public Organizations, let alone the new ad hoc worker and peasant organizations, from establishing a permanent administrative role. Legalistic concern with the details of democratic procedures delayed new elections to the zemstvos, but it is unlikely that this was of crucial significance since by 1917 peasant attitudes towards the zemstvos were deeply negative.[8] Nor, given the disappearance of the traditional

[4] N. G. Dumova, *Kadetskaia partiia v period pervoi mirovoi voiny i Fevral'skoi revoliutsii* (Moscow, 1988), pp. 122–7.
[5] H. J. White, 'The Ministry of Internal Affairs and Revolution in the Provinces', unpublished research seminar paper (CREES, Birmingham, 1988), p. 6.
[6] *op. cit.*, pp. 9–10.
[7] Gill, *Peasants and Government in the Russian Revolution* (London, 1979), pp. 25–6.
[8] W. G. Rosenberg, 'The zemstvo in 1917 and its fate under Bolshevik rule', in Emmons and Vucinich, *Zemstvo*, pp. 383–5, 397–8; D. Atkinson, 'The zemstvo and the peasantry', in *op. cit.*, pp. 123–4; Gill, *Peasants and Government*, pp. 98–9.

police, were the government's efforts to formalize the position of the militia, to establish a full-time service and a central inspectorate, ill-considered. That the new ministers failed to consolidate control of the country is to be explained not by their legal and administrative record but on the one hand, by their lack of coercive power, and on the other by their broader political and social policies.

The Provisional Government and the use of force

In the traditional liberal view, the Provisional Government's supposed lack of coercive power was largely a lack of willpower. Successive cabinets simply failed to grasp the nettle, to take measures to enforce discipline in the army, halt peasant encroachment on private land, put the soviets in their place, and crush the Bolshevik party. Where the liberal ministers were concerned, this was in part another reflection of their political ineptitude. Until the middle of April, nationalist feeling both in the country and specifically in the army was intense. Indeed, at that stage 'nationalism . . . had risen like a tidal wave threatening to engulf the Bolsheviks.' 'Had the Provisional Government been composed of skilful and realistic politicians, they might well have used this brief period for exploiting the nationalist sentiment to put the Soviet in its place.'[9]

Even more culpable were the moderate socialists who joined the cabinet in early May. They positively encouraged sedition in the army. Not only did they fail to rescind the Petrograd Soviet's fateful Order No. 1 issued during the February days, but they compounded the error when on 11 May Kerensky, as War Minister, promulgated a Declaration of Soldiers' Rights. Inspired by the unrealistic principle that 'mutual relations of servicemen, while strictly maintaining military discipline, must be based on the feeling of dignity of citizens of free Russia, and on mutual confidence, respect and courtesy', the Declaration did further grievous damage, primarily by allowing servicemen to join political organizations. Moreover, the moderate socialists repeatedly restrained the government from using the army to assert its authority. During the April demonstrations against Miliukov they countermanded General Kornilov's initiative to clear the streets of the capital by force. In June they refused to take action against the Bolshevik party despite its blatantly seditious plans to stage an anti-government demonstration. Following the violent disturbances of the July Days, they prevented decisive measures being adopted: although *Pravda* was closed, Trotsky arrested and Lenin driven into hiding, the steps taken were not followed through. Only when mass insubordination and cowardice had ruined the June offensive was Kerensky persuaded, with the greatest difficulty, to restore the death penalty for military offences. Even then his conversion to the cause was half-

[9]Ulam, *Russia's Failed Revolutions*, pp. 341, 325.

hearted and in any case it was too late. Throughout, the moderate socialists persisted in seeing the Bolsheviks as erring comrades and in abiding by the slogan 'No Enemies to the Left!' They were preoccupied, instead, by the spectre of counter-revolution, of a rerun of the reaction which followed the French revolutions of 1789 and 1848. Yet in reality, 'there is not a jot of evidence to support [their] fear, unless by counter-revolution is meant introduction of order in the rear and restoration of fighting capacity at the front.'[10] The Kornilov affair, which they insisted upon seeing as the long-feared military counter-revolution, was no such thing. Kornilov was not a monarchist, and far from conspiring against the Provisional Government he believed until the last minute that his preparations for a show of force in Petrograd had the consent of the Prime Minister, Kerensky.[11]

The Soviet version, by contrast, sees a determination to use force crystallize very early in the life of the Provisional Government. The Kadet leadership, egged on by organizations representing the industrial and commercial bourgeoisie, army officers, and landowners, as well as by the embassies of the Allied powers, rapidly became convinced that the army must be used to halt the revolution. The party in the country, in part because of the influx of 'March Kadets' from the far Right, moved steadily towards the same conclusion. By the time of the cabinet crisis at the end of April, Miliukov and the right wing of the party considered coalition futile and began to prepare the ground for counter-revolution. By 18 July Miliukov was openly calling for a military dictatorship. As for the moderate socialist leaders, it was only because they lent the Provisional Government their ill-gotten prestige that these reactionary machinations had any chance of success. At times, no doubt, their fear of forfeiting all mass support, and their anxiety that even they might be swept away by the Right, led them to waver over the extent of repressive measures. But the dominant Menshevik, Tsereteli, began to urge the use of force against the Bolsheviks from June. Both the Mensheviks and the SRs threw their full weight behind preparations for a military offensive, thereby buttressing the authority of officers and paving the way for counter-revolutionary action. And from July, their determination to prop up the bourgeois government led them ever deeper into collusion with counter-revolution.

At first, in the Soviet view, the Provisional Government was inhibited by the constraints of dual power. But as the moderate socialists

[10] Schapiro, *1917*, p. 102.
[11] See G. Katkov, *Russia 1917: The Kornilov Affair. Kerensky and the Break-up of the Russian Army*, (London, 1980) for a detailed account. In some respects Katkov stands outside the mainstream of the liberal tradition. His major work, *Russia 1917: The February Revolution* (London, 1967), was idiosyncratic in the vital role it attributed both to German efforts to foster revolution in Russia and to masonic ties among members of the Provisional Government.

used their influence to subordinate the soviets to the government, and as ministers became ever more alarmed at the momentum of the revolutionary movement, their attempts to use force became increasingly open. In the countryside, for example, whereas from March to June punitive detachments against peasants were used 17 times, the number rose to 39 in the next two months, and to no less than 105 in September and October.[12] In the capital, they seized upon the July demonstrations to march in troops from the front and launch vicious repression against the masses: although the demonstrations had been peaceful, the number killed and wounded exceeded 700.[13] The bourgeois press campaign against the Bolsheviks reached the point of frenzy, mass arrests were attempted, and censorship was restored to prevent Bolshevik literature from reaching the army.

The culmination was the Kornilov affair itself. Under intense pressure from the Kadets, Kerensky agreed to go along with Kornilov's ruthless programme to crush the soviets and install a dictatorship. Kerensky himself, in typically fickle petty-bourgeois fashion, drew back from his deal with Kornilov at the last minute through fear of the masses and personal pride. But the Kadets were deeply implicated in the conspiracy. At Kornilov's request, the Kadet cabinet ministers agreed to resign on 27 August in order to provoke a cabinet crisis and provide the Supreme Commander with *carte blanche* to construct a new government.[14] Miliukov's complicity was exposed to the world when the Kadet *Rech'* appeared on 30 August with a large blank space in place of the triumphant leading article he had written to welcome Kornilov. And even after the masses under Bolshevik leadership had reduced the plot to a fiasco, the Kadets began to lay plans for a renewed resort to force. If the Provisional Government and the fellow-travelling moderate socialist leaders failed to crush the revolution, it was because they lacked the means and not because of moral scruple or for want of trying.

In the light of revisionist work, plans for the use of force appear more fragmented than in the Soviet account. True, the Provisional Government moved in its first three weeks in office from a reluctant and ambiguous sanctioning of force in the countryside to clear authorization for commissars to summon troops.[15] Yet, given the level of disorder in the countryside, the number of occasions on which it was used was remarkably small. The measures taken after the July Days stunned workers by their ferocity, and yet they lost momentum very rapidly. The restoration of the death penalty at the front was seen at

[12] A. D. Maliavskii, *Krest'ianskoe dvizhenie v Rossii v 1917g. Mart-Oktiabr'* (Moscow, 1981), pp. 21–2, 244–5, 352–4.
[13] P. A. Golub *et al.*, *Istoricheskii opyt trekh rossiiskikh revoliutsii* (3 vols, Moscow, 1985–7) III, p. 204.
[14] Dumova, *Kadetskaia partiia*, pp. 197–8.
[15] Gill, *Peasants and Government*, pp. 26–7.

the time as a momentous departure from the spirit of the February revolution, yet despite mass disobedience in the army, it led to only about a dozen death sentences, and not all of these were carried out.[16] By the time of the Kornilov affair, Kadet alarm and frustration was intense. Whether the affair was 'counter-revolutionary' is a matter of definition. Kornilov did not seek to restore the monarchy and Kerensky had given him good reason to believe that he was working with the consent of the Provisional Government.[17] But the implications of his programme went beyond restoring military authority and would have involved a fundamental reversal in the direction of the revolution. The precise depth of Kadet complicity remains unclear, but their speeches and articles – and the rapturous reception they gave Kornilov at the Moscow State Conference two weeks before his move – conveyed full sympathy. 'This, after all, was certainly the direction in which Kadet efforts to consolidate Russia's right-wing forces were headed.'[18] Yet the long-awaited intervention by the military collapsed ignominiously.

In part, this tentative record reflected divided counsels among liberals and the presence of a significant minority who consistently urged greater conciliation of mass discontent. It reflected, too, the moderate socialists' determination (grossly underrated in the Soviet account) to avoid any steps which might lead to counter-revolution. Yet the implication that the government was inhibited merely by lack of will and foresight is misleading. By examining the question from below, revisionist work has demonstrated just how limited was the potential for the Provisional Government to use coercion, however willing ministers might have been. Above all it has brought home the irresistible upsurge by the army's rank and file against their officers' authority. The option of using front-line troops – let alone the even more deeply radicalized garrison troops – in a sustained drive against workers, peasants and mutinous regiments was lost not in October, not with the Kornilov affair, not even in the fateful June offensive. It had been lost in the course of the February revolution. Traditional authority had been smashed beyond repair.[19] In March, when Alekseev tried to resist rank-and-file encroachments on military statutes, the other generals, as well as the new War Minister, Guchkov, reluctantly persuaded him that resistance was futile.[20] At the end of April, when Guchkov himself looked to the front for reliable units to use against the soviets, he was forced to the same conclusion. The authority of the

[16] A. K. Wildman, *The End of the Russian Imperial Army* (2 vols, Princeton, N.J., 1980, 1987) II, pp. 129–33.
[17] See J. L. Munck, *The Kornilov Revolt: A Critical Examination of Sources Research* (Aarhus, 1987) for the most detailed examination of the affair.
[18] W. G. Rosenberg, *Liberals in the Russian Revolution. The Constitutional Democratic Party, 1917–1921* (Princeton, N.J., 1974), p. 228.
[19] Wildman, *Russian Imperial Army* I, pp. 289–90, 374–6.
[20] *op. cit.*, I, pp. 258–64; II, p. 18.

High Command and the officer corps in general had come to rest on the voluntary consent of their men. They were compelled to place their hopes in the new committees thrown up from below. Nor was the authority of the committee men themselves – largely sympathetic to the moderate socialists – more than conditional. When they put it to the test by urging the restoration of military discipline and full support for the June offensive, the upshot was wholesale mutiny.[21] When rumours of a move against revolutionary Petrograd by the High Command swirled across the front in late July and August, the reaction of the rank and file was one of fury. From the moment the Tsar fell, the largely peasant rank and file were determined that this meant an early peace; as the summer wore on they were determined too that it meant land. If the Provisional Government's fate rested on its ability to mobilize the army against those who supported both causes, it was doomed from the start.

The Provisional Government and the land question

Where the Provisional Government's land policy is concerned, all sides agree that its steady refusal to accede to peasant impatience for the immediate transfer of private land was suicidal. Peasant incursions had reached serious proportions by as early as May, and in some areas even earlier. Apart from a brief decline during harvest, they became ever more widespread and, from September, increasingly violent. Besides seizing land and ceasing to pay rent, groups of peasants helped themselves to the timber, the livestock, the machinery, and the crops of private estates. Given that the government either could not or would not use force to resist peasant pressure, intransigence was bound to alienate peasants both in the countryside and in the army.

What is open to question, however, is the explanation for this intransigence. In the traditional liberal view, it was another instance of the government's internal division, legalistic myopia and political ineptitude.[22] In principle, all the coalition parties accepted the need for far-reaching land reform. The Kadets, led by professional men far removed from the landowning nobility, had a more radical land policy than any of their western counterparts.[23] They readily accepted the need for compulsory alienation of much noble land, with due compensation, and for a massive transfer to the peasantry. But the majority of ministers were adamant that this must await the convening of the Constituent Assembly. So profound an invasion of private property rights required the fullest democratic sanction and must be

[21] *op. cit.*, II, pp. XIV, 73–111.

[22] J. L. H. Keep, *The Russian Revolution. A Study in Mass Mobilization* (London, 1976), pp. 162–3.

[23] J. Fleishauer, 'The Agrarian Program of the Russian Constitutional Democrats', *Cahiers du monde russe et sovietique* XX (1979), pp. 173–201.

carried out in a legal, orderly and systematic way. Premature action was certain to lead both to individual injustice and to severe disruption of agriculture on the large estates. The only action they took, therefore, was to establish a hierarchy of Land Committees to gather the necessary statistical data from the different regions of the country. Typically, the cabinet was not in fact united. Chernov, the SR Minister of Agriculture in the first two coalitions, pursued an independent line in defiance of his colleagues. He tried to transfer control of private land to the lower-level land committees, which were dominated by peasants, in the hope that this would allay peasant impatience. But more fundamental was the fact that the government as a whole, faced by a mounting wave of illegal land seizures, could think of nothing more constructive than to issue futile appeals for patience and goodwill. Even when it was manifestly clear that the peasants would not wait, it stuck blindly to its refusal to pre-empt the Constituent Assembly. The government thereby passed up a golden opportunity, simply by accepting the inevitable and handing over the land, to cut the ground from under the Bolsheviks.[24]

That it failed to do so was, in the Soviet view, inevitable. On this, as on all its policies, the government was guided by the Kadets, the party that had become the mouthpiece for landowners, both those from the nobility and the growing number from bourgeois backgrounds.[25] Not only were they determined to uphold the rights of private landowners, but they were alarmed that any breach here might spill over into a general attack on the right of private property.[26] Their insistence on compensation was no mere detail. It plainly showed where their loyalties lay and reflected their fear that confiscation would undermine the banks, to which a high proportion of estates were mortgaged. The depth of the government's commitment was fully exposed both by its resort to such force as it could muster, and by its constant prevarication and delay. Much quoted is Lenin's remark that the peasants were in effect being told, 'Wait until the Constituent Assembly for the land. Wait until the end of the war for the Constituent Assembly. Wait until total victory for the end of the war.'[27] As for the moderate socialists, they affected the picture little. The Mensheviks failed utterly to respond to the revolutionary drive of the peasants. The SRs, notwithstanding Chernov's typically ineffectual and totally inadequate gestures, betrayed their peasant constituency.[28] By propping up a

[24] R. Charques, *The Twilight of Imperial Russia* (London, 1958), pp. 247–8.
[25] On the efforts of landowners to organize and press their case upon the Provisional Government, see T. V. Osipova, 'Vserossiiskii soiuz zemel'nykh sobstvennikov (1917)', *Istoriia SSSR* (1976) 3, pp. 115–29.
[26] Golub, *Istoricheskii opyt* III, p. 38.
[27] Lenin, *Polnoe sobranie sochinenii* XXXIV, p. 57.
[28] K. V. Gusev, *Partiia Eserov: ot melko-burzhuaznogo revoliutsionarizma k kontr-revoliutsii* (Moscow, 1975), p. 116.

bourgeois government, they too became defenders of the landowners. The Provisional Government's policy arose not from moral principle, still less from misjudgement: it arose from the very nature of the class interests it represented.

Revisionist work has cast light on the government's motivation primarily by examining the formation of Kadet party policy. The Kadets, while exercising less than the outright mastery of the government attributed to them in Soviet historiography, did take the leading role in Lvov's two cabinets and exercised an effective veto over the policies of Kerensky's coalitions. They firmly and consistently insisted that the land question must await the Constituent Assembly. At an administrative level; they used their hold on the executive committee of the Chief Land Committee to stymie Chernov's initiatives; tension over the land question lay at the root of their decision to resign and bring down the First Coalition in early July; and their determination to postpone land reform was one of the major barriers to the formation of the Second Coalition.[29] These actions reflected the express will of the party. During 1917 a healthy network of local committees developed and no less than four party congresses – in March, May, July and October – were summoned to thrash out policy. The question of responding more quickly to peasant land hunger was explicitly discussed, and the case for doing so argued clearly and forcefully by a minority of leftist Kadets. Yet they were soundly defeated on each occasion, and indeed as the year progressed the prevailing tone at successive congresses became more rather than less rigid. Not only were local committees affected by an influx of those who had earlier supported the now defunct parties to the Right of the Kadets, but as peasant and worker radicalism intensified, and the level of violence rose, traditional Kadets tended increasingly to side with landowners and employers. From July a 'civil war mentality' began to take hold and the leadership actively strove to attract the support of the All-Russian Union of Industry and Trade, the Union of Landowners, army officers and the High Command in particular.[30] Even when the fiasco of the Kornilov affair briefly gave control of the party's Central Committee to moderates convinced that concessions must be made, they proved unable to stem the rightward drift.

The Kadet party was too broad a church to justify the Soviet view that it was simply the mouthpiece of landowners and employers. At the May congress no less than a third of voting delegates favoured dropping compensation for landowners. But the intransigence of the Kadets in the Provisional Government was not the arbitrary whim of a few bumbling politicians in Petrograd: it was deliberate and considered party policy.

[29] Gill, *Peasants and Government*, pp. 92, 96; Rosenberg, *Liberals*, pp. 182–4.
[30] Rosenberg, *Liberals*, pp. 204–11.

The Provisional Government, the urban economy, and the working class

No less politically disastrous than the Provisional Government's failure to solve the land question was its failure to sustain the urban economy. Although the economic history of 1917 is one of the least well-researched dimensions of that year – in part because of the collapse of the statistical services – there is broad agreement over some of the major problems. The incipient trade breakdown which had helped to bring down the Tsar greatly accelerated after February. The railways, already severely dislocated by the needs of the army, began to give way altogether amidst the disruption of 1917 and the number of locomotives in working order dropped precipitately. This exacerbated the shortage of fuel and raw materials reaching industrial centres and caused a downward spiral in industrial production. The scarcity and high cost of manufactures further reduced the incentive for peasants to market their grain: there was too little to buy with the roubles it fetched. As a result, although the curtailment of exports meant that in theory grain production was sufficient for the country's needs, food shortages in grain-deficit provinces, in the army, and above all in the cities became progressively more acute. Declining tax revenues could not begin to match the government's enormous wartime expenditure, a 'Liberty Loan' floated in April fell flat, and foreign credit became increasingly difficult to secure. The government's resort to massive deficit spending fuelled rampant inflation. The overall result was immense economic hardship for almost all sections of the population and, of greatest political significance, for the urban working class who became ever more bitterly critical of the government.

Here, too, the traditional liberal view blames government incompetence and division for the woefully inadequate measures it took to mitigate the economic disruption caused by the war. Ministers accepted the need for a state monopoly of grain and established a hierarchy of food committees to which producers were obliged to sell their surplus at fixed prices. But the upper-level committees were staffed by urbanites with little understanding of the village, while the lower-level ones, which were responsible for collection, were dominated by peasants who had no wish to sell their grain. This reluctance to sell was also in large measure the government's fault: although it saw the need to ensure an adequate supply of the manufactures peasants wanted at acceptable prices, which alone would give them the incentive to sell, it never got round to doing so.[31] At the end of August, in a typically ill-considered panic move, it doubled the price of grain, thereby greatly accelerating inflation while achieving only a brief and limited increase in grain procurement. Nor was the government any more efficient in organizing the distribution of grain: nation-wide rationing was announced on 29 April, but the administrative

[31] Schapiro, *1917*, pp. 65–6.

arrangements were bedevilled by confusion and delay, five weeks elapsed before detailed instructions on the issuing of ration cards were forthcoming, and another three before food committees were told to assess the needs and resources of their area.

An important factor contributing to this pitiful record was the acute division within the government. Even after the moderate socialists consented to form a coalition, they withheld genuine co-operation. Although the socialists and liberals favoured very similar policies to deal with the crisis, focusing on the extension of government control over supply and distribution of food, fuel and all the major commodities, effective action was vitiated by their 'savage competition' over who should run the relevant supervisory committees. The Mensheviks in particular could not free themselves from their doctrinaire hostility to representatives of 'the bourgeoisie'. By their constant 'innuendoes, accusations and bitterness' they poisoned the atmosphere of the cabinet and made resolute government impossible. If only the Mensheviks had been practical politicians and recognized the critical need for wholehearted co-operation with the liberals, all might have been well.[32]

Not least of the offences committed by the moderate socialists was their contribution to the extreme militancy of labour, a third feature of economic breakdown stressed in traditional liberal accounts. Egged on by the simplistic class analyses of the socialist parties, and suddenly freed from traditional constraints, the workers became more and more unreasonable and anarchic. Carried away by 'apocalyptic' and 'intoxicating hopes of a new golden age', they abandoned all self-discipline and advanced wildly unrealistic claims. They demanded huge wage increases, the immediate introduction of the eight-hour day, and the transfer of various management functions to their factory committees. And they backed up their demands with intimidation by armed militia bands and crippling strikes. 'Even prosperous and well-disposed firms faced collapse if they were to concede all the demands put forward simultaneously on behalf of their employees.'[33] Industrial production spiralled downwards as factories, already desperately short of fuel and raw materials, were forced to contract and even close down.

In the Soviet view, the economic disaster was rooted in a crisis of capitalism. It was incurable without socialist revolution and the transfer of power to a government able to institute state planning and control in the interests of all. The failure of the Provisional Government's grain monopoly was inevitable given its commitment to private enterprise and the profit motive. On the one hand, it opened the door to an orgy of speculation in which the banks and merchants indulged. On the other, pressure from industrialists against the imposition of

[32] The case is argued in detail in Basil, *Mensheviks*.
[33] J. L. H. Keep, *The Russian Revolution. A Study in Mass Mobilization* (London, 1976), pp. 67–8.

state control over the production and pricing of manufactures ruled out any chance the government would honour its promise to meet peasant needs.

Nor was this failure the result of division within the cabinet. Since the Mensheviks and SRs were determined to prop up the bourgeoisie and its government, they offered no effective opposition. Their abject subservience to their capitalist colleagues was fully exposed by their record in labour relations. They joined in demands for wage restraint while employers reaped huge profits, and they repeatedly refused adequate wage rises for workers in state enterprises. Moreover, Skobelev, the Menshevik Minister of Labour, failed to enshrine the eight-hour day, make strikes legal, introduce meaningful social insurance, or establish a minimum wage, and the narrow restrictions which the first Provisional Government tried to impose on factory committees were not rescinded. Across the whole range of labour legislation the Mensheviks caved in to increasingly organized pressure from employers transmitted through the ministries of Trade and Industry and of Finance.[34]

Given such intransigence on the part of government and employers, and given the precipitate fall in real wages, the demands of the proletariat were in no sense 'unreasonable' or the cause of industrial decline. On the contrary, a major source of that decline was the conscious and deliberate campaign by employers, especially from July onwards, to use the weapon of the lock-out against labour.[35] They sought to bring the proletariat to its knees by closing factories on the pretext of shortages of fuel and raw materials, and to discredit the entire revolution by intensifying economic decline and popular misery. As the instrument of capital, the Provisional Government was inherently incapable of solving the economic crisis.

Revisionist work has lent a measure of support to the Soviet view on this dimension of the debate. Where the grain monopoly is concerned, there was administrative muddle and delay, as liberal historians stress.[36] But a major cause of this was the lack of enthusiasm both on the part of the Kadet minister responsible for establishing the monopoly, A. I. Shingarev, and among merchants and landowners appointed to the higher-level food committees.[37] Likewise, there is clear evidence of fierce if ill-coordinated pressure on the cabinet by industrialists against the introduction of controls on the production and pricing of manufactures and against proposals for a steep increase

[34] P. V. Volobuev, *Proletariat i burzhuaziia Rossii v 1917 godu* (Moscow, 1964), pp. 173, 191–214, 321–51.

[35] *op. cit.*, pp. 313–20.

[36] Gill, *Peasants and Government*, pp. 46–64, 75–89.

[37] Z. Galili y Garcia, 'The Menshevik Revolutionary Defencists and the Workers in the Russian Revolution of 1917', (Ph.D. Dissertation, Columbia University, 1980), pp. 162–5, 414–15.

in direct taxation.[38] And in the absence of such regulation and the provision of reasonably-priced manufactures, the government's grain monopoly was bound to founder on the rock of peasant refusal to sell their produce for worthless roubles.

Given this inherent deficiency in the policy pursued by liberal ministers to steady the economy and procure adequate grain, traditional liberal reproaches against the Menshevik and SR leaders for failing to throw their full weight behind it are beside the point. In fact, contrary to both Soviet and traditional liberal portrayals, Menshevik economic policy differed sharply from that of the Kadets. Leading Menshevik economists pressed upon the government a sustained and carefully-argued case for a far-reaching programme of state regulation. Indeed it is the steadfast refusal by the liberals within the cabinet to respond to Menshevik demands for comprehensive economic regulation which demonstrates most clearly that its dilatory approach was a matter of conscious policy rather than incompetence and confusion.[39] Very much the same applies to Menshevik attempts to reform labour law, almost all of which were smothered by liberal opposition.[40]

On the question of responsibility for factory closures, revisionist work has endorsed neither the traditional liberal nor the Soviet view. It has tended, instead, to stress the defensive motivation of both sides of industry. During the early weeks after February, most employers were highly conciliatory; closures of smaller firms throughout the year tended to be forced on them by shortages and high wage demands rather than being wilful acts of management; and it was when profits began to fall sharply during the second half of the year, and employers concluded that concessions were failing to dampen labour militancy, that some major employers began to make concerted efforts to discipline labour by resorting to lock-outs.[41] The pattern of labour militancy followed a similar trajectory. In March and April, revisionists have found workers remarkably disciplined and moderate. Productivity rose in the early weeks, and 'the most striking aspect of the workers' activity was their temperateness, their concern for good order, and their readiness to accept the authority of the rehabilitated management and the Soviet.'[42] Only from the middle of the year did factory committees become markedly more assertive and extend their role to monitoring all actions of management. When viewed from below, however, it is clear that this increasing radicalism was less

[38] op. cit., pp. 166–71, pp. 554–76.
[39] op. cit., pp. 591–3.
[40] op. cit., pp. 510–35.
[41] D. Mandel, The Petrograd Workers and the Fall of the Old Regime; The Petrograd Workers and Soviet Seizure of Power (2 vols, London, 1983–4) II, p. 151; Galili y Garcia, 'Menshevik Revolutionary Defencists', pp. 535–54.
[42] Galili y Garcia, 'Menshevik Revolutionary Defencists', p. 147.

the product of utopian hopes and socialist propaganda than of the workers' own dire predicament. With real wages falling fast, and factories being subject to repeated interruptions because of shortages and what appeared to be deliberate lock-outs, workers took the initiative in seeking out fuel and raw materials and trying to maintain production.[43] Like the actions of employers, these steps were a response to rather than a root cause of industrial breakdown. Indeed, it may have been because of the presence in the capital of the most energetic factory committees and trade unions that unemployment rose more slowly there than elsewhere.[44] But as conditions deteriorated, the popular demand for co-ordinated state action to arrest the decline became ever more insistent. The government failed to cater for the needs of workers and paid the political price.

The Provisional Government and the nationality problem

Controversy over national conflict within the former Empire and the role it played in bringing down the Provisional Government has been less clearly focused. In part this is because of the sheer complexity of the myriad conflicts which erupted as traditional authority collapsed and economic crisis inflamed relations both between Great Russians and the minorities, and between one minority and another. Demands for varying degrees of autonomy – cultural, administrative, military and political – arose from all around the periphery, from the Baltic to the Caucasus, from the Poles and Finns, from the Muslim areas and the Ukraine. The Provisional Government resisted this centrifugal process as best it could. In occupied Poland, where its leverage was minimal, the government promised independence, hoping to encourage Polish commitment to the war effort. In all other cases, including that of Finland which had long enjoyed privileged status, it insisted that the Constituent Assembly alone had the right to resolve the issue. The Kadets were particularly intransigent, and it was their hostility to the compromise reached at the end of June between more conciliatory ministers and the Ukrainian Rada (or Soviet) which triggered their resignation from the First Coalition.

In traditional liberal eyes, these bitter national divisions were in origin quite distinct from class conflict and arose from man's natural loyalty to his own cultural and ethnic group. Kadet intransigence, for example, was an expression of the long tradition of deeply-rooted, elemental Russian nationalism to which they were heir. Predominantly Great Russians themselves, they were wholeheartedly committed to Russia's territorial integrity and Great Power status, and the war only intensified their horror of separatist movements of any kind.

---

[43] S. A. Smith, *Red Petrograd. Revolution in the Factories 1917–1918* (Cambridge, 1983), pp. 146–9.
[44] *op. cit.*, pp. 168–9; Mandel, *Petrograd Workers* II, pp. 215–16.

Likewise, minority nationalism expressed the natural aspirations of these increasingly self-conscious national and ethnic groups to assert their own identity and to run their own affairs. The clash between the nations of the old Empire provided a major source of the Provisional Government's weakness: in some areas national conflict proved more important than class struggle. Thus in the eastern borderland native resentment was directed not so much against the landlord as against the Russian colonist.[45] The Ukrainian demand for autonomy created the basis for a short-lived alliance of convenience with the Bolsheviks against the Provisional Government.[46] Equally, the Bolsheviks drew much of their strength from the nationalism of the predominantly Great Russian army and urban work-force. Indeed the October revolution itself was 'as much a Great Russian chauvinist uprising across Russia which had little to do with notions of class' as it was a class struggle.[47]

In Soviet eyes, on the other hand, to treat the two forms of conflict as mutually independent is artificial. National conflict was a product of class conflict. The Great Russian chauvinism of the Kadets gave expression to the interests of an imperialist bourgeoisie ruthlessly exploiting the minority nationalities beneath its sway. Minority nationalism was a complex amalgam. In part it reflected the attempt of the native bourgeoisie – and in the more backward areas such as Central Asia, of semi-feudal landlords – to assert their own interests and to manipulate popular feeling in order to smother class conflict within their own nation. The rival ambitions of the bourgeoisie of different nations somewhat divided the ruling class, although partial accommodation between the Provisional Government and local nationalist leaders was achieved as the mounting revolutionary movement drove them together. On the other side of the barricades, mutual interest in throwing off the yoke of both the Russian and the native ruling classes provided a firm bond uniting the oppressed peoples of every nationality in the country.[48]

Revisionist work has made a start on unravelling the complex interplay between national and class conflict. National divisions clearly deepened the Provisional Government's problems. The fractured composition of the country's middle classes weakened their political coherence more than Soviet accounts acknowledge.[49] Minority demands for political autonomy contributed to the central government's

---

[45] R. Pipes, *The Formation of the Soviet Union: Communism and Nationalism, 1917–1923* (Cambridge, Mass., 1964), p. 51.
[46] *op. cit.* pp. 67–73.
[47] S. Blank, 'The Bolshevik Party and the Nationalities in 1917: Reflections on the Origin of the Multi-National Soviet State', *Sbornik* 9 (1983), p. 14.
[48] Golub, *Istoricheskii opyt* III, pp. 123–31.
[49] A. J. Rieber, *Merchants and Entrepreneurs in Imperial Russia* (Chapel Hill, N.C., 1982), pp. 421–2.

loss of authority. Within the army, the desire among many minority national groups for the formation of separate national units was a significant source of grievance against both the government and the High Command, who resisted what they saw as a threat to military cohesion.[50] Where national and class lines coincided, social polarization was exacerbated by national hostilities. In Latvia, where largely Latvian workers and peasants confronted a predominantly German upper class, mass radicalism was particularly fierce.[51] But revisionist analyses of workers, peasants and soldiers alike present a remarkably common pattern of radicalization in which national divisions were of distinctly secondary importance.[52] This is not to deny the presence of ethnic and national friction within the lower classes. In Petrograd, for example, when rumours spread that the government intended to evacuate some factories, Russian workers picked out the small minority of Chinese workers in their midst as prime candidates for unemployment.[53] In Baku, tension between Russians, Armenians and Muslims was acute. But even here, national divisions were overlaid by those of class until after October.[54] The main battle lines of 1917 were drawn not between one nation and another but between officers and soldiers, landowners and peasants, employers and workers.

The Provisional Government and the Constituent Assembly

Among the most insistent reproaches addressed by traditional liberal historians to the Provisional Government is its failure to convene the Constituent Assembly quickly. This is seen as further evidence of ineptitude. From the moment the government took office, it had proclaimed its commitment to move as rapidly as possible to the summoning of a Constituent Assembly. This body, to be elected by universal, equal, direct and secret ballot, would have provided a focus of legitimacy which the Provisional Government palpably lacked. With the disappearance of the monarchy, the absence of such a focus facilitated the breakdown in respect for authority in general and that of the government in particular. It bred popular anarchy and opened the door to a Bolshevik coup. Moreover, local elections demonstrated that a general election held early in the year would have returned an

---

[50] M. Frenkin, *Zakhvat vlasti Bolshevikami v Rossii i rol' tylovykh garnizonov armii. Podgotovka i provedenie Oktiabr'skoi miatezha* (Jerusalem, 1982), chap. 4. Frenkin established his reputation as an independently-minded Soviet scholar during the 1960s. This volume, and his other major work, *Russkaia armiia i revoliutsiia 1917–1918* (Munich, 1978), were published after his emigration to the West and reflect an increasingly radical rejection of the Soviet approach to the revolution.

[51] For the most detailed treatment of Latvia, see A. Ezergailis, *The 1917 Revolution in Latvia* (Boulder, Cal, 1974); see also Wildman, *Russian Imperial Army* II, pp. 49–53.

[52] *op. cit.* I, pp. 100–4; Gill, *Peasants and Government*, pp. 157–69.

[53] Smith, *Red Petrograd*, pp. 172–3.

[54] R. G. Suny, *The Baku Commune 1917–1918. Class and Nationality in the Russian Revolution* (Princeton, N.J., 1972), pp. 102–46, 344–9.

overwhelming majority for the coalition partners. Once elected, they would have been in a position to address the country's problems with real authority. Instead, however, the Provisional Government in its noble but myopic way permitted preparations to drag on. Anxious that all should be satisfied the elections were fair, it set up an unwieldy Special Council to make the arrangements. This attempt to organize from scratch a flawless ballot of a vast, scattered and semi-literate population – in wartime at that – was quixotic. By the time the Assembly eventually met in January 1918 the Bolsheviks had seized power and were able to disperse it by force. 'Bad luck', 'foolishness' and characteristic concern for legal nicety had betrayed the Provisional Government.[55]

In the Soviet view, this delay in summoning the Assembly was the result of deliberate policy on the part of the Kadets. Their claim to be democrats, of course, rested on their commitment to parliamentary rule and universal suffrage. They were well aware of the cloak of legitimacy that a Constituent Assembly would confer on a new government. And from their first days in office they saw the value of being able to hold out the promise that the Assembly would meet: it enabled them to fob off the demands they dreaded from workers, peasants and the national minorities by arguing that all major reforms must await the Assembly. But from the start the liberals knew their own electoral prospects were bleak – a point rammed home by local elections from May onwards. They therefore engaged in a game of cat and mouse. The first cabinet, while announcing with a flourish that it would convene a Constituent Assembly 'as soon as possible', took care to name no date. The Kadets ensured that their men dominated the Special Council and spun out discussion of the detailed arrangements. Only in mid June, when the moderate socialists in the First Coalition took fright at growing support for the Bolshevik slogan of 'All Power to the Soviets', was a date for the elections (17 September) at last set. Even then the Kadets opposed the decision, used their supporters in the Special Council to urge delay, and successfully insisted that local arrangements were to be in the hands of dumas and zemstvos still to be elected, thereby making postponement almost inevitable.[56] After the collapse of the First Coalition they made further postponement one of the conditions of their participation in a new coalition, and thus managed to put off the evil day until 12 November. The ostensible enthusiasm of the SRs and Mensheviks, too, was less than whole-hearted, the latter in particular fearing the peasants might prove counter-revolutionary. And in any case, their general subservience to the Kadets inhibited them from insisting on swift elections. As early as 1 June the Bolshevik representative on the Special Council had

[55] Ulam, *Russia's Failed Revolutions*, p. 374; Schapiro, *1917*, pp. 69–70.
[56] O. N. Znamenskii, *Vserossiiskoe uchreditel'noe sobranie. Istoriia sozyva i politicheskogo krusheniia* (Leningrad, 1976), pp. 105–10.

pointed out the contrast with the brisk action of the French Provisional Government of 1848, which within little over two months of the fall of Louis-Phillipe had convoked a Constituent Assembly.[57] In Russia's case, pleas of 'technical difficulties' were mere pretexts for the government's determination to delay the Assembly.

On this question, revisionist analysis of the Special Council and of Kadet attitudes has largely borne out the Soviet view.[58] It is true that in March a few right-wing Kadets called for immediate elections both to overcome the problem of 'dual power' and in the belief that this might favour their party by disenfranchising soldiers.[59] And Kadet concern to ensure the authority of the Assembly by arriving at fair and popularly-accepted regulations was genuine. But very soon they became intensely anxious that the Assembly would turn out to be extremely radical and would make 'unwise' decisions, not least on the war. Their representatives on the Special Council began to 'work with such exactitude as to force a delay'. Most Kadets hoped that the Assembly would not meet before the end of the war.[60]

The Provisional Government and the war

One final – and critical – controversial feature of the Provisional Government's record is its failure to extract Russia from the war. In retrospect, the case for doing so in the government's own interests seems strong. The war at once exacerbated its problems and created enormous obstacles to tackling them. Hatred for the war was radicalizing the army and making it ever less serviceable as an instrument of firm government authority. While the war was in progress, to transfer land to the villagers was virtually unthinkable since it would provide an almost irresistible temptation to the millions of peasant-soldiers at the front to come home and claim their share. Rather than bringing all the different nations of the Empire together, the army was becoming a breeding ground for minority nationalist sentiment. And the war's effect on the budget and the economy, on transport, civilian production and the flow of grain, was crippling. Above all, the army's will to fight, as the June offensive so plainly demonstrated, had gone beyond recall. Why, instead of cutting its losses and withdrawing, did the Provisional Government carry on with the war to the point of its own destruction?

In the traditional liberal view, three prime motives lay behind the government's perseverance. First, there was the sheer weight of Russian nationalist sentiment. Militant nationalism had been the most fundamental motivation of the Progressive Bloc's challenge to the

[57] op. cit., p. 76.
[58] L. Kochan, 'Kadet policy in 1917 and the Constitutional Assembly', *Slavonic and East European Review* XLV (1967), pp. 83–92.
[59] Rosenberg, *Liberals*, pp. 88–9.
[60] op. cit., pp. 146–7.

Tsar. It had been in the hope that the revolution would rally the country behind the war effort that many liberals had thrown their lot in with it. Miliukov's staunch commitment to winning Constantinople and control of the Straits may have been unpopular with Petrograd workers, but he spoke for the Kadet party and the great majority of educated Russians. Their love for their country at once ruled out a shameful surrender and made them hungry for the fruits of victory. Second, they were committed by solemn treaty to the Allies. The Tsar's government had undertaken to enter no negotiations for a separate peace until the war was won, and the Provisional Government felt bound in honour to uphold this commitment.[61] Third, the government feared that should Russia's war effort collapse, the Entente as a whole would face defeat and Germany would be free to establish unshakeable domination over the continent and reduce Russia to a second-rate power. This third anxiety was shared by the socialists in the coalition, especially since they believed a triumph for the Kaiser might lead to the return of the Romanovs. But, as in every other field, the moderate socialists pursued a contradictory policy. They accepted the need to maintain the army as a fighting force and to launch the June offensive, yet at the same time they carried on constant propaganda for peace and against the supposedly imperialist goals of their own 'bourgeoisie', thereby contributing to the decline in the army's morale. Like its other policies, the government's persistence in the war may, therefore, have been misguided and mismanaged but 'it was dictated by principle.'[62]

From the Soviet point of view, the government's nationalism merely gave expression to rapacious imperialist designs. Russia's bourgeoisie was driven by lust for the new territory, markets and windfall profits that victory would bring. And behind the talk of moral obligation to the Allies were a thousand threads binding the government to British and French imperialism: the Allies never tired of stressing that further loans depended upon Russia's sustained contribution to the war. Even if the ministers had wanted to, this bourgeois government representing the interests of capital was inherently incapable of abandoning its annexationist goals.[63] Moreover, the gathering revolutionary storm provided an additional motive for persisting in the war. Their only hope of survival lay in using the army as an instrument with which to crush the revolution. Only victory offered the hope of shifting the balance of forces, restoring the authority of the High Command, and enabling them to confront the demands of the masses from a position of strength. Peace and demobilization, on the other hand, would silence their chauvinist demagogy and leave them helpless before the

[61] Schapiro, *1917*, p. 102.
[62] *op. cit.*, p. 217.
[63] Dumova, *Kadetskaia partiia*, pp. 143–50.

forces of the revolution.[64] Even in September and October, when defeat stared them in the face and the government harboured treacherous plans to hand over revolutionary Petrograd to the Germans, they could not change course. The few Kadets who suggested that an early peace might regain credit for the government and enable it to concentrate its energies against the revolution failed to carry the day.

As for the moderate socialists, in the Soviet view their determination to support the bourgeois government deprived them of an independent voice in foreign affairs. Their 'revolutionary defencism' was a thin veil for the imperialist ambitions of their masters. Their feeble efforts to convene an international socialist peace conference in Stockholm were futile: not only were the pseudo-socialist foreign parties they invited thoroughly committed to the war, but western workers would only respond to the peace campaign of a revolutionary government engaged in smashing capitalism at home. The fine phrases of the moderate socialists, of Chernov and Tsereteli, about 'peace without annexations and indemnities' were meaningless as long as the bourgeoisie held power. Indeed, they were worse than useless since for a time they deceived less politically-conscious workers and peasants into believing in their determination to secure peace. The Provisional Government's pursuit of the war, then, was not a matter of poor political judgement, idealism or loyalty to the Allies. It was inherent in the imperialist nature of the regime.

Revisionist work has had difficulty in assessing the relative merits of traditional liberal and Soviet explanations for the government's perseverance in the war. In assessing the government's motivation, it is all but impossible to weigh the role played by innate nationalism and lofty principles as against economic ambitions and domestic concerns, or by the anxiety of liberal ministers to align Russia with the western democracies and secure aid from them as against foreign 'imperialist' pressure. What has been brought home, however, is just how widespread and fervent was support for the war among the middle and upper classes. From March to October provincial representatives of the Kadet party gave solid backing to Miliukov's defence of Russia's long-standing war aims in general and her right to Constantinople in particular. They were unshaken by the April crisis over popular opposition to these goals. Influenced, no doubt, by the optimism conveyed both by the liberal press and by the majority of government ministers, they greeted the June offensive with unqualified joy. As late as 21 October, four days before the Bolshevik uprising, when the War Minister, A. I. Verkhovsky, admitted Russia was no longer in a condition to fight and should seek peace, Kadet leaders helped persuade Kerensky to sack him.[65] The commitment of moderate socialists

---

[64] A. P. Zhilin, *Poslednee nastuplenie (iun' 1917 goda)* (Moscow, 1983), pp. 11–13.
[65] Rosenberg, *Liberals*, pp. 257–8.

to peace, on the other hand, appears much more urgent than the Soviet version allows. But their impact on the formation of government policy was limited. Leading Foreign Ministry officials were decidedly unsympathetic to their moves for peace. The ambassador in London went out of his way to convey to the British Government that the Provisional Government was hostile to the Soviet's idea of a socialist conference in Stockholm, and would not consider itself bound by any decision made there.[66] And although Tereshchenko, the non-party liberal who was Foreign Minister from Miliukov's fall until October, struck a much more conciliatory pose than his predecessor, he too was 'an ardent nationalist'. He bowed to the pressure of the Petrograd Soviet and the moderate socialists and sought an inter-Allied conference designed to revise their annexationist war aims. But Tereshchenko himself hoped the revision of war aims would persuade the soldiers that Germany alone was the aggressor and that they must continue to fight, rather than that it would lead directly to peace; and at no stage did he renounce the goal of controlling the Straits.[67]

In any case, it quickly became clear that Russia lacked the leverage to insist the Allies move towards a compromise peace, and the Provisional Government refused to consider suing for a separate peace. Even if they had been willing to do so in principle, there evidently were powerful domestic motives for rejecting the idea. These were made particularly plain in government and liberal enthusiasm for the June offensive. For one thing, as Tereshchenko explained to the French ambassador, it would provide an excellent opportunity to consolidate government authority in the capital by despatching the bulk of the unruly Petrograd garrison to the front.[68] More generally, 'the commitment of troops to battle was [seen as] a way of generating patriotism, consolidating support for the authority of the Provisional Government, smothering social conflict, and triggering a new willingness for sacrifice. It also justified the Kadet desire to postpone social reforms, and even to delay the Constituent Assembly.'[69]

Conclusion

In the light of revisionist research, therefore, while the Soviet account of the Provisional Government's failure appears over-schematic, that of the traditional liberal approach appears superficial. The failure was not the result of administrative incompetence, reluctance to use force, misplaced faith in flowery speeches and popular patience, economic

[66] R. Wade, *The Russian Search for Peace. February–October 1917* (Stanford, Cal., 1969), pp. 108–15.
[67] *op. cit.*, pp. 76–8.
[68] L. E. Heenan, *Russian Democracy's Fateful Blunder. The Summer Offensive of 1917* (New York, 1987), pp. 54–5.
[69] Rosenberg, *Liberals*, pp. 167–8.

illiteracy, legal perfectionism, or divisions within the government. There is truth in each of these charges, and yet they all miss the point. No statesmen, no cabinet, even if it possessed the quintessence of liberal wisdom and combined the talents of Gladstone, Cavour and Lloyd George could have achieved the goals the Provisional Government pursued. From February workers, soldiers and peasants had drained government of the power to prevent them transforming relations with management, ending the war, and seizing the land. The Provisional Government tried to do just that.

Since the policy of resisting mass demands was doomed, revisionist attention has focused on the possibility that the coalition partners might have pursued a much more radical line. The case has been made that this was an option for the Kadets. There was, after all, an articulate left wing within the party which consistently urged full co-operation with the moderate socialists. And would not the party's political goal of constitutional democracy have been best served by acceding to popular impatience for social reform? The Kadets, so the argument runs, could have directed their energies 'not to attack the moderate socialists or the Soviet, but to support them', and 'used their considerable argumentative powers to contain any possible right-wing opposition to this course.'[70]

The argument turns on the Kadets' ability to carry the High Command, landowners and industrialists with them. If they failed, their hypothetical move to the Left would have had little more significance than that of the Radical Democratic party which dissident Left Kadets helped form in July. It would have cost them the support of the Right, thereby depriving them of independent political weight, and it would have made little impact on the social polarization which it sought to overcome. Yet their prospects of carrying those groups with them were bleak. The 'argumentative powers' needed to persuade the High Command to abandon the war, especially before the June offensive, and landowners to hand over their property without compensation, would have been little short of miraculous. There was more room for compromise over the issues dividing employers and workers than there was over peace and land. German and French industrialists at the end of the war would show much greater flexibility – and political astuteness – in making partial concessions to workers' demands than did their Russian counterparts.[71] But revisionist work on Russia's industrialists, merchants and entrepreneurs underlines just how remote were the chances in 1917 that they would respond in disciplined fashion to a Kadet-led policy of far-reaching concessions. They remained deeply fractured along regional, ethnic and cultural lines, and the gulf

---

[70] op. cit., pp. 467, 469.
[71] See C. S. Maier, Recasting Bourgeois Europe (Princeton, N.J., 1975) on western developments after the war; Volobuev, Proletariat i burzhuziia, pp. 185ff. points out the contrast.

separating them from the professionals and technical specialists of the Kadet party remained significant.[72] During 1917, it is true, in the face of working-class pressure both forms of division were being overcome. But even then the divisions between Moscow's commercial and industrial leaders, and those of Petrograd and the South were not bridged. In any case, the closing of ranks that took place was motivated precisely by determination to resist working-class demands and state regulation. The conflicts of interest involved in 1917 were too profound to be settled by even the most eloquent of arbiters.

[72] Rieber, *Merchants and Entrepreneurs*, pp. 405–26.

7 THE FAILURE OF THE MODERATE SOCIALISTS

In both traditional liberal and Soviet accounts of 1917, the treatment accorded the moderate socialist parties is one of scorn. The former, as we have seen, reproach the Mensheviks and SRs for supporting the Provisional Government in a half-hearted fashion, whereas the latter reproach them for supporting it at all. But neither school entertains seriously the possibility that they could have pursued a successful independent line of their own. And there is a good deal of common ground between the explanations which the two schools offer for their failure to do so.

The liberal view

In the traditional liberal view, it can be traced in the first instance to the deep divisions within both parties. Each was split between Centre, Left and Right factions, opinions ranging from virtual anarchism to the mildest of reformism, from extreme internationalism to fierce nationalist support for carrying the war to outright victory. Moreover, both parties lacked the stomach for power and 'neither had a Lenin capable of knocking heads together and leading a unified phalanx'.[1] Moreover, the moderate socialists were blinkered by an abstract, bookish approach to political realities. 'Weaned on the histories of the French and English revolutions' they were mesmerized by the mythical danger of counter-revolution from the army.[2] They thus devoted great energy to undermining the authority of the officer corps, while at the same time ostensibly supporting the defence of the country. At the root of their contradictory behaviour lay their slavish adherence to doctrine. As good Marxists the Mensheviks, whose intellectual superiority gave them ascendancy over the muddled SRs, remained convinced throughout 1917 that since Russian capitalism was in its infancy, a bourgeois government must come to power and preside over a sustained period of capitalist development. Until there had been enormous growth in her productive power and the size of her proletariat, she would not fulfil the conditions for socialism laid down by Marx. Socialists, therefore, should abstain from power while organizing the masses to exert maximum pressure for concessions from the

[1] A. Ulam, *Lenin and the Bolsheviks* (London, 1969), p. 438.
[2] Ulam, *Russia's Failed Revolutions* (London, 1981), p. 316.

government. Hence their steadfast refusal to take power, their extreme reluctance to form a coalition with 'the bourgeoisie', and their refusal even once in government to offer the liberals genuine support. 'Ideology came first and practical politics came last, if at all.'[3]

The Soviet view

In the Soviet view, the Mensheviks adhered to a lifeless interpretation of Marx which mistook the letter for the spirit, while the SRs lacked any coherent revolutionary theory at all. Both parties were ill-organized and wracked by division, and the SRs in particular casually enrolled thousands of *intelligenty*, officials, officers and petty traders whose views differed little from those of the Kadets.[4] These deficiencies, though, rather than being a matter of chance or poor leadership, reflected the inherent dilemma of 'petty-bourgeois' parties. Like the petty bourgeoisie itself, they were torn between the twin poles of the bourgeoisie and the proletariat. Their search for a 'middle line' was therefore doomed from the start. Having turned their backs on the proletariat in February, their radical rhetoric amounted to no more than 'deceit' and 'demagogy'. Their supposed fear of counter-revolution was mere rationalization for what in practice was simply support for the bourgeoisie. From July the leadership of both parties crossed over fully to the side of reaction. As the revolution followed its 'law-governed' course, support for them dwindled and their membership fell away. The peasants, soldiers and more backward workers who had initially followed them saw through their false promises and phrasemongering and rallied behind the party of the proletariat.[5]

The revisionist view

Revisionist work has been able to provide greater insight into the eclipse of the Mensheviks and SRs than either of these approaches. It has done so by taking the two parties rather more seriously. After all, both were led by lifelong revolutionaries who had proved the depth of their commitment to radical social change: the delegates to the Menshevik All-Russian Conference in May 1917, for example, had on average been arrested three-and-a-half times and spent four-and-a-half years in prison and exile.[6] The Mensheviks saw themselves as the

[3] J. D. Basil, *The Mensheviks in the Revolution of 1917* (Columbus, Ohio, 1983), p. 72.
[4] K. V. Gusev, *Partiia Eserov: ot melko-burzhuaznogo revoliutsionarizma k Kontrrevoliutsii* (Moscow, 1975), p. 97.
[5] L. M. Spirin and K. V. Gusev, eds, *Neproletarskie partii Rossii. Urok istorii* (Moscow, 1984), pp. 280–309.
[6] Z. Galili y Garcia, 'The Menshevik Revolutionary Defencists and the Workers in the Russian Revolution of 1917', (Ph.D. Dissertation, Columbia University, 1980), p. 433.

authentic spokesmen for the proletariat and the assertion of working-class interests as their *raison d'être*. The SRs made the same claim in respect of all working people, and their programme counterbalanced Menshevik preoccupation with urban workers by making its centre-piece the free transfer of all private land into the hands of the peasantry. The great majority of both parties denounced the war as imperialist, rejected all annexationist goals, and were committed to the earliest possible democratic peace. Moreover, the overwhelming support which the two parties enjoyed during the early months after February indicated a close correlation between their policies and popular aspirations.

Nor do the explanations offered by traditional liberal and Soviet historians for their failure to implement their policies and retain mass support carry full conviction. It is true that both parties contained widely differing factions, and in the case of the SRs in particular, party structure was amorphous and conditions of membership ill-defined. But no less remarkable than their internal divisions was the close co-operation between the main body of the two parties, despite differences of ideology, programme and tradition, and the massive electoral victories they achieved. Moreover, the implied contrast with Bolshevik unity and structural coherence during 1917, as we shall see, is easily overstated.[7] The notion that the moderates lacked effective leadership, too, is not entirely convincing. True, it is difficult to escape the conclusion that for the SRs Chernov was a decidedly mixed blessing. His prestige as a founding father and the author of the party programme guaranteed his pre-eminence, and yet he repeatedly failed to assert himself.[8] But the same can hardly be said of the Mensheviks. The Georgian Menshevik Tsereteli, their key figure in 1917, had all the attributes of a man born to lead. He had established his credentials when leading the Social Democratic fraction in the Second Duma, and the long years in prison and prolonged exile which followed had added lustre to his name. He was a man of magnetic personal charm, he possessed formidable powers of oratory and persuasion, he exuded confidence in his own judgment, and he had a very clear conception of the line he intended to follow.[9] Moreover, on his arrival from exile in Siberia in mid March, he quickly gathered around himself a tightly-knit cohort of Soviet leaders who formed an inner cabinet, the so-called 'Star Chamber'. They met regularly, in private, to agree upon their strategic line and they succeeded for several months in

[7] See below Chapter 9, pp. 193–8.
[8] O. Radkey, *The Agrarian Foes of Communism. Promise and Default of the Russian Socialist-Revolutionaries, February–October, 1917* (New York, 1958), chap. 7. Radkey's detailed work on the SRs is of distinctly pre-revisionist vintage, but in some respects it foreshadowed later approaches.
[9] W. H. Roobol, *Tsereteli – A Democrat in the Russian Revolution. A Political Biography* (The Hague, 1976), pp. 64–5, 100.

carrying both the EC and the Soviet plenum with them. The fact that Chernov and his SR colleagues tended to take their cue from Tsereteli enabled him to provide unified and forceful leadership of the moderate socialist bloc as a whole.[10]

In any case, the precipitate decline in the moderate socialists' popularity among soldiers and workers, evident from July, suggests that their failure was one neither of organization nor of leadership, but rather of policy. Yet the view that they were doomed by doctrinaire belief that February was a bourgeois revolution is unsatisfactory. The very cornerstone of the SR party was precisely their belief in peasant-based socialism and in Russia's freedom to avoid the pattern of development outlined by Marx. The Mensheviks did see the revolution in traditional Marxist terms, and were agreed that, at any rate in the absence of western revolution, Russia was too backward for the immediate introduction of socialism. But the policy implications of this view were far from self-evident, as was amply demonstrated by the fierce disputes among the Mensheviks. The Menshevik Internationalists, who seized the initiative on the EC during the first three weeks after February, encouraged direct confrontation with the liberal Provisional Government and a mass campaign to overturn its foreign policy and spread fraternization at the front.[11] Tsereteli and his newly-arrived comrades from Siberia played a key role in tilting the balance against such a *démarche*.[12] At the end of April the Mensheviks were split down the middle over the issue of entering a coalition with the liberals. The fact that the majority eventually decided to do so showed that they were ready to flout doctrine, in this case Engels's hallowed warning that socialists who took office before conditions were ripe for socialism would arouse expectations they could not fulfil. When Martov, the pre-war Menshevik leader, returned from exile in early May, he was bitterly critical of almost every aspect of the policy the party had adopted. By the beginning of July he was calling for a decisive break with the Kadets and the Allies, the formation of a socialist-dominated government, an end to all further offensives, immediate transfer of the land, and forceful state regulation of the economy.[13]

Moreover, undue emphasis on the constraints of moderate socialist ideology – and the Soviet accusation that they consciously betrayed the masses – obscures just how radical the policies adopted by Tsereteli

---

[10] Galili y Garcia, 'Menshevik Revolutionary Defencists', pp. 319–26; Roobol, *Tsereteli* pp. 102–3.
[11] A. K. Wildman, *The End of the Russian Imperial Army* (2 vols, Princeton, N.J., 1980, 1987) I, p. 355.
[12] Roobol, *Tsereteli*, pp. 100–1, 111–20; Galili y Garcia, 'Menshevik Revolutionary Defencists', pp. 280ff.
[13] I. Getzler, *Martov: A Political Biography of a Russian Social Democrat* (London, 1967), pp. 150–67.

and the main body of Mensheviks and SRs were. Chernov's entry into the cabinet in early May as Minister of Agriculture was interpreted by most SRs as the signal for a swift response to peasant land hunger.[14] Chernov's intention was to entrust all private land to the land committees, envisaging that peasant domination of the lower-level committees would ensure their control over the land. Equally, he sought to ban the sale of land lest private transactions be used to place some private land beyond the reach of the Constituent Assembly.[15] When the Menshevik Skobelev became Minister of Labour at the same time, he confidently announced a long list of the labour reforms he intended his new ministry to introduce: full legal backing for the eight-hour day, full freedom to strike, the establishment of a labour inspectorate, a comprehensive system of labour protection, and broad social legislation including immediate measures to aid the unemployed.[16] For Menshevik economists, a major attraction of forming the coalition was their belief that a socialist presence in the cabinet would make it possible to force the government to adopt the detailed plans they had worked out for comprehensive state control over production, distribution, prices, and profits. They saw these measures as a wartime necessity rather than a programme for transition from *laissez-faire* capitalism to socialism but, the question of who should administer them apart, in the short-term they were not far removed from Bolshevik demands for economic regulation.[17] Likewise, majority opinion in both moderate socialist parties envisaged the coalition pursuing peace with the utmost vigour. With Miliukov ousted, they believed, the government would now insist that the Allies open the way to general peace by dropping their annexationist goals. At the same time, it would lend support to the EC's vigorous efforts to organize an international socialist conference in Stockholm which would coordinate pressure on all belligerent countries to end the war.[18]

The moderate socialists, in short, fully accepted that Russia's 'objective conditions' permitted profound social and political change. Had they succeeded in implementing their programme, the political outcome of the revolution would have been very different. But they were determined to do so in alliance with the more 'progressive' sections of privileged and middle-class society. These two goals, as we have seen in examining the Provisional Government, proved to be incompatible. 'Bourgeois' opposition, both within and outside the cabinet, blocked

[14] Radkey, *Agrarian Foes*, chapter 5.
[15] G. Gill, *Peasants and Government in the Russian Revolution* (London, 1979), pp. 91–2.
[16] Galili y Garcia, 'Menshevik Revolutionary Defencists', pp. 507–8.
[17] *op. cit.*, pp. 561–70; S. A. Smith, *Red Petrograd. Revolution in the Factories 1917–1918* (Cambridge, 1983), pp. 151–5.
[18] R. A. Wade, *The Russian Search for Peace. February–October 1917* (Stanford, Cal., 1969), pp. 51–64, 74–88.

Chernov's land reforms, Skobelev's labour reforms and the Soviet plan for economic regulation, and the coalition proved unable to bring about peace. Equally, mass impatience was far greater than the moderate socialists supposed. From May, the level of peasant unrest and seizure of land, machinery and stocks rose steeply. From May, too, industrial conflict intensified and the number of strikes soared. By July frustration at the government's failure to implement the Soviet's plans for regulating the economy provoked mounting demands for 'All Power to the Soviets'. And the soldiers' impatience for peace was demonstrated by the mass mutiny which devastated the June offensive. No significant section of the 'bourgeoisie' would support policies sufficiently radical to gain popular acceptance.

Yet the Soviet view that the moderate socialists' failure to implement their policies, and their eclipse, were 'law-governed' is difficult to uphold. Even within the terms of the Soviet interpretation itself, the options before them were open at various points in the year. Indeed it is their failure to exercise these options that excited such indignation in Lenin at the time and in Soviet historians ever since. They could have formed a soviet-based government in April, when Lvov and his colleagues threatened to resign, or at the beginning of July when the Kadets resigned, or early in September when Kerensky and the Kadets were discredited by the Kornilov affair. Equally, they could have made their entry into coalition dependent on stringent conditions – be it immediate land reform or rigorous state regulation of the economy. The option most often stressed in revisionist analyses was that of refusing to support the fateful June offensive, and insisting instead that the army merely hold the line while the war in the West ground to its end.[19] Each option would have led, no doubt, to confrontation with privileged society. The crucial question, therefore, is why they baulked at such confrontation, why the moderate socialists came to believe both that it was necessary and that it was possible to achieve their goals in alliance with 'progressive' elements of the bourgeoisie. It is on this question, on the misconceptions of Tsereteli and his colleagues, that revisionist analysis has focused.

Two primary and mutually-reinforcing considerations convinced them that such an alliance was necessary. First, there was their fear of counter-revolution. This fear had less to do with bookish analogies with the fate of western revolutions than with their own experience in 1905 and especially in 1917 itself. Right-wing longing for forcible repression of the soviets was, of course, discernible from March onwards, strident and explicit from July. But the moderate socialists were also extremely wary of the danger that patriotism among rank-

[19] L. E. Heenan, *Russian Democracy's Fateful Blunder. The Summer Offensive of 1917* (New York, 1987), p. 129; Wildman, *Russian Imperial Army* II, xiii-xv; see also Radkey, *Agrarian Foes*, p. 482.

and-file soldiers could be turned against the revolution. The EC had to compose the Soviet Peace Appeal of 14 March very carefully to take account of the thunderous applause with which soldier delegates to the Petrograd Soviet greeted patriotic rhetoric.[20] From the middle of the month the soldiers' patriotism was further impressed upon the Soviet leaders by numerous demonstrations and delegations of soldiers both from Petrograd and from the front. These delegations denounced workers for lack of patriotism in being more concerned to secure the eight-hour day and higher wages than to supply the front. All too easily, it seemed to the socialists, the attempts of the liberal and right-wing press to play upon this emotion could pay political dividends.[21] On hearing of mass desertion from the front after the June offensive, the prominent Menshevik F. I Dan spoke for many in warning that 'counter-revolution could find its most reliable support in a deserting army.'[22]

The moderate socialists took vigorous steps, underrated in Soviet accounts, to parry the supposed danger. In late March they launched an energetic and successful campaign to defuse the soldiers' criticism of workers and ensure that the troops at the front looked for political leadership to the Petrograd Soviet rather than to their officers or Miliukov and his colleagues.[23] Following the collapse of the June offensive, concern at the resurgence of confidence on the Right led moderate socialists on soldiers' committees to revert to an attitude of deep suspicion towards officers.[24] And Mensheviks and SRs of all hues threw their weight against Kornilov at the end of August. But throughout they also felt it essential to avoid the isolation of the working class by preventing the consolidation of a solid right-wing bloc embracing the whole of the bourgeoisie. Hence their determination to co-operate with the more progressive elements of the middle class.

The second reason they saw such co-operation as essential arose from their view of the problem of the war. The moderate socialists ruled out a separate peace. In international terms, they believed it would lead to Germany's outright victory over the western Allies and hand her continental hegemony. It would thereby undercut pressure for peace from the international proletariat, and enable the Kaiser to reduce Russia to satellite status and crush the revolution.[25] In domestic terms, they were convinced it would be extremely unpopular both among the rank and file of the army, whose patriotism had been so strongly impressed upon them in March and April, and among all sections of the 'bourgeoisie'. It would therefore split 'the vital forces of

[20] Galili y Garcia, 'Menshevik Revolutionary Defencists', pp. 280–3.
[21] *op. cit.*, pp. 180–8.
[22] *op. cit.*, p. 750.
[23] Wildman, *Russian Imperial Army* I, pp. 291–331.
[24] *op.cit.* II, pp. 158–60.
[25] Wade, *Search for Peace*, p. 90.

the nation', drive a wedge between socialists and progressive liberals, and play straight into the hands of the Right.[26] But if a separate peace was out of the question, the alliance with the western powers and the defence capability of the army would have to be sustained while pressure was brought to bear for a general peace. Neither the Allies nor the officer corps would have confidence in a purely socialist government. Therefore 'revolutionary defence', as well as prevention of counter-revolution, demanded co-operation with the liberal and 'progressive' bourgeoisie.

It was one thing to be convinced of the need for such co-operation, another to be convinced it was possible. As Tsereteli remarked shortly before the formation of the First Coalition, had they concluded the bourgeoisie were irreconcilably hostile to their goals, the moderate socialists would have been forced to agree with Lenin and say: 'There is no salvation for Russia except in the desperate attempt to at once proclaim the dictatorship of the proletariat and the peasantry.'[27] But the evidence of the early months of 1917 made them optimistic. In part this optimism rested on the conciliatory attitude of Russia's privileged elements. The first Provisional Government's commitment to the summoning of a Constituent Assembly and thorough democratization of local government seemed to provide important common ground. On the question of land reform, although a conflict over compensation clearly lay ahead, the Kadet programme acknowledged the need for drastic redistribution. In the army, most officers quickly came to terms with the need to recognize and work with soldiers' committees. Even on the most divisive issue, that of foreign policy, the April crisis seemed to demonstrate that intransigent imperialists like Miliukov and Guchkov were heavily outnumbered by more enlightened liberals in the cabinet who were willing to abide by the Soviet's policy of pursuing an early peace without annexations or indemnities. Perhaps most important of all was the amenable attitude of employers in the immediate aftermath of February, especially in the capital. On 10 March the Society of Factory and Works Owners in Petrograd agreed to the eight-hour day, the recognition of factory committees, and the establishment of conciliation chambers. To the delight of the moderate socialists, the employers acknowledged the virtue of the reduction in the working day as an 'historically necessary measure', 'capable of ensuring the future spiritual development of the working class, by providing for self-education and trade-union organization, and of establishing correct lawful relations between labour and capital.'[28] Although Moscow's employers proved less amenable, in most areas

[26] Roobol, *Tsereteli*, pp. 87–9; Galili y Garcia, 'Menshevik Revolutionary Defencists', pp. 722–3.
[27] R. P. Browder and A. F. Kerensky, *The Russian Provisional Government 1917* (3 vols, Stanford, Cal., 1961) III, p. 1265.
[28] Quoted in Smith, *Red Petrograd*, pp. 66–7.

swift concessions and steep wage rises seemed to bode well for a measure of co-operation from industrialists.[29] The moderate socialists appreciated that this willingness to give ground reflected pressure from below rather than sheer goodwill on the part of privileged Russia. But it convinced them that sustained co-operation between 'all the vital forces of the nation', symbolized by the Committees of Public Organizations in provincial towns, was possible.

No less important was their understanding of the mood among workers, peasants and soldiers. The sharp drop in the number of strikes during March and April suggested that the demands of workers would not exceed what employers would be prepared to grant. Workers would use the new freedom to organize the disciplined trade-union and labour movement the Mensheviks had tried so hard to create after 1905. In the army, the evidence of patriotism combined with allegiance to the Soviet expressed from the end of March suggested willingness to defend the front while every effort was made to conclude an early, general peace. And so far as the peasantry were concerned, the relatively low level of rural unrest during March and April seemed to indicate that they would be prepared to await an orderly transfer of land.

In each case, moderate socialist optimism was confirmed by the complexion of the bodies which sprang up to represent mass aspirations. In March, April, May and June the upper tiers of workers', soldiers' and peasants' soviets, of the soldiers' committees, and of the land committees presented a most reassuring picture of the mood of the masses. The Petrograd Soviet, the All-Russian Soviet Conference of late March, and the subsequent congress of early June voted solidly in support of combining radical social change with coalition. The All-Russian Peasant Congress of May accepted the need to organize the transfer of land through the Constituent Assembly. Congresses of soldiers' committees at the front endorsed 'revolutionary defencism' and the June offensive.[30] The Moscow duma elections of late June, too, gave overwhelming support to the SRs and Mensheviks. There were discordant notes but the moderate socialist leaders were confident that expressions of extreme radicalism, be it the refusal of the Kronstadt Soviet to acknowledge the coalition government or the demonstrations of 18 June in the capital, were out of step with the rest of the country.

In retrospect, the understanding of the moderate socialist leaders appears deeply flawed. Where their fear of the Right was concerned, they were unable to see that the depth of disaffection among the troops had in fact rendered would-be counter-revolutionaries impotent. Taken aback by the soldiers' expressions of patriotism, they under-

[29] Galili y Garcia, 'Menshevik Revolutionary Defencists', pp. 131–57.
[30] Wildman, *Russian Imperial Army*, II, pp. 24–31.

rated the rank and file's loathing for officers and military discipline, and impatience for peace and land reform.[31] In their reading of the international situation and their peace plans, they exaggerated the influence Russia could exert both over Allied governments and over western socialists. They failed to see that the USA's entry into the war in April reinvigorated western determination to fight on and made German victory unlikely.

Equally, their optimism about co-operation between privileged society and the masses was misplaced. They exaggerated the significance of compromise between political leaders in a situation of acute socio-economic strife and social polarization in which state power was at a minimum. They underrated employers' resentment against labour's demands, the intensity of officers' frustration with the breakdown of traditional military discipline, and the depth of hostility, both within and outside the cabinet, to Chernov's efforts at land reform. Even more significantly, they underrated the impatience of the peasantry, the determination of soldiers not to go on the offensive again, and the process radicalizing the workers. Their understanding of the mass mood tended to be based on the upper echelons of the various popular representative hierarchies. They looked to the All-Russian Congress rather than to local soviets, to the Petrograd Soviet rather than to the district soviets in the capital, to the trade unions rather than the factory committees, to the provincial land committees rather than village assemblies, to conferences of soldiers' committees rather than to those closest to the rank and file. In each case, as revisionist work on workers, peasants and soldiers has demonstrated, the higher-level bodies tended to be less sensitive to popular opinion than lower ones.[32] Elections to them were less frequent, and more of their membership tended to be *intelligenty* – be it radical journalists, village teachers, or junior officers – at one remove from the mass constituency. The supreme expression of this tendency was the gulf that opened out between the CEC elected in June by the All-Russian Congress of Soviets, which the moderate socialists dominated, and popular opinion in factories, trenches and villages.

It is in terms of this misconception, then, that the failure of the moderate socialists must be seen. It is this which led them to invest their political capital and prestige in a coalition which did not respond to mass demands, thereby forfeiting much of their mass support from early in the summer onwards. The more they urged patience, the more

---

[31] Ferro, 'The Russian Soldier', *Slavic Review*, 30 (1971), pp. 483–512; Wildman, *Russian Imperial Army* I, pp. 378–9.

[32] Smith, *Red Petrograd*, pp. 200–08; R. A. Wade, *Red Guards and Workers' Militias in the Russian Revolution* (Stanford, Cal., 1984), pp. 122ff; O. Figes, *Peasant Russia, Civil War. The Volga Countryside in Revolution (1917–1921)* (Oxford, 1989), pp. 40–6; Gill, *Peasants and Government*, pp. 28–36, 114–31; Wildman, *Russian Imperial Army* II, pp. 31–72.

their influence waned. SRs in the villages discovered that unless they defied their party's leaders and endorsed direct action by the peasants, the peasants turned their backs on them. In the cities rank-and-file Mensheviks and SRs found allegiance to their party leadership an increasing electoral liability and virtually incompatible with active participation in the most militant workers' organizations, such as the militia and factory committees, which socialist ministers repeatedly denounced. Nowhere was their loss of influence more dramatic than in the army. The crucial step here was their decision to throw their weight behind the June offensive. Military plans for the offensive were in train long before the coalition was formed, and support for it was implicit in their entry into the government. Moreover, they were persuaded by Kerensky and their coalition partners that only a resurgence of military strength would increase Russia's leverage and enable her to force both the Germans and her allies to respond to her peace appeals. Party leaders and moderate socialists on soldiers' committees therefore rallied to Kerensky's campaign to reinvigorate the army. They urged garrision soldiers to go to the front and those already there to restore discipline and follow their officers into battle. 'This could not possibly have been more at odds with the mood of the soldier masses.'[33] In the eyes of the rank and file their erstwhile leaders had turned round and betrayed them. The fury of the Petrograd garrison was expressed in the July Days, while at the front the moderate socialists suffered a very sharp drop in prestige and influence. A rapid and sustained decline in popular support had set in.

Yet the moderate socialist leaders did not revise the basic assumptions formed in the early months of the revolution. The extent of their loss of mass support was only slowly borne in upon them. They saw the embittered mood of the workers, soldiers and sailors who took part in the July Days as peculiar to Petrograd. After all, troops from the front had readily come to their aid, and in the immediate aftermath, the Bolsheviks suffered a sharp set-back and wide currency was given to the accusation that Lenin and his anti-war party were in the pay of the Germans. Even when from August and September soviet and local duma elections began to register unmistakably an alarming swing towards the Bolsheviks, the moderate socialists tended to see this in terms of the masses' naïvety and backwardness rather than as a rational search for an alternative approach to their own. Arbitrary land seizures, mass disruption of the army, and rejection of compromise with employers and the bourgeoisie as a whole, they were convinced, threatened chaos, civil war and counter-revolution. Moreover, their bitterness against their Bolshevik rivals, whose 'demagogy' they held responsible for the 'extremism' of the masses, created a major barrier against revising their policies.

[33] op. cit., I, p. 379.

Equally, they clung to their belief that co-operation with 'progressive' elements of propertied society was essential. True, their optimism steadily drained away. They became ever more disillusioned with the Kadets who, after breaking up the First Coalition on 2 July, explicitly refused to form a second coalition on the basis of the radical social reforms proposed by the moderate socialists. Worse still, the most sympathetic liberals outside the Kadet party, such as N. V. Nekrasov and Tereshchenko, would not form a coalition without Kadet participation. Thus it was only by the device of liberal and socialist ministers agreeing to differ on their respective programmes that the Second Coalition was formed, under Kerensky, on 25 July. Following the Kornilov affair at the end of August, most moderate socialists concluded that further co-operation with the Kadets was impossible. Yet in September they were unable to persuade even the most 'progressive' middle-class elements, the democratic and technical intelligentsia of local government and the co-operatives, to join them in a new coalition which would exclude the Kadets. At the same time, since the danger of civil war and counter-revolution seemed only to grow as the intransigence of the Kadets intensified, and a separate peace remained abhorrent, they continued to resist the idea of an all-socialist, soviet-based government. Therefore, although many felt unable to support the feeble Third Coalition formed by Kerensky on 27 September, in which Kadets were again included, they were unable to offer any alternative. They had reached an impasse.[34]

A minority of left-wing Mensheviks and SRs had rejected the strategy of their leaders from the start. While their leaders proved unable to develop an alternative strategy, the number of rank-and-file Mensheviks and SRs who did so grew with each month that passed. By the beginning of July, Left SRs were beginning to emerge as an organized faction within the SR party, and on the morrow of the October revolution they broke away. By then Martov and the Menshevik Internationalists were making deep inroads into what had once been a solid majority of their party favouring Tsereteli's policies. Both Left factions moved more and more closely into line with mass demands. But their association with the discredited moderate leadership was not readily forgotten. The party most closely identified with the rejection of coalition, the formation of a soviet government, and 'peace, bread and land' was that of the Bolsheviks.

[34] Galili y Garcia, 'Menshevik Revolutionary Defencists', pp. 755–72, 803–17.

8 THE BOLSHEVIKS, THE MASSES, AND OCTOBER

The centrepiece of the debate over the revolution concerns the Bolshevik victory. In a sense all the questions considered hitherto only serve as a backdrop to this issue. It is because of their bearing upon October that the long-term trends of pre-war tsarist society, the dynamics of February, and the explanations for the failure of both liberals and moderate socialists are so fiercely disputed. And it is in their conflicting evaluations of and explanations for the political triumph of Lenin's party that the respective schools of thought are most bitterly divided.

The Soviet view

In the Soviet view, the Bolshevik triumph was based upon its success in winning the support of nothing less than a majority of the population. That this proved possible bore out Lenin's flawless Marxist analysis of the correlation of class forces in Russia in the age of imperialism. By its very nature, of course, by virtue of its unswerving adherence to revolutionary socialism, the party represented the interests of the proletariat. As Lenin insisted, however, to succeed the revolution required the support of the great mass of the population. On their own, workers accounted for only some 10 per cent of the population. Yet the potential constituency of the party extended far beyond that. For the party espoused the interests of the non-proletarian masses: it was committed to peace, to the confiscation of private land, to decisive state intervention to arrest economic decline, and to the principle of national self-determination. These were precisely the goals of the petty bourgeoisie. Moreover, there was in fact no way they could be achieved except through the medium of the party of the proletariat. The bourgeoisie stood in diametric opposition to them; the petty-bourgeois parties, while nominally committed to a similar programme, adamantly refused to form a democratic, soviet-based government to implement it. The only way forward for the petty bourgeoisie lay in supporting the creation of a proletarian government.

Objectively, then, the party represented the interests of the great majority of the nation. The nature of the class conflict rendered Russia ripe for socialist revolution with popular support. The problem lay in converting this objective fact into conscious 'subjective' commitment on the part of the masses. The task was gigantic. The manifest failure of the Bolsheviks' rivals to solve any of the country's problems, of course, generated spontaneous discontent among the masses. But the illusions sown by the barrage of bourgeois propaganda and the hypocritical promises of the moderate 'socialists', the efforts of their enemies to silence and slander the Bolsheviks, the low level of literacy in the army and the countryside, and the political backwardness even of many workers – all this presented huge obstacles to winning the masses over to the side of the proletariat. It was the glory of the Bolshevik party that it overcame each of these obstacles and forged a new mass consciousness.

That it did so brilliantly vindicated Lenin's theory of the role and organization of the vanguard party, the 'party of a new type'. Throughout the revolutionary year the party retained the structure on which he had insisted. On the one hand, the post-February conditions of open struggle enabled it to develop its democratic processes more fully – the election of officials, thorough mass consultation, and frequent conferences at both regional and national level. On the other hand, the party remained centralized and ideologically homogeneous. Unlike the amorphous petty-bourgeois parties, it did not accept new members indiscriminately but only on the recommendation of two existing members and subject to confirmation by the local party organization. In terms of organization, it remained strictly hierarchical. From the primary cell upwards, all took their lead from the policy propounded by the Central Committee. And from his return to Russia in April onwards that policy was the work of Lenin. Throughout, the party was guided by his profound understanding of the class forces at play, of the bankruptcy of the bourgeois revolution, and of the manner in which it would 'grow over' into socialist revolution.

In the course of 1917 the principled stand and organizational strength of the party enabled it to bring home the meaning of events to the masses. Through a sustained campaign of patient propaganda and political education the party gradually put its message across. By September the party was publishing 75 different newspapers and journals, in 8 different languages. The print run of *Pravda*, the central organ of the party, soared to 90,000 by July and over 200,000 by October.[1] Bolshevik activists energetically denounced the counterrevolutionary machinations of the bourgeoisie and its government, they exposed the impotence and hypocrisy of the petty-bourgeois parties, and they argued the case for socialist revolution in every available forum.

Naturally the most complete victory was won among the proletariat. In factory committees, in working-class clubs, in public meetings and demonstrations, in the trade unions and the soviets – everywhere the

[1] P. A. Golub *et al.*, eds, *Istoricheskii opyt trekh rossiiskikh revoliutsii* (3 vols, Moscow, 1985–7) III, p. 144.

party's spokesmen, its slogans, its programme gathered ever more support. As political and class consciousness developed among wider and wider sections of the working class, so they rallied to the Bolsheviks. Between February and October the membership of the party rose from 24,000 to some 350,000.[2] About 60 per cent of the new members were workers, and in the major industrial centres such as Petrograd workers constituted over 80 per cent of the membership.[3] Apart from those who actually became members, the mass following of the party among workers swelled out of all recognition. In the late summer it gained majority support in the soviets not only of Petrograd and Moscow but of most of the country's industrial centres. In the elections for the Constituent Assembly held in November, 9 of the 10.4 million workers voting supported the Bolsheviks.[4] By October the Bolsheviks enjoyed the allegiance of all but a small fraction of Russia's proletariat.

Progress was slower in the army. But the substantial minority of worker-soldiers provided the basis for a network of party cells through which Bolshevik ideas, the party programme, and literature specifically addressed to soldiers exerted growing influence over the peasant majority. The efforts of the Bolshevik military organizations were supplemented by numerous delegations of workers sent to the front to counteract the misleading propaganda of the government and High Command. Both urban garrisons and many front-line regiments stationed close to industrial centres came under the direct influence of proletarian radicalism. The growing tendency for soldier soviets to merge with worker soviets further increased proletarian and party strength. The success of the Bolsheviks' campaign was manifest. By October they had ousted the SRs and Mensheviks from many of the lower-level soldiers committees and were rapidly gaining control over the higher ones. The elections to the Constituent Assembly demonstrated that over half the men in both army and navy were firmly behind the Bolsheviks.[5]

Bringing the peasantry in the countryside under the party's influence presented an even greater challenge. The 15 per cent of the peasantry who were well-to-do naturally sided with the bourgeoisie. The 20 per cent 'middle peasants', though strongly attracted by Bolshevik policies on land and peace, were too deeply committed to their property to be reliable allies of the proletariat. But the great mass of the peasantry, some 65 per cent, were rural proletarians or semi-proletarians whose interests coincided with those of the workers.[6] The trouble was that

[2] op. cit., III, p. 134.
[3] Kh. M. Astrakhan, *Bolsheviki i ikh politicheskie protivniki v 1917 godu* (Leningrad, 1973), p. 140.
[4] Golub, *Istoricheskii opyt* III, pp. 76–7.
[5] P. A. Golub, *Partiia, armiia i revoliutsiia: Otvoevanie partiei bol'shevikov armii na storony revoliutsii. Mart 1917–fevral' 1918* (Moscow, 1967), pp. 204–6.
[6] Golub, *Istoricheskii opyt* III, pp. 96–7.

politically they were extremely backward, and the number of Bolshevik organizations in the villages was very limited. Nevertheless, the party succeeded in winning them over to its programme for the confiscation of all noble, church and private land, for the nationalization of the land and its transfer into the hands of peasant soviets and other democratic organs. As with the soldiers, the example of working-class radicalism exercised a profound effect upon the peasantry, facilitated by the fusion of more and more peasant soviets with those of workers and soldiers. At the same time, the ideas of the party were spread by worker activists sent to the countryside; by militant soldiers and sailors returning to their native villages; and by party activists, including Lenin himself, taking every opportunity to address conferences and congresses of peasant representatives. Both the resolutions of these assemblies, and the rapid intensification of peasant assaults on noble land bore testimony to the party's success. In the words of Lenin, 'Here was objective proof, proof not in words but in deeds, of the people coming over to the side of the Bolsheviks.'[7]

A similar process took place both among the urban petty bourgeoisie and the national minorities. The greatest inroads were made where the party was most active and the proletarian presence strongest. The strata of artisans and petty traders, of clerks, white-collar workers and members of the intelligentsia were increasingly drawn away from the reactionary policies of the Provisional Government. Likewise, despite every effort by the forces of reaction to exploit nationalist feeling in order to subdue class struggle, Bolshevik commitment to the right of self-determination steadily gained influence over the myriad national freedom movements. The peasantry of the oppressed minorities repudiated compromise and set about resolving the land problem 'in the spirit' of the Bolshevik programme.[8] Support for the Bolsheviks was demonstrated by their control of the urban soviets not only of Great Russia but of White Russia, the Ukraine, Latvia, Estonia and the northern Caucasus. At the Second All-Russian Congress of Soviets, delegates from the national minorities joined in proclaiming soviet power. In the elections to the Constituent Assembly the national parties won a mere 10 per cent of the vote of the garrison troops, while the Bolsheviks won 57.8 per cent.[9] And in the aftermath of October the swift and largely peaceful transfer of power to local soviets bore out the nationwide support for the Bolsheviks.

Thus as the revolution unfolded, the party's stand raised mass consciousness and attracted ever wider support. The Mensheviks and SRs,

[7] op. cit., III, p. 106; Lenin, Polnoe sobranie sochinenii (55 vols, Moscow, 1958–65) XXIV, p. 400.
[8] Golub, Istoricheskii opyt III, p. 131.
[9] op. cit.

by betraying democracy and supporting the bourgeoisie, alienated their petty-bourgeois constituents. Both parties suffered a haemorrhage of support, and Left factions within each party were drawn closer and closer to Bolshevik positions. It was increasingly borne in upon soldiers and sailors, artisans and the urban petty bourgeoisie, peasants and the oppressed nationalities that only by rallying behind the Bolsheviks and the proletariat could they achieve their goals. By October Bolshevik slogans, policy and strategy enjoyed the support of a majority of the entire population.

At the same time as it raised mass consciousness and rallied the people to its banner, the party took the leading role in organizing the masses. It was under its guidance that the popular democratic institutions were formed and consolidated. Party activists were in the vanguard of developing factory committees, organizing the workers' militia, strengthening the committees of soldiers and sailors, and co-ordinating the nation-wide network of soviets. At every turn the party's leadership was vital. By instilling discipline into the ranks of its followers, by restraining them from co-ordinated, premature *démarches* against the government, and by concentrating their attention on the crucial issue of power it welded together an irresistible revolutionary movement.

The October revolution itself displayed to the full both the organizational strength of the party and the brilliance of Lenin's leadership. He realized that the July Days marked the end of 'dual power', the final betrayal of the revolution by the Mensheviks and SRs, and the beginning of a concerted attempt to establish a counter-revolutionary dictatorship. 'He was able swiftly and precisely to evaluate the new situation, to give a scientifically-based prognosis of the further development of the class struggle . . . and to plan the most appropriate methods and means of struggle against the counter-revolution. And again, as at every sudden historical turning-point, the creative power of Lenin's genius was displayed.'[10] Following the Kornilov affair, the Bolsheviks made one final effort to persuade the petty-bourgeois parties to allow the revolution to develop peacefully by themselves forming a soviet-based government. They refused. Lenin thereupon prepared the party for armed insurrection against the Provisional Government.

He chose the moment with consummate skill. To have acted before the party had the support of the majority of the people would have been adventurism. To delay could be fatal. The forces of reaction were already planning a further attempt at a military coup. Kerensky's government might at any minute surrender the revolutionary capital to the Germans. Apathy and despair could spread among the masses. But in October the time was ripe. At its historic meeting on 10 October, the

[10] *op. cit.*, III, p. 308.

Central Committee adopted Lenin's resolution to prepare an armed insurrection. Under Lenin's personal direction, preparations were put in hand. Party leaders in Moscow and other major centres were alerted, while in the capital the party concentrated overwhelming force. Behind the Red Guard, armed, trained and co-ordinated under the party's leadership, stood the most reliable garrison units, sailors of the Baltic Fleet and troops from the northwest front. On the morning of 24 October the Central Committee resolved to mobilize all its forces. Operating through the legal form of the Petrograd Soviet's Military Revolutionary Committee, it overthrew the Provisional Government with hardly a drop of blood shed, and delivered power to the soviets.

The popular nature of the revolution was demonstrated by the swift, triumphant spread of Soviet power across the country. In only 16 out of 97 major centres did the Bolsheviks and their allies have to resort to force to effect the transfer of power.[11] Elsewhere support for the revolution rendered its opponents helpless. When the new government disbanded the Constituent Assembly, where the elections had yielded an artificial Right SR majority out of step even with their own peasant constituents, there was minimal protest. The Bolsheviks' victory was thus in the truest sense democratic and popular, the political expression and culmination of explosive class struggle.

The liberal view

In the traditional liberal view, the Bolshevik victory was anything but popular and democratic. The party was and remained a conspiratorial minority, whose active membership 'consisted in the main of intellectuals.'[12] Their success is to be explained in the first instance by their superior organization. A highly centralized body of professional revolutionaries had been Lenin's ideal ever since he wrote *What Is To Be Done?* in 1902. The tightly-knit, military-style organization he created stood in stark contrast to its feeble, fractured, ill-organized rivals. It provided the perfect instrument through which a small group of the most radical intelligentsia could exploit Russia's difficulties. Moreover, Lenin and his co-conspirators enjoyed all the advantages of utter ruthlessness. To achieve revolution they would stop at nothing. They had no compunction about inciting violence, defying democratic principle and risking civil war provided they could capture power. No wonder they prevailed against rivals paralysed by scruples and principle.

What gave this ruthless minority its opportunity was the chaos which

[11] I. I. Mints, *Istoriia Velikogo Oktiabria* (3 vols, 1977–9, 2nd edn) III, pp. 637–8.
[12] J. L. H. Keep, *The Russian Revolution. A Study in Mass Mobilization* (London, 1976), p. ix.

reigned during 1917. Following the February revolution, in part as a result of Bolshevik rabble-rousing, Russian society slid into a state of anarchy. The workers' totally unrealistic demands and their assertion of workers' control 'was bound to create anarchy, mass unemployment and impoverishment.'[13] Peasants went on the rampage in the country-side, carving up noble land and machinery, thereby fatally disrupting the grain trade and perpetuating Russia's backwardness. In the army and navy defeatism spread, officers were lynched and military dis-cipline collapsed. As the authority and administration of the Pro-visional Government disintegrated, power lay in the street at the mercy of any organized group of determined men.[14] The situation presented the perfect opportunity for Lenin and his clique.

The liberal tradition has dismissed the notion that the Bolsheviks enjoyed widespread popularity. Only in the capital did they briefly achieve a substantial following. But the capital, as the political, social, legal and economic centre of the country, was in every sense atypical, and between February and October the course of events there 'tended to become more and more estranged from the revolutionary tide in the rest of the country.'[15] Until very late in the year, their following in the nation at large was restricted to a narrow minority among the working class, itself a small fraction of the total population. In the army their support was patchy and ephemeral. They never made any significant progress among the peasantry, who remained staunchly loyal to the SRs. And despite enjoying all the advantages of office, in the one free election open to all classes, that for the Constituent Assembly, the party gained only 25 per cent of the seats.

That they were able to create the illusion of mass support owed more to intrigue, subterfuge and infiltration than genuine popularity. The key lay in the structure of the mass institutions – factory committees, workers' militia, trade unions, soldiers' committees and above all the soviets – which came into being during 1917. They were tailor-made for the party's purposes, inherently vulnerable to the Bolsheviks' superior organization and articulateness. From the spring of 1917 these organizations showed a strong tendency to concentrate power in the hands of officials. 'Common to all soviets was a form of organiz-ation that permitted them to be influenced – indeed, manipulated – by the radical activists who assumed leading positions in their executive committees or other standing bodies.'[16] Their electoral rules were arbitrary and ill-defined and ensured in each case that rank-and-file deputies exercised the feeblest control over the executive. 'The plenum's function was not to take decisions but rather to mobilize

[13] op. cit., p. 158.
[14] A. Ulam, Lenin and the Bolsheviks (London, 1969), pp. 449–99.
[15] R. Pethybridge, The Spread of the Russian Revolution. Essays on 1917 (London, 1972), p. 179.
[16] J. L. H. Keep, The Debate on Soviet Power (Oxford, 1979), p. 19.

support for the leadership and to confer upon its actions the sanction of an affirmative popular vote.'[17] The activists, the 'junior cadres' within these institutions rapidly gained control over them. And these 'junior cadres' were in turn creatures of the leadership, less educated, less sophisticated, but made in their own image and likeness, imbibing their 'jargon' and 'world view'.[18] The rank and file who followed them did so 'out of a vague sense of solidarity, without any clear idea of the objectives pursued by those who aspired to direct them.'[19] And despite their untiring efforts, even at its very height the Bolsheviks' popularity was distinctly limited. The Second All-Russian Congress of Soviets which met on 25 October yielded the narrowest of majorities for the Bolsheviks and their allies. It was only because the peasantry were grossly underrepresented, and the moderate socialists withdrew, that they were able to claim that their conspiracy had been approved by the soviets.

Such limited support as they did attract was drawn from the *Lumpenproletariat*, from the dregs of society. Their vital constituency were 'the more ignorant among the population.'[20] The naïvety and political innocence of the Russian masses was crucial to the Bolsheviks' success. There was simply 'no such thing as mass political consciousness in Russia in 1917.'[21] The ideas of the peasantry and soldiers were childlike and utopian. With their 'total lack of political experience or understanding of what was happening . . . [they were] an easy prey to the agitators.'[22] The workers 'were intoxicated by hopes of a golden age'; 'driven to near-despair by the economic crisis, their nerves kept on edge by incessant propaganda, they responded uncritically to the appeals of a party that promised untold blessings once "soviet power" had been achieved.'[23] 'In 1917 emotion and irrational bias swayed most Russians.'[24] Ignorant, politically immature, with no grasp of the real issues at stake, they were guided not by rational goals of their own but by the vagaries of rumour, by rabble-rousing, propaganda and demagogy. 'Fantasies of uninhibited self-rule were combined with unexpressed longings for a firm directing hand . . . a naïve and contradictory outlook [which] gave great leverage to any party which could combine an ultra-democratic image with an authoritarian core.'[25]

Moreover, for all the claims made about Lenin's profound and

---

[17] *op. cit.*, p. 19.
[18] Keep, *Mobilization*, p. 141.
[19] *op. cit.*
[20] L. Schapiro, *1917. The Russian Revolutions and the Origins of Present-Day Communism* (Hounslow, 1984), pp. 78, 214.
[21] Pethybridge, *The Spread*, p. 196.
[22] Schapiro, *1917*, pp. 64, 92.
[23] Keep, *Mobilization*, pp. 67, 95, 157.
[24] Pethybridge, *The Spread*, p. 142.
[25] Keep, *Debate*, p. 18.

scientific analysis of the class forces at play, for all his skill at couching his propaganda in Marxist terminology, he and his comrades were in fact opportunists of the first order. From his earliest days as a revolutionary, Lenin had been a Jacobin, a voluntarist temperamentally at odds with the whole historical message of Marxism.[26] His strategy owed precious little to Marxism and everything to an insatiable lust for power. Perceiving the possibility of undermining the Provisional Government and installing a Bolshevik dictatorship, he abandoned the cardinal tenets of Marxism. On his return in April, to the horror even of his most loyal Bolshevik lieutenants, he proclaimed the bourgeois revolution complete and the socialist revolution on the agenda. This was in flagrant defiance of the very kernel of Marx's ideas: that only an advanced capitalist society can yield the economic and social conditions for socialism – massive productive power and a vast, sophisticated proletariat. Despite the overwhelming preponderance of the petty bourgeoisie, despite the primitive state of the economy outside a few urban islands, Lenin proclaimed Russia ripe for socialism.

Lenin's opportunism involved the party in the most crude deception. To destabilize the Provisional Government the Bolsheviks pandered to mass ignorance, impatience and utopianism. Stealing the clothes of radical SRs, they urged the peasants to seize noble land and carve it up among themselves. To undermine the army, they agitated for total democratization, the election of officers, the destruction of military discipline, and fraternization with the enemy. To curry favour among the national minorities they portrayed themselves as champions of the right of each nation to self-determination. To encourage working-class radicalism, they championed workers' control. Furthermore, the central political slogan of the Bolsheviks – 'All Power to the Soviets' – was designed to appeal to a semi-anarchist popular urge to have done with all authority. Yet each policy, each promise blandished before the ignorant masses was supremely cynical. Too late would the peasantry discover that the ultimate goal of the Bolsheviks was to destroy their private landholding in favour of state-run collective farms; too late would the soldiers learn that once in power the Bolsheviks would create an army every bit as hierarchical as its imperial predecessor; too late would the national minorities find that the principle of 'self-determination' would be promptly overridden by the higher principle of proletarian internationalism once the Bolsheviks were in power; too late would the workers realize the Bolshevik determination to ride roughshod over workers' control and subject them to harsh discipline; and too late would the people of Russia as a whole realize that the soviet system and every democratic process

[26] R. Pipes, 'The Origins of Bolshevism: The Intellectual Evolution of Young Lenin' in R. Pipes. ed., *Revolutionary Russia* (London, 1968), pp. 26–62.

would be smashed 'under the blow of the centralist Bolshevik hammer.'[27] 'In the last resort, Bolshevism proved to be less a doctrine, than a technique of action for the seizing and holding of power by the Bolshevik party.'[28]

The October revolution itself epitomized the Bolshevik approach. The timing and execution of the *coup d'état* demonstrated to the full both Lenin's political acumen and his ruthlessness. It was an act of supreme opportunism. The Bolsheviks could never secure power through a democratic route. But the prevailing chaos, the decomposition of the Provisional Government, the demoralization of their rivals and the apathy and disillusionment of the masses gave them their chance. By forcibly seizing power 'in one very special city of Russia' they could create a bridgehead from which to impose their control over the rest of the country.[29] Fully conscious that the chance might never recur, Lenin harried his hesitant colleagues into action. Feigning fear lest Petrograd be surrendered or Kerensky attempt a military assault on the Left, he insisted that they strike at once, without any form of popular sanction. Launching the *coup* on 24 October, they deliberately and consciously pre-empted the Second All-Russian Congress of Soviets which assembled on 25 October. This fully exposed the emptiness of their democratic pretensions, of their professed wish that all power should pass to the soviets. They knew, of course, that it was essential to mask their true intentions, to deceive even most of their own followers. Hence the care taken, at the prompting of Trotsky and others, to present the action of the party as that of the Petrograd Soviet rather than of the party. The inner circle of Bolsheviks marshalling the Red Guards for the *coup d'état* operated under the cloak of the Military Revolutionary Committee of the Petrograd Soviet which had been set up ostensibly to defend the revolution against a second Kornilovite *démarche*. And even then, 'there was no pro-Bolshevik enthusiasm in the population, only apathy.'[30]

The sequel to the seizure of power immediately confirmed its authoritarian, anti-democratic nature. Even within the party, the common assumption was that the new government would be an all-socialist coalition rather than a one-party dictatorship. Martov and the Internationalist Mensheviks urged just such a coalition. The railwaymen staged a strike for the same goal. Yet Lenin was immovable. Having secured power, the Bolsheviks would never let it go. All opposition was denounced as counter-revolutionary. The Cheka was created on the very morrow of the *coup* to silence criticism by force. And gradually Bolshevik authority was imposed on the provincial soviets as opposition deputies were intimidated or forcibly ejected,

[27] Pethybridge, *The Spread*, p. 210.
[28] L. Schapiro, *The Origin of the Communist Autocracy* (London, 1977, 2nd edn), p. 14.
[29] Pethybridge, *The Spread*, p. 180.
[30] Ulam, *Lenin and the Bolsheviks*, p. 483.

hostile assemblies disbanded, new elections manipulated, and recalcitrant peasant bodies merged with more pliant worker soviets. When the Constituent Assembly elections of November yielded a resounding defeat for the new regime, it was summarily disbanded and the party proceeded to create a brutal dictatorship.

The libertarian view

In the libertarian view, the Soviet and liberal accounts of the Bolshevik victory are both fundamentally misconceived. The liberal view grossly distorts the nature of the social upheaval which overcame Russia during 1917. The revolution was truly popular and profoundly democratic. No less misleading is the role which Soviet orthodoxy attributes to the Bolshevik Party. Lenin and his comrades were the illegitimate beneficiaries of the autonomous action of the masses.

The revolution of 1917 was the product of popular revolt against oppression. It was accomplished 'not by any political party, but by the people themselves.'[31] Time and again the self-proclaimed leaders of the revolution were taken by surprise by the initiative welling up from below – in January 1905, in February, April and July 1917. The masses were not enticed into revolt by superior leaders. Their extreme radicalism was not the product of manipulation and brainwashing by the Bolsheviks, as the liberal view would have it, nor was it the fruit of enlightenment brought to them by the Bolsheviks, as the Soviet view contends. The goals for which they strove were their own. They responded only to what fulfilled their own aspirations; the rest they rejected. In this sense, not only February but the whole social upheaval of 1917 was 'spontaneous' – unorchestrated, unplanned but consciously willed, deliberately carried through by millions upon millions of ordinary people. The peasants sought to solve the 'agrarian question' in their own way and by themselves, while 'the autonomous action of the working class seeking totally to alter the conditions of its existence' was 'the most fundamental feature' of the period.[32]

Moreover, the action taken by the masses was neither destructive nor chaotic. Protest which Soviet historians treat as 'spontaneous', undisciplined and unreflecting, and which liberals see as the mindless product of envy and hatred, is hailed by libertarians as creative in the truest sense. The masses were motivated by something deeper than poverty, envy and desire for revenge. They sought to assert their human dignity. They sought to overthrow that which oppressed, degraded, humiliated them. They sought to seize control over their own lives. 'The revolutionary masses by their own initiative began,

[31] A. Berkman, *The Russian Tragedy* (Montreal, 1976), p. 13.
[32] M. Brinton, *Bolsheviks and Workers' Control 1917 to 1921. The State and Counter-Revolution* (Montreal, 1975), p. vii.

long before the October days, to put into practice their social ideals. They took possession of the land, the factories, mines, mills and tools of production. They got rid of the more hated and dangerous representatives of government and authority. In their grand revolutionary outburst they destroyed every form of political and economic oppression.'[33]

At its height, the mass movement struck at the very roots of hierarchy and subordination, it challenged authoritarian relations at the point of production. During the revolution the masses advanced from defence of their own interests against management and external authority towards full control over their own working lives, over the production process itself. Libertarian attention has been focused in particular upon the factory committees established during 1917.[34] Initially limited in their aims, the committees became increasingly assertive and interventionist. Their scope broadened throughout the period, moving from collective defence against the barbaric and arbitrary methods of tsarist factory management towards fully-fledged self-management. 'The shop and factory committees were the pioneers in labour control of industry with the prospect of themselves, in the near future, managing the industries entire.'[35] For most workers, the factory committee movement 'was not just a means of combating the economic sabotage of the ruling class or a correct tactical slogan . . . [but] was the expression of their deepest aspirations . . . instinctively they sensed that who managed production would manage all aspects of social life.'[36]

There was a parallel if less sophisticated movement on the land. The peasantry were determined to drive off the landlord and the government agent, to reintegrate into the commune those who had separated from it, and to establish the autonomy of the village. They were motivated not merely by economic desperation or the levelling instinct, but by a desire to build an egalitarian society imbued with their own values. In the countryside, the creative potential of peasant revolution was most fully developed under the umbrella of the Makhnovist movement in the Ukraine between 1918 and 1920. Here the peasantry defied the Reds and Whites alike and asserted full control over their own lives in a network of freely-organized, co-ordinated and disciplined communes. 'The movement of the revol-

[33] Berkman, *Russian Tragedy*, pp. 36–7.

[34] Recent libertarian studies of the factory committees owe a considerable debt to specialists who do not share many of their assumptions. See in particular P. Avrich, 'The Bolshevik Revolution and Workers' Control in Russian Industry', *Slavic Review* 22 (1963), pp. 47–63 and 'Russian Factory Committees in 1917', *Jahrbücher für Geschichte Osteuropas* (1963) 11, pp. 161–82.

[35] Berkman, *Russian Tragedy*, p. 58; G. P. Maximoff, *The Guillotine at Work. Twenty Years of Terror in Russia* (Chicago, Ill., 1940), pp. 348–51.

[36] Brinton, *Bolsheviks and Workers' Control*, p. 20; Maximoff, *Guillotine*, p. 62.

utionary peasants became organized and unified, and realized ever more precisely its fundamental constructive tasks.'[37]

It was this mass drive for true liberation which provided the revolution with its momentum and direction, which *was* the revolution. Yet, for all their creative achievement, the masses proved unable to carry through their challenge to final victory. They lacked the experience, the firmly established organizations, and the ideological clarity necessary to sustain it to the end. The constraints of the tsarist era had stunted their ideological and organizational development. The institutions they set up had 'no historical tradition, no competence, no notion of their role, their task, their true mission.'[38] Even the factory committee movement was 'unable to proclaim its own objectives [workers' self-management] in clear and positive terms.'[39] During 1917 they had not the time to consolidate their own institutions, to entrench direct democracy and forestall bureaucratization. The result was that they were 'taken in tow' by the political parties. The parties of the intelligentsia had been set up before the workers created their own institutions, and although the soviets had been an authentically working-class creation, in 1917 the intelligentsia succeeded in maintaining a stranglehold on key posts within them.

This was what made it possible for the Bolsheviks to take advantage of the mass movement. Unlike the newly-created representative bodies of peasants and workers, the party was firmly established when the revolution broke out. Its centralized, disciplined structure had the edge over the democratic organizations in the hands of the masses. 'Confronted with an "efficient", tightly-knit organization of this kind . . . it is scarcely surprising that the emerging Factory Committees were unable to carry the revolution to completion.'[40] Thus although the primary allegiance of the masses was to their factory committees, their village assemblies, their soviets, none the less the Bolsheviks were able to exploit the support they attracted to establish their own dictatorship.

Such support as they did enjoy, moreover, was won by deception. They skilfully echoed the aspirations of the masses. They tailored their slogans to match the masses' own goals. They hailed factory committees and workers' control, they championed the immediate transfer of the land to the peasants, an end to the war and traditional hierarchical authority in the army, and the dismantling of the bourgeois State. This espousal by the party of broadly libertarian aims amounted to conscious or unconscious demagogy. For in reality Bolshevik ideology was permeated by elitism and authoritarianism. Indeed, 'the fundamental

---

[37] Voline, *The Unknown Revolution 1917–1921* (Montreal, 1974), p. 569; P. Arshinov, *History of the Makhnovist Movement 1918–1921* (London, 1987), pp. 148–65.
[38] Voline, *Unknown Revolution*, p. 187.
[39] Brinton, *Bolsheviks and Workers' Control*, p. xiii.
[40] *op. cit.*

characteristic of Bolshevik psychology was distrust of the masses, of the proletariat' – and to an even greater extent of the peasantry.[41] 'At heart the Bolsheviks had no faith in the people and their creative initiative.'[42] Behind a mystifying veil of revolutionary Marxism, they constituted 'the last attempt of bourgeois society to reassert its ordained division into leaders and led and to maintain authoritarian social relations in all aspects of social life.'[43] They represented the interests not of the proletariat but of the intelligentsia.

The cleavage between the goals of the masses and those of the Bolsheviks was fundamental. Lenin and the Bolsheviks had never intended that workers should actually run the factories in which they worked. For them, workers' control by factory committees provided useful leverage against the bourgeoisie. But the notion of refounding social relations on the basis of self-management had no place in their plans. The Decree on Workers' Control of November 1917 envisaged the committees doing no more than 'checking' management: management itself would continue to exercise authority from above. For the Bolsheviks, socialism meant the nationalization of private property and its control by their own appointees. For them, it was enough that property be at the disposal of a 'workers'' State which they themselves would run. But in the libertarian view, the role of the workers in this form of 'socialist' society would differ little from their role in capitalist society: they would fulfil orders handed down from above.[44]

Peasants and workers, on the other hand, rightly saw the solution to their problems in taking direct command of production themselves. The only hope of overcoming the economic crisis which the Provisional Government was so manifestly incapable of mastering lay precisely in relying upon grass-roots initiative. Unfettered peasant communes were in the best position to restore agriculture and respond to urban needs. Freely-elected factory committees were in the best position to judge the requirements of their industries; to sustain the morale and self-discipline of workers; and to find ways of restoring the disastrous breakdown in trade between town and countryside.[45] Against Bolshevik scorn for the inability of workers to cope with the complexities of large-scale industry, libertarians point to the feverish commitment of workers, to their genuine success at working out for themselves the problems of supply, of food, of relations with the peasantry. To Bolshevik accusations that factory committees disrupted socialist planning and began to look upon their own factory as private property, they point to the vigorous efforts of the factory committees to co-ordinate their efforts, to provide common guide-

[41] Berkman, *Russian Tragedy*, 41; Arshinov, *Makhnovist Movement*, pp. 67–78.
[42] Berkman, *Russian Tragedy*, p. 16.
[43] Brinton, *Bolsheviks and Workers' Control*, p. 85.
[44] *op. cit.*, pp. 15ff.
[45] Voline, *Unknown Revolution*, pp. 289–301, 369.

lines, to co-operate with each other. As early as 2 April a conference of Factory Committees of Petrograd War Industries had been convened. The factory committees of Kharkov followed suit in May. A series of conferences representing all the capital's factory committees met in May–June, August, September and October. At the October conference plans were drawn up for an All-Russian Conference of Factory Committees which met on the eve of the October revolution. Far from being an obstacle to co-ordinated planning and distribution, self-management provided the soundest basis for it.[46] But this ran counter to the whole thrust of Bolshevism.

The ideological cleavage was reflected in the unbridgeable gulf which divided the Bolsheviks from the masses. 'The few Bolshevik cadres of working-class origin soon lost real contact with the class.' Those workers who supported it 'could not control the party. The leadership was firmly in the hands of professional revolutionaries.'[47] The duplicity, authoritarian ideology, and centralized organization of the party made it the ideal vehicle for the imposition of rule by the intelligentsia. As soon as it was in a position to do so, the party moved to curtail self-management. It subordinated the factory committees to the trade unions, established rigid party control over the trade unions, and concentrated managerial power in the hands of a centralized state bureaucracy. And once the State had asserted the right to appoint management from above, the division between officials and workers at the bench rapidly widened. At the same time, the new regime did all it could to gain control over the peasantry and to replace the free federal structures of the communes with hierarchical bodies directed by the party.

The overthrow of the Provisional Government in Petrograd in October amounted to little more than a reverberation of the action taken by workers, peasants and soldiers across the country. Yet instead of dealing the deathblow to state power and external authority, it marked the point at which power began to slip from the hands of the masses. The masses' challenge had been sufficient to sweep away tsarism and nobility, to dispossess the bourgeoisie and all but destroy the existing State. But it proved unable to prevent the reassertion of authority in a guise less easy to expose than tsarism or capitalism but no less oppressive: Bolshevism.

[46] Berkman, *Russian Tragedy*, p. 58; Brinton, *Bolsheviks and Workers' Control*, pp. 2–14, 18–21; see also the discussion in C. Sirianni, *Workers' Control and Socialist Democracy. The Soviet Experience* (London, 1982) pp. 104–18, 185–97.
[47] Brinton, *Bolsheviks and Workers' Control*, p. xii.

9 THE BOLSHEVIK VICTORY REVISITED

In the light of revisionist research, all three of the traditional accounts of the Bolshevik victory are seriously inadequate. While facets of each are borne out, none of them provides a satisfactory explanation for October. On the face of it, the approach with which revisionist work has most in common is that of the libertarians. Like the libertarians, it has emphasized the need to view events from below. The collapse of coercive authority placed an unprecedented premium upon the aspirations of workers, peasants and soldiers. Since their obedience could no longer be compelled, they could pressurize, frustrate and indeed destroy those – be it officers, managers, landlords, officials or politicians – nominally in charge of them. Their wishes and hopes had a direct political significance they had not had before. For revisionists, therefore, as for libertarians, the outcome of the revolution cannot be understood without studying these wishes and hopes, without delving into the experience and the motives of ordinary men and women during 1917. Despite confirming significant aspects of the libertarian portrayal of the masses, however, revisionist research takes the analysis considerably further. On the one hand, by bringing to bear a wealth of evidence not tapped by libertarian writers, it explores in much greater depth the dynamics of mass radicalization during 1917. On the other, it casts new light on the relationship between this radicalization and the triumph of the Bolsheviks.

Mass radicalization

Central to revisionist findings is the perception that the actions of workers, soldiers and peasants during 1917 can be understood in their own terms, with little reference to the blandishments directed at them from above.[1] The masses were of course assailed by appeals and instructions, programmes and promises proffered by rival political leaders. But what stands out is that once the February revolution had destroyed traditional authority over them, they acted upon their would-be leaders as much as being acted upon by them. No less than their social superiors, ordinary men and women were guided primarily by values and aspirations of their own. They sought to assert these values and to solve the problems that confronted them. Moreover, when viewed from the vantage point of the factory bench, the trench,

[1] For a useful summary of revisionist work on the view 'from below', see R. G. Suny, 'Toward a Social History of the October Revolution', *American Historical Review* 88 (1983), pp. 31–52.

the village, the solutions they adopted emerge as neither wild nor unthinking. In large measure their actions represented rational responses to the predicament they faced. The driving force behind their intervention, their organizational activity and the shifts in their political allegiance was an essentially autonomous and rational pursuit of their own goals.

So far as the peasantry are concerned, overriding all other issues was the question of the land. They sought relief, as they had made abundantly clear in the course of the revolution of 1905–7 and in the elections to the first two Dumas, in the redistribution of the imperial demesne, State land and the large estates. The land, they insisted, should belong to those who worked it. Private landowners would retain no more than the area of land they could work with their own labour, absentee landlords would be dispossessed, and the authority of the commune reasserted over the 'Stolypin' peasant. Rebellion in the countryside was not instigated or provided with its ideas from outside. Party activists, radicalized soldiers returning from the army, and the example of the industrial working class played a decidedly secondary role in stimulating peasant militancy. It welled up from within the village itself.[2]

Nor can their action be dismissed as anarchic or ignorant. The invasion and subdivision of gentry estates was generally planned, organized and co-ordinated through the village commune. Behind the shifting pattern of peasant protest and rebellion there was both a short-term and a long-term economic logic. The immediate objects of peasant intervention – crops, timber, equipment or land itself – were not chosen at random but varied according to local needs and seasonal factors.[3] Nor was the reassertion of the peasant commune, the determination to parcel out the property of private landowners among peasant households, and the reversal of trends towards socio-economic differentiation necessarily economically retrogressive. Comparative studies with agriculture in Denmark and elsewhere have been used to demonstrate the economic potential of autonomous peasant agriculture and the small-scale family farm.[4] When viewed from the village, action that seemed to property-owners and officials the product of ignorance and external agitation was neither. Even the peasants' resort to violence, the attacks on landowners and their

[2] M. Ferro, *The Russian Revolution of February 1917* (London, 1972), pp. 121–30.
[3] O. Figes, *Peasant Russia, Civil War. The Volga Countryside in Revolution (1917–1921)* (Oxford, 1989), pp. 40–61; G. Gill, *Peasants and Government in the Russian Revolution* (London, 1979), pp. 141–9, 157–69. Although Gill's study of the Provisional Government's handling of the peasant problem complements other revisionist studies, much of his treatment of the peasantry as such adheres more closely to the traditional liberal approach. See the exchange between Gill and J. H. Kress over 'The Mainsprings of Peasant Action in 1917', *Soviet Studies* xxx (1978), pp. 63–86; xxxi (1979), pp. 574–80; xxxii (1980), pp. 291–6.
[4] R. Bideleux, *Communism and Development* (London, 1985), pp. 12–18.

families, the burning down of manor houses, was no 'orgy of mindless destruction'. It represented their determination not only to transform the traditional pattern of landownership and authority in the countryside but to ensure that it could never be re-established.

Moreover, peasant horizons were not limited to the vital but mundane issue of land redistribution. Revisionist analysis of the early twentieth-century peasantry has brought out the much wider scope of their aspirations, their yearning not merely to overcome their desperate land shortage but to transform the social environment in which they lived. The best documentation of these aspirations derives from the array of village petitions drawn up in the course of the revolution of 1905–7. Their motivation and demands remained very much the same a decade later. They demonstrated not a troglodyte ignorance of the world about them, but an insatiable thirst for news, for newspapers, for information, for knowledge. They questioned, they argued, they thought. 'At the centre of this immense process of communication was not propaganda sent or brought from elsewhere, but rather a grandiose and spontaneous effort at political self-understanding and self-education by millions of illiterate and half-literate villagers. In an endless, slow, often clumsy and ill-informed and ever-heated debate, masses of peasants looked at their life and environment anew and critically. They conceived and expressed what was often unthinkable until then: an image of a new world, a dream of justice, a demand for land and liberty.'[5] Beyond their demand for land were repeated calls for efficient and just courts, for an end to arbitrary authority and its replacement by officials elected by themselves, for free education.

True, a summary picture of the peasant drive against private landownership obscures both variations in the tempo of revolt and the tensions among the peasantry. The fiercest militancy and the highest level of violence was in central Russia where private landholding was concentrated and population density greatest.[6] Equally, in addition to attacks by peasants within the commune upon the minority who had withdrawn from it, there were ominous conflicts between peasants of different provinces and villages as concern about grain stocks led to clashes over the shipment of grain. But despite this, the common ground shared by peasants in all regions was manifest. As soon as the old regime was overthrown, peasants began to articulate their own aspirations through resolutions and petitions in villages across the country. From the spring, on a growing scale, they proceeded to take direct action at the local level to solve the problems that confronted them.[7] The goals, the methods and the rhythm of peasant actions during 1917 were their own.

[5] T. Shanin, *Roots of Otherness: Russia's Turn of Century* (2 vols, London, 1985, 1986) II, pp. 130–1.
[6] Gill, *Government and Peasants*, pp. 157–61.
[7] D. J. Raleigh, *Revolution on the Volga: 1917 in Saratov* (Ithaca, 1985), pp. 174–89.

Revisionist analysis of developments in the army paints a picture closely analogous to that of the countryside. The major goals of the rank and file of the soldiery were evident from the moment the February revolution broke out. Apart from sharing the expectation of the peasantry, from whom the great majority of soldiers were drawn, of swift and drastic land reform, their aspirations were focused on two issues. First, they immediately made ·plain their determination to transform their relations with their officers. The Petrograd Soviet's Order No. 1 was drawn up on the insistence of soldiers in the capital and expressed demands which had already been clearly articulated in the revolution of 1905–7. The Order accelerated pressure for the purge of unpopular officers, the assertion of soldiers' rights to humane treatment and polite forms of address, and the election of committees to represent them. But that pressure, rooted in a profound sense of alienation from privileged society, arose at the front and in garrisons across the country independently of any outside stimulus.[8]

Second, they yearned for an early end to the war. This was made plain by the speed with which in late March/early April front-line soldiers rallied behind the Petrograd Soviet in its conflict with the first Provisional Government over the search for peace, and by the overwhelming refusal to support the June offensive. There is little mystery in the desire for peace. It arose from battle fatigue and war-weariness, after three years of fighting; from desperate food shortages; from loss of faith in officers, in the High Command, in the possibility of defeating the enemy. No more than peasant land hunger can the soldiers' anti-war feeling be explained in terms of external agitation. The sources make it difficult to define with any precision the impact of Bolshevik propaganda: from midsummer militantly anti-war soldiers began to call themselves 'bolsheviks' and to be identified as such in officers' reports, even when they had no formal connection with the party. Certainly, to hear their demands articulated and to see them in print encouraged soldiers to press them. Undoubtedly the arrival of radicalized garrison troops accelerated the spread of resistance at the front. But there does not appear to have been a close correlation between the spirit of revolt and Bolshevik presence.[9] The depth and breadth of war-weariness in the army, the overwhelming desire on every front for peace, demonstrated that it was first and foremost a product of their own experience. By October, so powerful was the demand for peace that 'had the Bolsheviks not been there to legitimize it, it would have sought and found some other resolution, because the impulse was not to be denied.'[10]

No more than in the case of the peasantry can the soldiers' actions be

[8] A. K. Wildman, *The End of the Russian Imperial Army* (2 vols, Princeton, N.J., 1980, 1987) I, chapter 7.
[9] *op. cit.*, II, pp. 64, 73.
[10] *op. cit.*, II, p. 225.

dismissed as ignorant or anarchic. Their demand for peace did not mean that they were willing wantonly to abandon the front to the enemy. Although the June offensive provoked mass mutiny, resistance to the German counter-attack with its threat that the enemy would sweep into the interior was fierce.[11] Equally, analyses of the very inadequate figures on the rate of desertions from the front suggest that contemporary impressions of wholesale self-demobilization were wildly exaggerated.[12] As in the countryside, there were significant variations in the pattern of revolt and tensions among different groups of soldiers. Garrison troops were initially more hostile to the war than those at the front. Relations between officers and men deteriorated more rapidly in the North and West than in the South-West and on the Turkish front. Pressure for the formation of separate national units became increasingly pronounced as the year proceeded and was often viewed with hostility by Russian soldiers. But by October the whole army was being swept by a 'virtual tidal wave . . . of self-assertion by the soldier mass in behalf of peace regardless of consequences or conditions, which now effaced all previous distinctions of behaviour and affected all types of units whatever their previous history, including cavalry, cossacks and artillery.'[13]

The lion's share of revisionist research has been devoted to the working class. The nature of their intervention during 1917 has been illuminated by penetrating beneath the image of a homogeneous proletarian herd. Russia's workers were not one uniform, grey mass but flesh-and-blood individuals, highly differentiated in terms of level of skill, cultural development, nationality and outlook. Rather than responding *en masse* to events, their reactions depended closely upon their own particular experience. Moreover, as before the war the most radical workers were not the most 'ignorant', the *Lumpenproletariat*, but rather the most sophisticated. Two broad strata of workers have been distinguished: on the one hand, those who were relatively highly paid, skilled, literate and urbanized, and on the other, the less skilled or unskilled, whose levels of pay and literacy were lower, and among whom were a high proportion of women and youths and of recent migrants from the countryside.[14] It was the former group, the so-called 'cadre' workers, who in 1917 were initially the most radical and politically active. It was they who took the initiative in setting up factory committees and workers' militia, and who were most actively involved in trade unions and local soviets. It was they who were most conscious of the interaction between economic problems and political

[11] *op. cit.*, ii, pp. 118–19, 122, 143.

[12] *op. cit.*, i, pp. 362–71; ii, pp. 230–1; M. Ferro, *October 1917. A Social History of the Russian Revolution* (London, 1980), pp. 83–5.

[13] Wildman, *Russian Imperial Army* ii, p. 225.

[14] S. A. Smith, *Red Petrograd. Revolution in the Factories 1917–18* (Cambridge, 1983), pp. 14–36.

power, and who began pressing earliest for the replacement of the Provisional Government by a government based on the soviets. The latter, less advantaged, group of workers were slower to organize, more volatile in their protests, and at first less concerned with political questions. In the course of the revolution, however, sustained radicalization drew the two groups of workers closer and closer together. Differences in terms of cultural level, branch of industry, and nationality, without disappearing, were gradually overlaid by a sense of common interest against employers, 'the bourgeoisie', a privileged society seen as the enemy. By October, a powerful bond of class consciousness had been forged among the great majority of workers.[15]

The essentially autonomous and rational nature of working-class protest has been brought home by tracing the changing forms their intervention took. The February revolution demonstrated and unleashed a deeply-rooted and powerful urge to transform the conditions they had suffered under tsarism. Their concern was to curtail the authoritarian structure of the tsarist factory, to halt the most direct assaults upon the dignity of workers, to enforce the eight-hour day, and to improve workers' wages and conditions. True, in the immediate aftermath of the February revolution there was a purge of factory managers which struck establishment figures as anarchic and destructive. Revisionist work, however, has stressed the selective nature of the purge and seen it as an expression of workers' profound resentment against the humiliation meted out by the tsarist factory order. 'This was no elemental *bunt*, no anarchistic rebellion against all authority, but a decisive rejection of unlimited, arbitrary power, experienced as an insult to the workers' self-respect.'[16]

The relative moderation of workers in the early weeks of the revolution was borne out by the role that the new factory committees sought for themselves. Their concern was to provide a collective mouthpiece for the defence of workers' interests, to obtain full information from management concerning the enterprise, and to 'supervise' or 'inspect' managerial decisions. They entered into collective bargaining with their employers, the incidence of strikes was low and they showed great concern for good order.[17]

It was as price rises cut grievously into real wages that workers became more radical. From May onwards, the number of strikes rose steeply as workers sought to bring pressure to bear on employers. Again, skilled workers led the way while the involvement of wider and wider strata of the semi-skilled and unskilled saw the strike graph peak

---

[15] D. Koenker, *Moscow Workers and the 1917 Revolution* (Princeton, 1981), pp. 358–9.
[16] D. Mandel, *The Petrograd Workers and the Fall of the Old Regime; The Petrograd Workers and Soviet Seizure of Power* (2 vols, London 1983–4) II, p. 100.
[17] Galili y Garcia, 'The Menshevik Revolutionary Defencists and the Workers in the Russian Revolution of 1917', (Ph.D. Dissertation, Columbia University, 1980), pp. 147–8.

in September. But in the course of the summer the nature of the strike movement underwent a significant shift. Initially, wages were the overriding issue, but increasingly these demands were accompanied by broader demands both for recognition of trade unions and factory committees, and for the right of workers to vet management decisions. This was a function of the problems which workers confronted. Collective bargaining over wages seemed increasingly inadequate as inflation ran out of control and wage agreements laboriously hammered out with employers failed to keep pace with price rises, and as workers were faced with the mounting threat of closures and unemployment. Indeed, among skilled workers, the incidence of strikes began to decline as early as August as they sought more effective solutions.[18] They intensified the drive to extend workers' supervision of employers and to verify employers' claims that raw materials could not be procured, that production must be run down, that workers must be laid off. That was the primary motivation behind workers' increasing encroachment on the sphere of management. The urge to assert workers' dignity in the work-place was caught up in essentially defensive action simply to keep the plant open. 'The policy of workers' control of production was first and foremost an attempt by factory committees to stem the tide of industrial chaos.'[19] The radicalization among workers, therefore, was neither the product of external manipulation, nor was it naïve and utopian. On the contrary, their behaviour 'suggests a working class that was both highly rational in its responses to the political and economic pressures of 1917 and extremely patient as well.'[20]

Mass politicization

The implication of revisionist work is that it is from below, in the increasingly radical challenge to traditional authority mounted by peasants, soldiers and workers, that the political outcome of the revolution is to be explained. The political struggle, the struggle for power both locally and nationally, was not an autonomous process somehow divorced from the masses' pursuit of their social and economic goals. On the contrary, in pursuit of those goals workers, soldiers and (to a lesser extent) peasants made an ever more direct and decisive impact upon the political struggle.

They did so because they discovered that without intervening politically, without replacing the authority of the Provisional Government in the countryside, in the cities and in the capital itself, with authorities who would heed their demands, they could not achieve many of their most cherished goals. Direct action at the local level was

[18] D. Koenker and W. G. Rosenberg, 'Skilled Workers and the Strike Movement in Revolutionary Russia', *Journal of Social History* 19 (1985–6), pp. 605–30.
[19] Smith, *Red Petrograd*, p. 146.
[20] Koenker, *Moscow Workers*, p. 359.

sufficient for peasants to take over the land and drive off traditional authority; for soldiers to transform relations with officers, frustrate an effective new offensive, and prevent government use of the army for internal purposes; for workers to destroy the old factory order and assert their immediate interests against employers. But there were limits to what such action by village committees, soldiers' committees and factory committees could achieve. It could not end the war and bring home the soldiers; it could not stem the economic decline or restore the flow of raw materials to the factory, and manufactures to the village; it could not secure food supplies for grain-hungry regions and starving cities. For these tasks, broader forms of organization were needed – to ration food, to co-ordinate economic recovery, to negotiate peace. This was the logic which lay behind the swelling popular demand for power to be transferred from the Provisional Government and its local agencies, which seemed unable or unwilling to carry out these tasks, to the new popular bodies with the widest competence, the soviets. This was the logic which underlay the rapid shift in political allegiance from socialist parties supporting the Provisional Government to those committed to a government responsible to the soviets. The masses chose spokesmen through whom they could impose their own solutions. Of the 670 delegates to the Second All-Russian Congress of Soviets elected in October, no less than 505 were committed to the transfer of all power to the soviets.[21]

In the countryside, the primary political impact of peasant radicalism was to undermine the authority of the Provisional Government. Within two months of the February revolution, initial faith in the government's commitment to peasant interests began to evaporate. The SR activists who dominated the All-Russian Peasant Congress of May and controlled its Executive Committee rapidly forfeited the confidence of their constituents as they urged the peasantry to support the Provisional Government and await the summoning of the Constituent Assembly with patience and restraint. The hierarchy of land and food committees established by the government suffered the same fate. Upper-level committees, where the urgency of peasant demands was filtered through and diluted by urban activists, quickly found themselves unable to control the radicalism of lower-level committees directly responsive to peasant pressure.[22]

In party political terms, the peasantry's search for more radical spokesmen was manifested primarily in the rapid increase in support for the emergent Left SRs. Since SRs and Left SRs formally belonged to the same party until the latter were expelled after the October revolution, it is not possible to quantify this shift with precision. In the

[21] A. Rabinowitch, *The Bolsheviks Come To Power. The Revolution of 1917 in Petrograd* (New York, 1976), p. 292.
[22] Figes, *Peasant Russia*, pp. 30–40; Gill, *Peasants and Government*, pp. 114–31.

Constituent Assembly elections in November, the party as a whole won an overall majority of seats, of which only 10 per cent went to Left SRs. Yet the evidence suggests that this grossly underrated the Left's support in the countryside. At the party Council in August, 40 per cent of the delegates were 'leftists'; at the second Soviet Congress in October, the SR delegates were almost evenly divided between 'leftists' and 'rightists'; and at the Extraordinary Congress of Peasant Deputies in November, which met while the Constituent Assembly elections were in progress, Left SRs outnumbered SRs by more than two to one.[23] A decidedly secondary, but nevertheless marked, manifestation of peasant radicalism was increased peasant support for the Bolshevik party. In areas close to the front and to major urban centres, where workers and soldiers pressed the claim of the Bolsheviks to be the most effective champions of drastic land reform and peace, significant inroads were made into the overall SR majority in the countryside.[24]

In the army, rank-and-file determination to force an immediate peace and land settlement upon the political leadership was reflected in an even sharper leftward swing. The political orientation of the soldiers was expressed both through elections to the new hierarchy of soldiers' committees and, in urban areas, to soviets of soldiers' deputies or workers' and soldiers' deputies. For a few weeks after February, liberal officers found it possible to win support on committees at army, corps and divisional level. As the tension between the Soviet and the first Provisional Government mounted, however, they were rapidly displaced by delegates sympathetic to the moderate socialist parties. In upper-level committees, the moderate socialists retained their position until the autumn. But from as early as May, both at the lower, regimental level and in the soldiers' sections of urban soviets, they found greater and greater difficulty in doing so.[25]

As we have seen, the issue which put their influence to the test was that of the June offensive. The support for the offensive offered by moderate socialist soldier delegates was viewed in the trenches – and in garrisons destined for the front – as a profound betrayal. Not only did it involve restoring much of the officers' authority, but it seemed to fly in the face of the Soviet's promise of an early peace. The débâcle of the offensive itself threw the committees into disarray. Renewed attempts by the High Command to restore discipline served only to intensify soldiers' suspicion. When the Kornilov affair broke, rank-

[23] O. Radkey, *The Election to the Russian Constituent Assembly of 1917* (Harvard, 1950), p. 72; O. Radkey, *The Sickle under the Hammer: The Russian Socialist Revolutionaries in the Early Months of Soviet Rule* (New York, 1963), pp. 290–1; Mandel, *Petrograd Workers* II, pp. 348–9.
[24] Radkey, *Election*, pp. 23–39.
[25] Wildman, *Russian Imperial Army* I, p. 372; II, pp. 31–5.

and-file intervention to prevent officers taking steps to support the Commander-in-Chief was immediate and overwhelming. The Kerensky government's subsequent retention of officers apparently implicated in the affair, and its continuing failure to bring peace, cut the ground from under the feet of the moderate socialist committee men. From September, through wave upon wave of demonstrations, delegations to the capital, and fresh elections to regimental committees and soldiers' soviets, the soldiers expressed overwhelming pressure for a new, soviet-based government committed to an immediate peace.[26] In party political terms, radical SRs made major inroads at the expense of their moderate comrades, but most dramatic was the increase in support for the Bolsheviks. By early November, they had secured formal control of the committee structure on the northern and western fronts, and were rapidly attracting support on the southwestern, Rumanian and Caucasian fronts. In the Constituent Assembly elections their vote from the armed forces exceeded that of the SRs, and both the Western Front and the Baltic Fleet yielded majorities of over 60 per cent for the Bolsheviks.[27]

The demand for a soviet government was taken up earliest and with greatest militancy in the cities. From the start, factory committee delegates showed acute awareness of the need for co-ordinated action to uphold the economy. Successive conferences of factory committees were among the earliest and most insistent voices calling for central planning of the economy. As the economic crisis intensified, food supplies dwindled, and strike action failed to yield sustained improvements, the demand for radical political action to stem the industrial decline was taken up by an ever greater proportion of workers. The State must curb the speculation which workers blamed for halting the flow of food, fuel and raw materials, prevent employers closing factories, and end the war. Since the Provisional Government failed to act, it must be replaced by one that would.

In the cities, it was through the Bolshevik party that workers pressed their demands for government by the soviets. While Menshevik and SR party membership declined, workers joined the Bolshevik party in tens of thousands. While the moderate socialist press languished from the summer, workers' contributions to the Bolshevik press poured in. Factory after factory adopted Bolshevik resolutions on the critical economic and political issues before them.[28] From May onwards a growing proportion of workers voted in local government elections for Bolshevik candidates.[29] By October Bolsheviks were in control of the

[26] op. cit., II, pp. 258ff.
[27] Radkey, Election, p. 80.
[28] Mandel, Petrograd Workers II, pp. 244–63; Koenker, Moscow Workers, chaps. 5, 6, 7.
[29] W. G. Rosenberg, 'The Russian Municipal Duma Elections of 1917: A Preliminary Computation of Returns', Soviet Studies XXI (1969), pp. 131–63.

soviets of most of the country's major industrial centres. Between the First All-Russian Congress of Soviets in June, and the second in October, the proportion of Bolshevik delegates rose, according to some estimates, from 17 per cent to 60 per cent.[30] In the Constituent Assembly elections, they gained an overwhelming majority of the votes cast by workers.

These facts cast doubt on the notion that the party owed its influence to manipulation of the bureaucratic tendencies of popular institutions. Such tendencies were certainly present in 1917. In the new mass organizations, electoral procedures were irregular and often ill-defined. The make-up of national and regional conferences and congresses was haphazard and far from perfectly representative. Yet it was in the upper echelons of land and food committees, of soldiers' committees, and of city-wide soviets and the trade unions that these tendencies were most pronounced. It was here that *intelligenty* were most prominent, that membership of the executive committee was often by co-option of personnel selected by the major socialist parties rather than by election, and that the plenum's hold over the executive was weakest. And during 1917, it was for the most part the moderate socialist parties, not the Bolsheviks, who benefited from their initial control of the executive, the agenda and the timing of elections, and from the indirect form of election to such bodies as the first All-Russian Congress of Soviets.

Lower-level organizations, on the other hand, regimental soldiers' committees and *volost'* peasant committees, were much more directly responsive to changes in rank-and-file attitudes and moved leftward much earlier.[31] In the cities, the most vibrant and economically powerful working-class organizations, the factory committees, were established on the workers' own initiative. They were directly elected, frequently re-elected and were immediately dependent for their effectiveness on the support of their constituents.[32] The workers' militia, too, were set up and maintained at the factory level on the workers' own initiative. SR and Menshevik leaders soon expressed disapproval of them, and the upper echelons of the Bolshevik party showed little interest in them until late in the year. In the eyes of workers and local Bolshevik organizations, however, they constituted an essential guarantee against a restoration of the old order, a means of bringing pressure to bear on employers, and an instrument for the maintenance of order in industrial and working-class districts. Their autonomy was jealously guarded and their responsiveness to instructions from above

---

[30] See J. Bunyan and H. H. Fisher, *The Bolshevik Revolution, 1917–1918, Documents and Materials* (Stanford, Cal., 1961), p. 110 for contemporary estimates of the make-up of the Second Congress.

[31] Figes, *Peasant Russia*, pp. 40–6; Gill, *Peasants and Government*, pp. 114–31.

[32] Smith, *Red Petrograd*, pp. 203–8; see also Smith's review article in *Soviet Studies* 30 (1981), pp. 454–9.

decidedly conditional.[33] Nowhere was 'bureaucratization' less developed, nowhere did the rank-and-file constituency retain closer control over their officials, nowhere were working-class aspirations more clearly articulated. And yet it was here at grass-roots level that Bolsheviks drew their strongest support.

This is not to deny that Bolsheviks often showed little respect for democratic processes. Early in 1917 there were important instances where unscrupulous disregard for party rules and democratic practice enabled Bolshevik activists to take over joint Menshevik–Bolshevik Social Democratic organizations.[34] There were instances, too, such as in the politically-valuable naval base at Kronstadt, where skilful manoeuvring by experienced Bolshevik cadres sent from Petrograd measurably advanced the party's position against far-Left rivals.[35] But the prime source of the party's leverage lay quite simply in the popularity of its policies.

The Bolshevik party in 1917
The upsurge in Bolshevik popularity was confirmed by explosive growth in the party's membership. Indeed the party was virtually recreated by a mammoth influx of new recruits. Membership figures must be treated with extreme caution, not least because in many areas the schism between Menshevik and Bolshevik organizations was not fully consummated until the summer. Nevertheless, an expansion from some 10,000 in February to some 250,000 or even 300,000 by October is not unlikely. Even in the upper reaches of the party, new members predominated: at the Sixth Party Congress in July no less than 94 per cent had joined the party since 1914 and most of them probably in the course of 1917. Equally significant is the social composition of the membership. All the indications confirm the Soviet view that a clear majority of members were workers, with a substantial minority of soldiers and sailors, while members of the intelligentsia were relegated to a small minority. Even so far as the upper echelons are concerned, an analysis of leading Bolshevik cadres in Moscow in 1917 reveals that the great majority were workers by social origin and half were workers by current occupation before the revolution.[36] Far

---

[33] This theme is central to R. A. Wade, *Red Guards and Workers' Militias in the Russian Revolution* (Stanford, Cal., 1984).
[34] See for example A. Ezergailis, 'The Thirteenth Conference of the Latvian Social Democrats, 1917: Bolshevik Strategy Victorious', in R. C. Elwood, ed., *Reconsiderations on the Russian Revolution* (Cambridge, Mass., 1976), pp. 133–53.
[35] I. Getzler, *Kronstadt, 1917–1921. The Fate of a Soviet Democracy* (Cambridge, 1983), pp. 40–66.
[36] W. Chase and J. Arch Getty, 'The Moscow Bolshevik Cadres of 1917: a Prosopographical Analysis', *Russian History* 5 (1978), pp. 84–105; R. Service, *The Bolshevik Party in Revolution. A Study in Organizational Change 1917–1923* (London, 1979), pp. 42–7.

from being an exclusive clique of radical intellectuals, the Bolshevik party had become a mass workers' party.

Equally, revisionist work has put in perspective the significance of the party's much-vaunted organization. Compared to the extremist groups who competed for radical support, the Bolsheviks undoubtedly enjoyed major organizational advantages. Left SRs existed under the shadow of the more moderate parent party until after October; the Menshevik Internationalists established no distinct party network of their own; and the anarchists failed to establish any nation-wide organization. But the Bolsheviks' own organizational prowess is easily exaggerated. The notion that the Bolshevik victory over the Provisional Government and the major moderate socialist parties was essentially one of organization rather than of policy, that it was 'military' rather than 'political', does not bear close scrutiny.

Far from being highly centralized and disciplined, the party during 1917 was 'internally relatively democratic, tolerant and decentralized.'[37] In the conditions of 1917 it could hardly be otherwise. For one thing, its administrative processes were rudimentary. It suffered from a severe shortage of experienced administrative personnel. Even the central secretariat, run jointly by Ia. M. Sverdlov and E. D. Stasova, was a makeshift affair with no more than half-a-dozen assistants. Far from drilling and disposing of the party's human resources at will, it could barely keep track of the local party organizations which sprang up in the course of the year. Moreover, the disruption to the railways and postal services severely impeded communication within the party. The flow of information to the centre was irregular and uncertain; the dissemination of *Pravda* to the localities was frequently interrupted; detailed instructions were seldom practical at all. As often as not, Sverdlov found himself issuing vague advice to operate according to local conditions, which left much initiative in local hands.

At the same time, the disciplinary sanctions at the leadership's disposal were minimal. Explicit orders to individual activists, whether to change location or take up new duties, were freely ignored. Even formal policy directives issued from the centre were followed only in so far as they corresponded to local Bolshevik opinion. Lower down the committee hierarchy, too, town committees found great difficulty in imposing their authority on suburban committees, which in turn were often disobeyed by individual cells. Frequent and fiercely contested elections gave the minority within each party body grounds for biding their time rather than choosing between submission and resignation. Indeed 'insubordination was the rule of the day whenever lower-party bodies thought questions of importance were at stake.'[38]

---

[37] Rabinowitch, *Bolsheviks Come to Power*, p. 311.
[38] Service, *Bolshevik Party*, pp. 52, 37–62.

Even in the cities, therefore, the party was anything but a stream-lined, military-style machine. Nor should the force at its command be exaggerated. Not until the autumn did the party's central organs make energetic efforts to co-ordinate and assert party control over the workers' militia and the Red Guard. And even by October, co-ordination was very loose. Armed workers' bands remained fiercely jealous of their independence, Bolshevik members were still in a minority, and to the end the Bolshevik leadership grossly underesti-mated the number of armed workers committed to Soviet power.[39] While the party cultivated strong links with militant regiments in the capital and with the sailors of the Baltic Fleet, in the army as a whole its organization was patchy and fragmented. Indeed, the most detailed revisionist analysis of the army concludes that 'if the Bolshevik cause had depended on its organizational capacities, its prospects were very dim in October 1917.'[40] And in the countryside the party's organized presence was minimal.

This is not to imply that the Bolshevik party was the passive recipient of mass support. Along with the whole Russian revolutionary tradition it played its part in providing the socialist vocabulary in terms of which workers, and to some extent soldiers and peasants, interpreted events and articulated their aspirations. The party used every means at its disposal to spread its ideas, to undermine confidence in the Provisional Government, to sharpen workers' suspicions of their employers and sense of their distinctive class interests. Its burgeoning press sustained a powerful propaganda drive directed at workers. In the army, after a brief retreat during the reaction which followed the July Days, the number of Bolshevik cells rapidly proliferated and its output of literature specifically addressed to soldiers swelled.

Yet the impact of the party's agitation and propaganda must not be misconstrued: it evoked so powerful a response precisely because it so accurately articulated the masses' own goals. But it did not create either those goals or the mass radicalism that went with them. In the countryside the role it played was for the most part peripheral. In the cities and in the army, popular opinion shifted sharply leftward even where the party failed to make headway. This was demonstrated both by the inroads which radical Mensheviks made into the position of Tsereteli and the moderate leadership, and by the rapid growth of the Left SRs. And at the front, as we have seen, there was no close correlation between organized Bolshevik activity and rank-and-file militancy.[41] The primary achievement of the party's propaganda drive lay neither in 'whipping up' popular discontent, nor in instilling political consciousness into the masses. It lay in identifying the party

[39] Wade, *Red Guards*, pp. 178–83, 194–5.
[40] Wildman, *Russian Imperial Army* II, p. 278.
[41] *op. cit.*, II, pp. 64, 73–7.

with the very policies on which the masses were determined. Bolshevik popularity rose not because the party held out 'a new vision of the revolution', but rather because they seemed to provide 'a more speedy and direct realization of the original one.'[42]

The making of Bolshevik policy

In the revisionist view, these departures from the received image of the party – its relatively open, mass, plebeian, flexible and internally-democratic character – were not incidental or irrelevant to its victory. They were crucial. For a key condition of the astonishing expansion of the party and growth in its popularity was its acute sensitivity to shifts in public opinion and to the fluctuating political situation in different parts of the country. What guaranteed this was precisely the *inability* of the leadership to impose its will upon the rank and file. Instead, the leadership found it essential to undertake a constant process of consultation. Each major turning-point in the party's orientation and strategy was fiercely debated at every level of the party. Through internal party elections and the numerous local, regional and national conferences mounted during the year, the mass membership exerted influence over policy formation. On joining the party, therefore, workers and soldiers did not suddenly cut their links with their own social milieu, adapt to some pre-established Bolshevik mold, and swear fealty to ready-made decisions handed down from above. They brought their own ideas and concerns to bear upon the leadership.

To stress the party's responsiveness to pressures from below is not to deny the significance of the lead given by Lenin. His prestige within the party was enormous; his pre-eminence among the leaders was manifest; his ability to combine theory and practice, to bring a Marxist analysis of the class struggle to bear upon the choices confronting the party, was unique. Clearly his personal radicalism played an important part in ensuring that the party he had done so much to create responded so readily to mass radicalism. On the other hand, he was in no position to impose policy upon the party. Again and again his colleagues on the Central Committee showed themselves fully capable of opposing him. A crucial condition for his success in pushing the party to the Left was that the party's democratic processes gave voice to rank-and-file pressure moving in the same direction. The single most important policy reorientation of the year, whereby in April conditional support for the Provisional Government was withdrawn in favour of outright opposition, reflected rank-and-file radicalism as much as Lenin's personal authority. In the elections to the April party conference, at which his April Theses were adopted, the relatively moderate leaders who had opposed his radical shift were swamped by more militant delegates.[43] He succeeded in carrying the party precisely

[42] *op. cit.*, I, p. 379.
[43] Service, *Bolshevik Party*, pp. 53–4.

because he articulated a tide of opinion which had begun to swell before his return, and independently of him. The stamp he set upon party policy reflected the close correspondence between his programme and the demands welling up from below.

Equally, for all Lenin's tactical skill, the notion that it was his flawless guidance which brought the party to victory is misleading. More than once the party's flexibility and the rank and file's readiness to respond more closely to the popular mood than to instructions from above saved the Bolsheviks from the potentially damaging consequences of tactical decisions made at the centre. Widespread working-class hostility to factionalism, for example, encouraged party activists to ignore the official decision in April to sever links with Mensheviks and abandon 'joint' Bolshevik–Menshevik committees. In many areas it was only once the Mensheviks' identification with the policies of the Provisional Government had brought home the profound differences between the two social democratic parties that the break was made. Likewise, in late June local committees from the most militant garrison regiments and factories in the capital, together with the party's newly-established Central Bureau of Military Organizations, responded to mass pressure and joined in the demonstrations of the July Days, forcing the hand of the reluctant Central Committee.[44] In areas where popular opinion was overwhelmingly hostile to a move against the Provisional Government, on the other hand, local Bolshevik leaders freely and furiously denounced the affair.[45]

An even more significant instance was over the tactical change Lenin demanded following the July Days. Since the Menshevik-SR leadership of the soviets had thrown their lot in with the 'counter-revolution', he insisted that the party should drop the slogan 'All Power to the Soviets!'. Instead, the focus of activity should be upon preparations for an armed uprising. There was resistance to his call both by an enlarged meeting of the Central Committee and by the Second Petrograd All-City Party Conference in mid July. Eventually, after heated debate and substantial amendment of the resolution put forward by the Central Committee, the Sixth Party Congress at the end of the month formally dropped the slogan.[46] Yet at the local level there was widespread refusal to implement a change in policy that ran counter to mass feelings.[47] The result was to soften what might have been a deeply damaging blow to the party's image as the champion of

---

[44] A. Rabinowitch, *Prelude to Revolution: The Petrograd Bolsheviks and the July 1917 Uprising* (Bloomington, Ind., 1968), pp. 233–4.
[45] R. G. Suny, *The Baku Commune 1917–1918, Class and Nationality in the Russian Revolution* (Princeton, N.J., 1972), pp. 104–6.
[46] R. Slusser, *Stalin in October. The Man Who Missed the Revolution* (Baltimore, 1987), pp. 162–205. A Soviet translation of Slusser's study has been announced.
[47] See for example D. J. Raleigh, *Revolution on the Volga*, p. 204.

soviet-based government, and to smooth the way for the resumption of the slogan in early September following the Kornilov affair and the sharp swing to the Bolsheviks in the major soviets.

This reappraisal casts grave doubt on the liberal and libertarian charge that the party's adoption of popular policies and slogans constituted cynical deception. Traditionally the charge has rested primarily upon an evaluation of Lenin's personal motivation. Even here, the evidence is at best inconclusive. Revisionist analyses of Lenin's thought have brought out the impact which mass activism made upon his own outlook, and have been readier to convict him of ill-founded optimism than insincerity.[48] He was convinced that the war represented the death throes of European capitalism; that the carnage, economic destruction, and intensified class hostility produced by the war had brought the continent to the point of socialist revolution; and that in all the major countries state monopoly capitalism had furnished a simplified financial and economic mechanism ideally suited to the transition from capitalism to socialism. The imminent prospect of socialist revolution in the advanced West transformed the prospects in relatively backward Russia, while the devastating crisis gripping her economy and society convinced him that socialism alone offered a resolution. At the same time, he saw in the popular radicalism of 1917 evidence that the masses themselves were moving to the same conclusion. In the process of overthrowing bourgeois society, with workers encroaching ever deeper upon the authority of management and peasants taking control of the countryside, the masses were undergoing a quantum leap in political understanding and experience.[49] Moreover, here the masses had thrown up political organs perfectly tailored to the socialist project – the soviets.

To dismiss as cynical demagogy his political strategy during 1917, his endorsement of workers' control, of direct land seizure by the peasantry, of the principle of national self-determination, of 'all power to the soviets' may, therefore, be unjustified. His vision of the future flowed from his analysis of 1917 and was closely based upon Marx's celebration of the decentralized and direct democracy of the Paris Commune of 1871. He spelled it out in *State and Revolution*, completed in the summer of 1917, and in numerous articles both before and immediately after October. First and foremost it demonstrated his enormous faith in the creativity and initiative of the masses, in their capacity for self-rule. It gave little prominence to the role of the party after the establishment of soviet power. Not that he believed its role would cease after the revolution. It would continue to provide

[48] N. Harding, *Lenin's Political Thought* (2 vols., London, 1977, 1981) ii, pp. 1–200; on Lenin's attitude to the national question, see A. Ezergailis, *The 1917 Revolution in Latvia* (Boulder, Cal., 1974), pp. 77–92.
[49] E. Kingston-Mann, *Lenin and the Problem of Marxist Peasant Revolution* (Oxford, 1983), pp. 173–5.

ideological leadership. But he exuded confidence that, given their heads, the masses would create precisely the multinational socialist society to which the party was dedicated. He looked to a soviet republic in which mass involvement in the dual legislative and executive powers of the soviets would efface the distinction between governors and governed. He anticipated the permanent replacement of police and army by the people's militia. He envisaged a framework which would combine central planning by a proletarian government with wide scope for peasants and workers to run their own affairs. It is true that he had no commitment to workers' self-management in the libertarian sense of the term, and that he enthused about the potential of large-scale industry. But he took it for granted that harmony would reign between a workers' state and workers on the factory floor, and that under socialism, investment in modern productive forces need impose no hardship on workers and peasants. The closely argued and internally coherent structure of the vision he set forth in 1917 points to the utopianism of his outlook rather than his adherence to a hidden agenda.

On the other hand, the sequel to October would reveal myriad problems that had remained unresolved in Lenin's thought. What if socialist revolution did not spread westward? What if the proclamation of soviet power did not pacify separatist aspirations among the national minorities? What if the peasantry showed no sign of moving voluntarily towards collective, socialist farming and instead of co-operating with a socialist government, refused to yield up grain for the cities? What if economic decline accelerated rather than abated after the establishment of soviet power, and the priorities of the 'proletarian' State and party on the one hand, and those of many workers on the factory floor on the other, diverged? What then would become of his insistence on maximum devolution of power, reliance upon the initiative of workers and peasants, support for workers' control and an 'end to bossing'? Early in 1918 he was to jettison much of his programme, and revert from a semi-anarchist vision of soviet power to alternative currents within the Marxist tradition and within his own thought which fostered the highly-authoritarian direction in which Bolshevism developed. This demonstrated how grossly he had underrated the problems that would confront the country and the government after the revolution. It demonstrated, too, how little store he set by democratic sanction; the lengths to which he would go to retain power in the hands of the party regardless of the collapse in its popularity; and his absolute conviction that the party knew best.

The implication of the revisionist portrayal of the party, however, is that whatever verdict is passed on Lenin's personal sincerity, an analysis of his thought is an inadequate base on which to rest the charge of Bolshevik cynicism. The party was neither at the beck and call of

Lenin nor was it an élite group of intellectuals divorced from the masses. Certainly *intelligenty* played a disproportionate role in upper-level party bodies, and monopolized the Central Committee. But the party, which had never conformed closely to Lenin's blueprint of a tightly-knit body of 'professional revolutionaries', was now light years away from that model. 'Bolshevism' in 1917 did not flow from a single fount but embraced many different currents of thought. Even before February the party had been far from ideologically homogeneous. The massive intake of new members after February brought in thousands of ex-Mensheviks, a smaller number of ex-SRs, and tens of thousands who had never belonged to any party and whose knowledge of Bolshevik tradition was minimal. It became 'a catch-all party for those radical Social Democrats who agreed about the urgent need to over-throw the liberal-dominated cabinet, establish a socialist government and end the war.'[50] Beyond this agenda, as the sequel to October would show, lay a host of questions – how to respond to German imposition of a unilateral peace settlement, to sustained pressure for autonomy from national minorities, or to the rival claims of factory committees and trade unions – to which 'Bolshevism' offered a variety of answers. The divisions that would soon splinter the mass alliance of 1917, therefore, cannot be traced to a rigid and fundamental division between 'Bolsheviks' on the one hand and 'the masses' on the other. The Bolsheviks of 1917 were not alien beings; they were neither demonic nor superhuman; the great majority were themselves workers and soldiers.

October

Revisionist analysis of the events of October itself bears out each feature of this reappraisal of the explanation for the Bolshevik victory. It recognizes the importance of Lenin's leadership but at the same time underlines the limits of the sway he held over the party; it highlights the vital role played by the party's flexibility and responsiveness to the mass mood; and it demonstrates the strength the Bolsheviks derived from their base within the soviets and from popular support for soviet power.[51]

So far as the decision to stage an armed uprising is concerned, the initiative was once again Lenin's. From mid September, from his hiding-place in Finland, he wrote urging the Central Committee to place an armed uprising on the order of the day. He insisted that it would be fatal to delay and rely upon the forthcoming Soviet Congress, scheduled for 25 October, to overthrow the Provisional Government. The government might mount a second Kornilov *Putsch* and prevent

---

[50] Service, *Bolshevik Party*, p. 49.
[51] The key work here is Rabinowitch, *Bolsheviks Come to Power*.

the Congress from assembling; it might surrender Petrograd to the Germans; it might provoke and crush uncoordinated popular uprisings. If the Bolsheviks failed to act, popular frustration might give way to despair and anarchy. But as on previous occasions, Lenin encountered fierce resistance from other Bolsheviks who read the situation differently. Far from treating his instructions as holy writ, his colleagues on the Central Committee firmly ignored his initial letters. As in April, it was only when word of his urgings reached lower-level bodies, notably the Moscow Regional Bureau and the Petersburg Committee, and the militant majority of both bodies brought pressure to bear on the Central Committee, that the tide began to turn. And even after the decision had been taken formally on 10 October and reaffirmed on October 16, the issue continued to be fiercely debated. The limits of Bolshevik discipline were epitomized by Lenin's senior colleagues, Zinoviev and Kamenev, who not only continued to dissent but publicly attacked the plan on 18 October. Two days later the Central Committee steadfastly refused Lenin's furious demands that they be expelled from the party.

Moreover, in the event Lenin's preferred strategy of an armed uprising organized directly through the organs of the party and timed to present the forthcoming Soviet Congress with a *fait accompli* was radically altered. The leadership undertook extensive soundings with lower-party bodies to assess the mood of workers and the garrison. These soundings established that, while support for a transfer of power to the soviets was overwhelming, there was widespread reluctance to 'come out', to risk all when the price of failure would be so high: workers implicated would lose their jobs, soldiers would be treated as mutineers, the fate of the revolution would be in jeopardy. Moreover, the leaders of the Bolshevik Military Organization, to whom Lenin looked to organize the uprising, warned and continued to warn as late as 20 October that they could not assemble sufficient force before the Congress was due to meet. Equally, it was clear that while support for a rising in the name of the Bolshevik party would be distinctly limited and lukewarm even among Red Guards, massive response could confidently be expected if the Provisional Government were either to move against the Petrograd Soviet or to attempt to prevent the Second Congress of Soviets from meeting. It was because the majority on the Central Committee, led by Trotsky, heeded these soundings and adapted the party's tactics accordingly that the Provisional Government was brought down with barely a shot fired.

Instead of seeking to overthrow Kerensky through the agencies of the party, they worked to undermine his government through those of the Petrograd Soviet. They integrated the party's decision to seize power with parallel moves by the Petrograd Soviet to defend the capital both against what seemed imminent German attack and against any assault on the Left by the government. The key institution, which gave the Bolshevik leaders an authority their purely party credentials did not carry even among militant soldiers, sailors and Red Guards, was the Petrograd Soviet's Military Revolutionary Committee (MRC). The Soviet had decided to establish this committee, charged with co-ordinating the defences of the capital, because of deep suspicion among soldiers and workers about Kerensky's motives for ordering much of the garrison to transfer to the front. The decision was taken on 9 October, before the party had decided upon an armed uprising. Only on 20 October did it become clear that the Mensheviks and mainstream SRs would not take part in the committee, and even then the Left SRs were prominently represented on it (indeed a Left SR took the chair). Among the Bolshevik MRC majority itself there was evidently a wide range of views about the committee's purpose, some sharing the Left SR assumption that its role was to defend the Left in preparation for the forthcoming Soviet Congress. Thus the MRC was no mere front for the party. Rather it represented a fusion between the determination of the Soviet to prevent any government *coup* against the Left, and the determination of its major Bolshevik figures, including Trotsky and the Bolshevik Military Organization leaders N. I. Podvoisky and V. A. Antonov, to undermine the Provisional Government.

Moreover, instead of bowing to Lenin's insistence that the government be overthrown before the Soviet Congress met, Trotsky and his colleagues operated according to a timetable whereby the government's overthrow would coincide with the assembling of the Congress and be immediately endorsed by it. Equally, in the light of the soundings that had been taken, they were at pains to ensure that the MRC's actions should be made in response to government moves. It was in view of the government's efforts to transfer garrison troops to the front that on 21–22 October the MRC asserted its own authority over the troops in defiance of the regular military command. It was when Kerensky ordered the closure of the Bolshevik press and the raising of the bridges linking working-class districts with the centre that on 24 October workers and soldiers supporting the Soviet directly challenged and overcame government orders. The result was a bloodless victory. Since Kerensky's efforts to mobilize military support in the capital and to summon aid from the front proved fruitless, there was no need to summon a mass uprising. Indeed throughout the October Days the Bolshevik leaders positively discouraged workers from taking to the streets. Mass meetings held on 22 October were deliberately held indoors to prevent disorder, and on 27 October *Pravda* featured a bold-type, front-page appeal to workers to refrain from strikes and demonstrations.[52] Through action fully endorsed in

---

[52] Mandel, *Petrograd Workers* II, p. 321.

mass workers' meetings, in garrison conferences and by the Soviet itself, the government had been emasculated.[53]

It was only in the early hours of 25 October, then, and partly under personal pressure from Lenin (who had just arrived at the Smolny Institute where both the Petrograd Soviet and Bolshevik headquarters were housed), that the MRC went onto the offensive.[54] Without the knowledge or approval of the leading Left SRs, subversion of the Provisional Government gave way to a planned seizure of power. Urged on by the MRC, soldiers and sailors together with Red Guards, whose mobilization 'seems for the most part to have come on local initiative' rather than central direction, took control of the major rail terminals, the Petrograd power station, the post office, the last bridge in government hands, the State Bank and the telephone exchange.[55] Even before the Admiralty and the Winter Palace were taken, Lenin drafted for nation-wide distribution the announcement that the Provisional Government had fallen and that power had passed to the MRC. With only hours to spare, his goal of presenting the Soviet Congress with a *fait accompli* had been achieved.

The manner in which the Bolsheviks came to power cast a long shadow. They had acted on 25 October without formal democratic sanction even from within their own party. As late as the afternoon of 24 October Stalin and Trotsky both assured a meeting of the Bolshevik deputies to the Congress that the MRC was not seizing power or pre-empting the Congress. They had consciously deceived fellow socialists whose commitment to the overthrow of the Provisional Government was no less strong than their own. On the evening of 24 October, under prompting from its Left SR members, the MRC issued a categorical denial that it was planning to seize power. It was the 'political hypocrisy' of the Bolshevik party, the action they took 'behind the back' of the Soviet Congress, that the moderate socialists cited as their reason for walking out of the Congress. Equally, their sense of outrage played its part in poisoning the negotiations for a 'homogeneous socialist government' which followed the seizure of power.

Yet in the light of revisionist research the October revolution emerges as very much more than a conspiratorial *coup d'état*. By then the central political issue was that of soviet power. It was popular support for this cause which doomed Kerensky and the Provisional Government and explains the ease with which armed resistance to the new order was overcome, even where (as in Moscow) it was more formidable than in the capital. Likewise, it was the moderate socialists'

---

[53] S. A. Smith, 'Petrograd in 1917: the view from below', in D. H. Kaiser, ed., *The Workers' Revolution in Russia, 1917. The View From Below* (Cambridge, 1987), pp. 78–9.
[54] Rabinowitch, *Bolsheviks Come to Power*, pp. 266–72.
[55] Wade, *Red Guards*, pp. 196–207.

opposition to the notion of an exclusively soviet-based government which, by October, had rendered them helpless. It had ensured that they would find themselves in a small minority in the Second Congress. The spectacle of force being used to remove the Provisional Government greatly intensified their bitterness against the Bolsheviks. But it is doubtful that this was the real cause of their decision to walk out. At the Northern Regional Congress of Soviets a fortnight before the seizure of power, finding themselves confronted by a majority favouring soviet power, they had staged a similar walk out. After October, their deputies reacted in exactly the same way in local soviets across the country when outvoted on the issue of adherence to the new soviet government. Nor was fury at the Bolshevik action the basic reason for their refusal to compromise with those moderate Bolshevik leaders who, in the days following 25 October, conducted the negotiations for a 'homogeneous socialist government'. The fundamental obstacle was their adamant objection to the formation of a government based exclusively upon the soviets. Over this issue, the moderate socialists had placed themselves at loggerheads with popular opinion.[56]

The Bolshevik victory in the struggle for power owed less to effective organization and military manoeuvre than Soviet, liberal or libertarian accounts would have it. The party owed its strength to its identification with the cause of soviet power. By October that cause enjoyed overwhelming support in the cities and the army, and tacit support in the villages. By virtue of its relatively flexible, open and democratic character, its sensitivity to mass opinion, its ability to respond to pressure from below, the party had established itself as the prime vehicle for the achievement of popular goals.

The sequel to October

This reinterpretation of the Bolshevik victory has prepared the ground for a thoroughgoing reappraisal of the sequel to October. For, in contrast to each of the traditional interpretations, revisionist work has shown that there was a profound discontinuity between the essentially popular revolution which brought the Bolsheviks to power, and the highly authoritarian regime which emerged. It has highlighted the fundamental change that overcame the organization, the composition and the social base of the new regime.

In the aftermath of October, the country suffered an economic collapse on the scale of a modern Black Death. To the dislocation which had overwhelmed the Provisional Government were added the repercussions of the precipitate military and economic demobilization which followed the proclamation of peace. The abrupt cessation of military orders brought much of industry to a complete halt. In the capital, no less than 60 per cent of the labour force was unemployed by mid 1918. At the same time, the breakdown of the trade nexus

[56] Mandel, *Petrograd Workers* ii, pp. 310–42.

between town and countryside, and between one region and another, already far advanced before October, became all but total. With the loss of the Ukraine to Germany, the problem of food supply in the cities and many parts of the countryside became desperate. The result was the collapse of the tacit alliance between workers, soldiers and peasants on the basis of which the Bolsheviks had come to power.[57]

Most ominous was the hostility which developed between city and countryside. With the rouble losing all value as a medium of exchange, and the production of manufactured goods hopelessly insufficient to secure adequate food supplies by barter, workers sought relief in forcible requisitioning of grain from the peasantry. The capital lost no less than a million inhabitants in the first six months after October as workers streamed from the cities in search of bread.[58] At the same time, economic catastrophe generated violent conflict within both countryside and city. The struggle to secure grain created fierce divisions between one region and another, between one village and another, and within individual villages.[59] Equally, with the wheels of industry grinding to a halt and bread rations falling below subsistence level, those workers who remained became engaged in bitter competition for jobs and for food. National divisions between workers, which had receded into the background in the common struggle for soviet power, were inflamed by economic deprivation.[60] The hundreds of thousands thrown out of work were profoundly disillusioned by the failure of the new order to alleviate their plight. Workers who retained their jobs spent much of their time in search of food, and industry was further undermined by mass absenteeism and demoralization. Desperate measures by factory committees to impose discipline alienated the rank and file.[61] Workers were pitted against workers, peasants against peasants, city against countryside, one national group against another. Under the impact of the 'balkanization' of the economy, the Bolshevik constituency of October fell apart.[62]

---

[57] W. Rosenberg, 'Russian Labor and Bolshevik Power after October', *Slavic Review* 44 (1985), pp. 213–38.

[58] For a more general discussion, see D. Koenker, 'Urbanization and Deurbanization in the Russian Revolution and Civil War', *Journal of Modern History* 57 (1985), pp. 424–50.

[59] These developments are central to Figes's excellent new study of the Volga countryside in the post-October and civil war periods, Figes, *Peasant Russia*.

[60] See for example Suny, *The Baku Commune*, pp. 171–233, 349–52.

[61] P. Flenley, 'Workers' Organizations in the Russian Metal Industry, February 1917–August 1918' (Ph.D. Dissertation, University of Birmingham, 1983); Smith, *Red Petrograd*, pp. 246–52.

[62] Two useful recent theses treating this process are T. J. Renehan, 'The Failure of Local Soviet Government, 1917–1918' (Ph.D. Dissertation, State University of New York, 1983); M. M. Helgesen, 'The Origins of the Party-State Monolith in Soviet Russia. Relations between the Soviets and Party Committees in the Central Provinces, October 1917–March 1921' (Ph.D. Dissertation, State University of New York, 1980), chaps. 2, 3.

The party of 1917 was poorly equipped to cope with the crisis that engulfed it. Well into 1918 it continued to be characterized by fierce divisions and internal dissent. There was a major internal struggle over acceptance of the Treaty of Brest-Litovsk. Orders from the centre continued to carry little weight. The new government's decrees on land and workers' control might be readily accepted, but where its wishes conflicted with local priorities, it was freely ignored even by local soviets securely in Bolshevik hands. It survived because the processes which atomized its constituency of 1917 also prevented the emergence of a coherent popular movement against it.[63] Instead of united rejection of the new regime, the struggle for bread and resources led different cities, villages, groups of workers and peasants who found themselves at a disadvantage locally to call for central intervention to aid them. The party's response to these calls was far from systematic. The armed force at its disposal was limited and undisciplined, while the state bureaucracy was severely disrupted and Bolshevik control over it tenuous. Yet by piecemeal intervention in local disputes, by responding to workers' demands that their enterprise be nationalized and supported by state funds, or to the demands of local soviets that their grain supplies be protected, the emergent party-state gradually acquired more leverage. Such intervention failed to halt the sharp decline in its popularity. But it enabled it to establish a new basis of authority which rested no longer on mass support but on a combination of force and patronage. Somewhat ironically, it benefited too from the outbreak of full-scale civil war in the summer of 1918. As White armies, with a measure of support from some moderate socialists, national minority groups and foreign governments, sought to reverse the verdict of October, the party became the key rallying point for workers determined to uphold it and for peasants whose loathing for the Whites was even greater than for the Reds.

The manner in which the party-state responded to the dual economic and military crisis radically transformed its relationship with its erstwhile popular base. The State itself undertook forcible requisitioning of grain from the peasantry. Workers' control over state-appointed managers was steadily cut back and a full panoply of sanctions introduced – work books, bonus incentives, piece-rates, dismissal, and labour camps – to prevent strikes and impose discipline. As economic deprivation found political expression, the party resorted ever more freely to the use of censorship, administrative sanctions, and force to stem incipient revivals by the Mensheviks and SRs. During 1918, the autonomy and democratic processes of the popular organizations thrown up in the course of the revolution were steadily undermined.[64]

[63] W. Rosenberg, 'Russian Labor', *Slavic Review, passim.*
[64] A. Rabinowitch, 'The Evolution of Local Soviets in Petrograd, November 1917–June 1918: The Case of the First City District Soviet', *Slavic Review* 46 (1987), pp. 20–37.

At every level and in every major institution the party gathered decision-making power. At the periphery the chairman of the local soviet took his instructions from the local party committee, while at the centre it was the Central Committee of the party, and its inner cabinet, the Politburo, which guided the Council of People's Commissars and through it the Soviet Congress.

The party itself was also transformed. From being a mass organization of workers it became a body predominantly made up of officials. Members were removed from the factory bench to take leading roles in institutions of all kinds – not only factory committees, trade unions, the various organs of the soviets and the full-time party apparatus, but the Cheka, the Red Army and the state bureaucracy. By 1922 over two-thirds of the party membership were administrators of one kind or another. Moreover, the internal structure of the party underwent a rapid process of centralization. On the one hand, confronted by civil war and economic disaster Lenin and his colleagues became impatient with internal party democracy. The party must provide the rigorous, ruthless command structure necessary to mobilize men, material and food from an increasingly impoverished society. On the other, ordinary members themselves encouraged the closing of ranks; policy disputes were restrained and local cells urged firmer direction from the centre in order to maximize the use of limited personnel and resources against the party's enemies. At the same time, the administrative burden placed upon party members and the rapid turnover in membership during the Civil War led to party cells meeting less and less often. Within each committee the authority of the secretary became increasingly pronounced, and it became common practice for these key posts to be filled by appointment from above rather than election from below.[65] As Bolshevik priorities shifted from political and ideological struggle to administrative, economic and military activity, the party became a highly-centralized and disciplined instrument at the disposal of the leadership. Power, so widely dispersed during 1917, now gravitated firmly towards the centre. The party-state structure which emerged during the course of the Civil War lent to the political process a degree of autonomy which was the very antithesis of the direct political intervention from below which had characterized 1917.

Conclusion

Although the distinctions between the rival schools of thought considered here remain apparent in studies of the post-1918 period, there is a much greater measure of common ground in the conclusions they draw. Revisionists accept that the party-state became all but insusceptible to pressure from below, making much of their work

[65] Service, *Bolshevik Party*, pp. 85–111.

compatible with both liberal and libertarian treatments.[66] Soviet
scholars are fast moving away from the orthodox account of the period
and beginning to grapple with the 'deformations' in Bolshevik rule
introduced during the Civil War.[67] But by reading history backwards,
by attributing to the party of 1917 characteristics it acquired during the
Civil War, the Soviet, liberal and libertarian traditions in their different ways have all distorted the process whereby the Bolsheviks came
to power. Each tradition mythologized the revolution. The impact of
the libertarian version was restricted to the world of the far Left. There
it fostered a simplistic view of the dynamics of working-class protest
and a caricature of the Bolshevik party during 1917 as a party of
intellectuals. It encouraged anti-Bolshevik polemic at the expense of a
broader analysis of the débacle which followed the seizure of power.
But the distortions of Soviet and liberal historiography exerted a much
more far-reaching and baneful influence.

The Soviet version became the basis of the Communist regime's
claim to legitimacy. It served to justify the assumption of sovereignty
by the party rather than the people. It encouraged authoritarian
disregard for the democratic rights of the proletariat and outright
contempt for those of the peasantry. It glorified centralization and
discipline within the party. It fostered the secretarian arrogance which
not only led to the one-party State in the Soviet Union itself but bore
much responsibility for splitting the European Left in the inter-war
years, thus opening the way to victory for the Nazis in Germany and
the Nationalists in Spain. It promoted a stultifying cult of Lenin and
clothed Marxism–Leninism in a cloak of ideological infallibility. It
locked the Soviet leadership into an ideological time-warp from which
they are only now escaping.

The liberal version became the basis for the conventional western
view of the revolution as the handiwork of a few fanatical intellectuals.
It fostered support for the ill-starred efforts of the Whites in the Civil
War. It reinforced the tendency always to regard politics as a largely
autonomous affair, a struggle which depends upon the skill and
resolution of rival leaders and in which 'the masses' serve as the mere
objects of politicians. It encouraged the inclination to see the root
cause of all challenges to the status quo in terms of conspiracy and
political sedition rather than autonomous mass social protest – a
shallow analysis which sustained narrowly military responses to countless nationalist and other popular movements in the post-war world. It
served to demonize Lenin and Marx alike, to popularize the notion

---

[66] E. Mawdsley, *The Russian Civil War* (London, 1987) contains a useful bibliographical
essay. The final section of the Selected Bibliography overleaf includes some of the most
important works on the civil war period by scholars adhering to each of the rival schools.
[67] For an early 'Leninist' reappraisal of the period, see R. Medvedev, *The October
Revolution* (London, 1979), written by the leading Soviet dissident historian of the
Brezhnev years.

that the whole European socialist tradition and especially its Marxist branch was inherently undemocratic, and to impoverish western intellectual life.

Revisionist work has exposed the shortcomings of each version. It has traced the process which led to mass radicalization and underscored the autonomous and rational nature of the intervention by workers, soldiers and peasants. It has demonstrated the decisive impact of that intervention upon the fate of the Provisional Government and of the moderate socialists. It has brought out the strength the Bolshevik party derived from its responsiveness to popular aspirations and anxieties, from its relatively decentralized, tolerant and ideologically heterogeneous make-up, and from its readiness to defy as well as to follow Lenin. It has highlighted the plebeian composition of the party, the mass popularity it enjoyed in October 1917, and the extent to which support for the party arose from its identification with the cause of soviet power. It has begun to analyse the devastating impact which precipitate military and industrial demobilization and 'economic balkanization' had upon the popular alliance of October 1917. It has underlined the speed with which the party forfeited mass support in the aftermath of the revolution and shifted its power base from soviet democracy to administrative and military coercion. It has revealed the transformation that overcame the internal structure and composition of the party in the course of the Civil War.

Revisionist work points to a radical reinterpretation of the Russian revolution. *Glasnost* and the opening of long-closed archives promise to bring fresh momentum to the effort to recover the real drama of 1917 from the myths that it inspired. But how far and how soon the labours of specialists will affect popular misconceptions remains to be seen. Old myths die hard.

SELECTED BIBLIOGRAPHY

This selected bibliography broadly follows the pattern of the main text. Although each work is cited only once, many are relevant to several sections.

I General

Most of the documentary collections available in English are stronger on political than social and economic dimensions of the revolution. The following are particularly useful:

The Bolsheviks and the October Revolution. Minutes of the Central Committee of the RSDLP (B), August 1917–February 1918 (London, 1974).

Browder, R. P. and Kerensky, A., *The Russian Provisional Government, 1917. Documents* (3 vols, Stanford, Cal., 1961).

Bunyan, J. and Fisher, H. H., *The Bolshevik Revolution 1917–1918: Documents and Materials* (Stanford, Cal., 1934).

Freeze, G. L., *From Supplication to Revolution: A Documentary Social History of Imperial Russia* (Oxford, 1988).

Golder, F., *Documents of Russian History 1914–1917* (New York, 1927).

McCauley, M., *Octobrists to Bolsheviks. Imperial Russia, 1905–1917* (London, 1984).

McCauley, M., *The Russian Revolution and the Soviet State, 1917–1921. Documents* (London, 1975).

The atmosphere of the revolution is best conveyed by the memoirs of participants. See in particular:

Chernov, V., *The Great Russian Revolution* (New Haven, Conn., 1936).

Kerensky, A. F., *The Kerensky Memoirs* (London, 1965).

Miliukov, P., *Political Memoirs, 1905–1917* (Ann Arbor, Mich., 1967).

Reed, J., *Ten Days that Shook the World* (Harmondsworth, 1977).

Shliapnikov, A. G., *On the Eve of 1917* (London, 1982).

Sukhanov, N. N., *The Russian Revolution 1917* (Oxford, 1955).

Trotsky, L. D., *History of the Russian Revolution* (3 vols, New York, 1932).

For a large-scale treatment which includes a generous selection of documents and has stood the test of time remarkably well, see:

Chamberlin, W. H., *The Russian Revolution, 1917–1921* (2 vols, New York, 1935).

Three accounts which in some respects foreshadowed revisionist work are:
Carr, E. H., *The Bolshevik Revolution, 1917–1923* (3 vols, London, 1950–3).
Deutscher, I., *The Unfinished Revolution: 1917–1967* (Oxford, 1967).
Kochan, L., *Russia in Revolution, 1890–1918* (London, 1966).

Three recent introductory studies which include brief accounts of 1917 and draw on revisionist work are:
Fitzpatrick, S., *The Russian Revolution* (Oxford, 1982).
Service, R., *The Russian Revolution 1900–1927* (London, 1986).
Williams, B., *The Russian Revolution 1917–1921* (Oxford, 1987).

For valuable comparative treatments of various themes, see:
Bideleux, R., *Communism and Development* (London, 1985).
Geary, D., *European Labour Protest 1848–1939* (London, 1981).
McDaniel, T., *Autocracy, Capitalism and Revolution in Russia* (Berkeley, Cal., 1988).
Skocpol, T., *States and Social Revolutions* (Cambridge, 1979).

II Historiography

Anderson, P., *Arguments Within English Marxism* (London, 1980).
Barber, J., *Soviet Historians in Crisis, 1928–1932* (London, 1981).
Buchholz, A., ed., *Soviet and East European Studies in the International Framework. Organization, Financing and Political Relevance* (Berlin, 1982).
Buldakov, V. P. and A.Iu Skvortsova, 'Proletarskie massy i Oktiabr'skaia revoliutsiia. (Analiz sovremennoi zapadnoi istoriografii)', *Istoriia SSSR* (1987) 5, pp. 149–63.
Byrnes, R. F., *Soviet American Academic Exchanges, 1958–1975* (Indiana, 1976).
Davies, R. W., *Soviet History in the Gorbachev Revolution* (London, 1989).
Elwood, R. C., 'How Complete Is Lenin's *Polnoe Sobranie Sochinenii?*', *Slavic Review* 38 (1979), pp. 97–105.
Enteen, G. M., *The Soviet Scholar-Bureaucrat. M. N. Pokrovskii and the Society of Marxist Historians* (Pennsylvania, 1978).
Heer, N. W., *Politics and History in the Soviet Union* (Cambridge, Mass., 1971).
Ioffe, G. Z., *Fevral'skaia revoliutsiia 1917g. v anglo-amerikanskoi burzhuaznoi istoriografii* (Moscow, 1970).
Ioffe, G. Z., "Velikii Oktiabr': transformatsiia sovietologicheskikh

kontseptsii i ego klassovo-politicheskaia sut", *Voprosy istorii KPSS* (1985) 6, pp. 72–86.

Laqueur, W. Z., *The Fate of the Revolution* (London, 1967).

Naumov, V. P., *Sovetskaia istoriografiia fevral'skoi burzhuazno-demokraticheskoi revoliutsii* (Moscow, 1979).

Spring, D., 'Soviet Historians in Crisis', *Revolutionary Russia* I (1988), pp. 24–35.

III Pre-war Russia

Atkinson, D., *The End of the Russian Land Commune 1905-1930* (Stanford, Cal., 1983).

Atkinson, D., 'The Statistics on the Russian Land Commune, 1905–1917', *Slavic Review* 32, (1973).

Atkinson, D., 'The zemstvo and the peasantry', in T. Emmons and W. S. Vucinich, eds., *The zemstvo in Russia. An experiment in local self-government* (Cambridge, 1982), pp. 79–132.

Avrekh, A. I., *Stolypin i Tret'ia Duma* (Moscow, 1978).

Avrekh, A. I., *Tsarizm i IV Duma, 1912–1914gg.* (Moscow, 1981).

Bater, J. H., 'Between Old and New: St Petersburg in the Late Imperial Era', in M. F. Hamm, ed., *The City in Late Imperial Russia* (Bloomington, Ind., 1986), pp. 43–78.

Bater, J. H., 'St Petersburg and Moscow on the eve of revolution', in D. H. Kaiser, ed., *The Workers' Revolution in Russia, 1917. The View From Below* (Cambridge, 1987), pp. 20–58.

Blackburn, D. and Eley, G., *The Peculiarities of German History: Bourgeois Society and Politics in Nineteenth-Century Germany* (Oxford, 1985).

Bonnell, V. E., *Roots of Rebellion: Workers' Politics and Organizations in St Petersburg and Moscow, 1900–1914* (Berkeley, Cal., 1983).

Bradley, J., 'Moscow: From Big Village to Metropolis', in M. F. Hamm, ed., *The City in Late Imperial Russia* (Bloomington, Ind., 1986), pp. 9–42.

Brooks, J., 'The zemstvo and the education of the people', in T. Emmons and W. S. Vucinich, eds, *The Zemstvo in Russia* (Cambridge, 1982), pp. 243–78.

Brooks, J., *When Russia Learned to Read. Literacy and Popular Literature, 1861–1917* (Princeton, N.J., 1985).

Bushnell, J., *Mutiny Amid Repression. Russian Soldiers in the Revolution of 1905–1906* (Bloomington, Ind., 1985).

Crisp, O. and Edmondson, L., eds, *Civil Rights in Imperial Russia* (Oxford, 1989).

Crisp, O., *Studies in the Russian Economy before 1914* (London, 1976).

Edmondson, L., 'Was there a Movement for Civil Rights in Russia in 1905?', in O. Crisp and L. Edmondson, eds, *Civil Rights in Imperial Russia* (Oxford, 1989), pp. 263–85.

Emmons, T., *The Formation of Political Parties and the First National Elections in Russia* (Cambridge, Mass., 1983).

Emmons, T. and Vucinich, W. S., eds, *The Zemstvo in Russia. An Experiment in Local Self-government* (Cambridge, 1982).

Ferenzi, C., 'Freedom of the Press under the Old Regime, 1905–1914', in O. Crisp and L. Edmondson, eds, *Civil Rights in Imperial Russia* (Oxford, 1989), pp. 191-214.

Frieden, N. M., 'The politics of zemstvo medicine', in T. Emmons and W. S. Vucinich, eds, *The Zemstvo in Russia* (Cambridge, 1982), pp. 315–42.

Fuller, W. C., *Civil–Military Conflict in Imperial Russia, 1881–1914* (Princeton, N. J., 1986).

Gatrell, P. W., *The Tsarist Economy 1850–1917* (London, 1986).

Gerschenkron, A., 'Agrarian policies and industrialization in Russia, 1861–1917', in M. M. Postan and H. J. Habakkuk, eds, *Cambridge Economic History of Europe* (Cambridge, 1965) vi, pt 2, pp. 706–800.

Geyer, D., *Russian Imperialism: The Interactions of Domestic and Foreign Policy, 1860–1914* (Leamington Spa, 1987).

Golub, P. A. *et al.*, eds, *Istoricheskii opyt trekh rossiiskikh revoliutsii. I. General'naia repetitsiia Velikogo Oktiabria. Pervaia burzhuazno-demokraticheskaia revoliutsiia v Rossii* (Moscow, 1985).

Gregory, P., *Russian National Income, 1885–1913* (Cambridge, 1982).

Haimson, L. H., ed., *The Politics of Rural Russia, 1905–1914* (Bloomington, Ind., 1979).

Haimson, L. H., 'The Problem of Social Stability in Urban Russia, 1905–1917', *Slavic Review* 23 (1964), pp. 619–42 and 24 (1965), pp. 1–22.

Hamm, M. F., ed., *The City in Late Imperial Russia* (Bloomington, Ind., 1986).

Hogan, H., 'The Reorganization of Work Processes in the St Petersburg Metal-working Industry, 1901–1914', *Russian Review* 42 (1983), pp. 163–90.

Hogan, H., 'Labor and Management in Conflict: The St Petersburg Metal-working Industry, 1900–1914', (Ph.D. Dissertation, University of Michigan, 1981).

Hosking G. A. and Manning, R. T., 'What Was the United Nobility?', in L. H. Haimson, ed., *The Politics of Rural Russia, 1905–1914* (Bloomington, Ind., 1979), pp. 142–83.

Hosking, G. A., *The Russian Constitutional Experiment: Government and Duma, 1907–1914* (Cambridge, 1973).

Johnson, R. E., *Peasant and Proletarian. The Working Class of Moscow in the Late Nineteenth Century* (Leicester, 1979).

Joll, J., *The Origins of the First World War* (London, 1984).

de Jonge, A., *The Life and Times of Grigorii Rasputin* (London, 1982).

Laverychev, V. Ia. *et al.*, eds, *Rabochii klass Rossii. 1907–Feveral' 1917g.* (Moscow, 1982).

Lieven, D. C. B., *Russia and the Origins of the First World War* (London, 1983).

McClelland, J. C., *Autocrats and Academics. Education, Culture and Society in Tsarist Russia* (Chicago, 1979).

McKay, J. P., *Pioneers for Profit. Foreign Entrepreneurship and Russian Industrialization 1885–1913* (Chicago, 1970).

McKean, R. B., 'Government, Employers and the Labour Movement in St Petersburg on the Eve of the First World War', *Sbornik* 12 (1986), pp. 65–94.

MacNaughton, R. D. and Manning, R. T., 'The Crisis of the Third of June System and Political Trends in the Zemstvos, 1907–1914', in L. H. Haimson, ed., *The Politics of Rural Russia, 1905–1914* (Bloomington, Ind., 1979), pp. 199–209.

McNeal, R., *Tsar and Cossack, 1855–1914* (New York, 1987).

Manning, R. T., *The Crisis of the Old Order in Russia: Gentry and Government* (Princeton, 1982).

Manning, R. T., 'Zemstvo and Revolution: The Onset of the Gentry Reaction, 1905–1907' in L. H. Haimson, ed., *The Politics of Rural Russia*, 1905–1914 (Bloomington, Ind., 1979), pp. 30–66.

Mosse, W. E., 'Stolypin's Village', *Slavonic and East European Review* 43 (1964–5), pp. 257–74.

Pavlovsky, G. A., *Agriculture on the Eve of the Revolution* (London, 1930).

Perrie, M., 'The Russian Peasant Movement of 1905–1907: Its Social Composition and Revolutionary Significance', *Past and Present* 55 (1972), pp. 123–55.

Ponomarev, B. P. *et al.*, eds, *Istoriia Kommunisticheskoi partii Sovetskogo Soiuza* (Moscow, 1982).

Ramer, S. C., 'The zemstvo and public health', in T. Emmons and W. S. Vucinich, eds, *The Zemstvo in Russia* (Cambridge, 1982), pp. 279–314.

Read, C., *Religion, Revolution and the Russian Intelligentsia 1900–1912* (London, 1979).

Rieber, A. J., *Merchants and Entrepreneurs in Imperial Russia* (Chapel Hill, N. C., 1982).

Roosa, R. A., 'Russian Industrialists and "State Socialism", 1906–17', *Soviet Studies* 23 (1972), pp. 395–417.

Rosenberg, W. G., 'Kadets and the Politics of Ambivalence,

1905–1917', in C. E. Timberlake, ed., *Essays on Russian Liberalism* (Columbia, Miss., 1972), pp. 139–63.

Schneiderman, J., *Sergei Zubatov and Revolutionary Marxism. The Struggle for the Working Class in Tsarist Russia* (Ithaca, 1970).

Shanin, T., *The Awkward Class* (Oxford, 1972).

Shanin, T., *The Roots of Otherness: Russia's Turn of Century* (2 vols, London, 1985, 1986).

Simms, J. Y., 'The crisis in Russian agriculture at the end of the nineteenth century: a different view', *Slavic Review* 36 (1977), pp. 377–98.

Startsev, V. I., *Russkaia burzhuaziia i samoderzhavie v 1905–1917 gg.* (Leningrad, 1977).

Swain, G., *Russian Social Democracy and the Legal Labour Movement* (London, 1983).

Thurston, R. W., *Liberal City, Conservative State: Moscow and Russia's Urban Crisis, 1906–1914* (Oxford, 1987).

Timberlake, C. E., ed., *Essays on Russian Liberalism* (Columbia, Miss., 1972).

Trapeznikov, S. P., *Leninism and the Agrarian and Peasant Question* (2 vols, Moscow, 1981).

Vinogradoff, E. D., 'The Russian Peasantry and the Elections to the Fourth State Duma', in L. H. Haimson, ed., *The Politics of Rural Russia, 1905–1914* (Bloomington, Ind., 1979), pp. 219–49.

Waldron, P., 'Religious Toleration in Late Imperial Russia' in O. Crisp and L. Edmondson, eds, *Civil Rights in Imperial Russia* (Oxford, 1989), pp. 103–19.

Weissman, N., 'Regular Police in Tsarist Russia, 1900–1914', *Russian Review* 44 (1985), pp. 45–68.

Yaney, G. L., *The Urge to Mobilize: Agrarian Reform in Russia, 1861–1930* (Urbana, Ill., 1982).

Zelnik, R., 'Russian Bebels: An Introduction to the Memoirs of the Russian Workers Semen Kanatchikov and Matvei Fisher', *Russian Review* 35 (1976), pp. 249–89, 417–47.

Zelnik, R., 'Russian Workers and the Revolutionary Movement', *Journal of Social History* 6 (1972), pp. 214–36.

IV The revolutionary intelligentsia

Acton, E., 'The Russian Revolutionary Intelligentsia and Industrialization', in R. Bartlett, ed., *Russian Thought and Society 1800–1917* (Keele, 1984), pp. 92–113.

Besançon, A., *The Intellectual Origins of Leninism* (Oxford, 1981).

Brower, D. R., *Training the Nihilists. Education and Radicalism in Tsarist Russia* (Cornell, 1975).

Brower, D. R., 'Student Political Attitudes and Social Origins: The

Technological Institute of St Petersburg', *Journal of Social History* 6 (1972–3), pp. 202–13.

Brym, R., *Intellectuals and Politics* (London, 1980).

Brym, R., *The Jewish Intelligentsia and Russian Marxism* (London, 1978).

Corrigan, P., Ramsay, H. and Sayer, D., *Socialist Construction and Marxist Theory* (London, 1978).

Elwood, R. C., 'Lenin and *Pravda* 1912–1914', *Slavic Review* 31 (1972), pp. 355–80.

Elwood, R. C., *Russian Social Democracy in the Underground. A Study of the RSDRP in the Ukraine, 1907–1914* (Assen, 1974).

Elwood, R. C., ed., *Vserossiiskaia Konferentsiia Ros. Sots.-Dem. Rab. Partii 1912 goda* (New York, 1982).

Engelstein, L., *Moscow 1905. Working-Class Organization and Political Conflict* (Stanford, Cal., 1982).

Fediukin, S. A., *Partiia i intelligentsiia* (Moscow, 1982).

Filippov, R. V., *Iz istorii narodnicheskogo dvizheniia na pervom etape 'khozhdeniia v narod'. 1863–1874* (Petrozavodsk, 1967).

Gerschenkron, A., 'The Problem of Economic Development in Russian Intellectual History of the Nineteenth Century', in E. J. Simmons, ed., *Continuity and Change in Russian and Soviet Thought* (Cambridge, Mass., 1955).

Gleason, A., *Young Russia. The Genesis of Russian Radicalism in the 1860s* (New York, 1980).

Gombin, R., *The Radical Tradition. A Study in Modern Revolutionary Thought* (London, 1978).

Gorelov, I. E., *Bol'sheviki v period reaktsii (1907–1910gg.)* (Moscow, 1975).

Harding, N., *Lenin's Political Thought* (2 vols, London, 1977, 1981).

Ivanova, N. A., *Struktura rabochego klassa Rossii 1910–1914* (Moscow, 1987).

Kassow, S. D., *Students, Professors, and the State in Tsarist Russia* (Berkeley, Cal., 1989).

Kingston-Mann, E., *Lenin and the Problem of Marxist Peasant Revolution* (Oxford, 1983).

Khoros, V., Pantin, I., and Plimak, E., *The Russian Revolutionary Tradition* (Moscow, 1988).

Konrad, G. and Szelenyi, I., *The Intellectuals on the Road to Class Power* (Brighton, 1979).

Lane, D., *The Roots of Russian Communism. A Social and Historical Study of Russian Social-Democracy 1898–1907* (Assen, 1969).

Lasswell, D. H. and Lerner, D., eds, *World Revolutionary Elites* (Cambridge, Mass., 1965).

Leikina-Svirskaia, V. R., *Intelligentsiia v Rossii vo vtoroi polovine XIX veka* (Moscow, 1971).

Leikina-Svirskaia, V. R., *Russkaia intelligentsiia v 1900–1917 gg.* (Moscow, 1981).

Lenin, V. I., *Polnoe sobranie sochinenii* (55 vols, Moscow, 1958–65).

Lenin, V. I., *Collected Works* (45 vols, Moscow, 1960–70). English translation of the 4th enlarged Russian edition.

McClennan, W., *Revolutionary Exiles: The Russians in the First International and the Paris Commune* (London, 1979).

Malia, M., 'What is the Intelligentsia?', in R. Pipes, ed., *The Russian Intelligentsia* (New York, 1961).

Nahirny, V., *The Russian Intelligentsia: From Torment to Silence* (New Brunswick, N.J., 1983).

Naimark, N., *Terrorists and Social Democrats. The Russian Revolutionary Movement under Alexander III* (Cambridge, Mass., 1983).

Perrie, M., *The Agrarian Policy of the Russian Socialist-Revolutionary Party from its Origins through the Revolution of 1905–1907* (Cambridge, 1976).

Perrie, M., 'The social composition and structure of the Socialist-Revolutionary Party before 1917', *Soviet Studies* XXIV (1973), pp. 223–50.

Pipes, R. E., 'The Origins of Bolshevism: the Intellectual Evolution of Young Lenin' in R. E. Pipes, ed., *Revolutionary Russia* (London, 1968), pp. 26–62.

Pipes, R. E., ed., *The Russian Intelligentsia* (New York, 1961).

Pipes. R. E., *Social Democracy and the St Petersburg Labour Movement* (Cambridge, Mass., 1963).

Pipes, R. E., *Struve. Liberal on the Left, 1870–1905* (Cambridge, Mass., 1970).

Pomper, P., *The Russian Revolutionary Intelligentsia* (Arlington Heights, Ill., 1970).

Pospelov, P. N. *et al.*, eds, *Istoriia kommunisticheskoi partii sovetskogo soiuza* (Moscow, 1967).

Pushkin, M., '*Raznochintsy* in the University: Government Policy and Social Change in Nineteenth-Century Russia', *International Review of Social History* XXVI (1981), pp. 25–65.

Rice, C., *Russian Workers and the Socialist-Revolutionary Party through the Revolution of 1905–07* (London, 1988).

Service, R., *Lenin: A Political Life. I The Strengths of Contradiction* (London, 1985).

Seton-Watson, H., 'The Russian Intellectuals', *Encounter* (September 1955), pp. 42–50.

Shatz, M. S., *Jan Waclaw Machajski. A Radical Critic of the Russian Intelligentsia and Socialism* (Pittsburgh, Pa., 1989).

Szamuely, T., *The Russian Tradition* (London, 1972).

Ulam, A., *In the Name of the People* (New York, 1977).

Volin, M. S., 'K voprosy ob izuchenii sostava bol'shevistskoi partii

nakanune i v period revoliutsii', in *Revolutsiia 1905–1907 godov v
Rossii i ee vsemirno-istoricheskoe znachenie* (Moscow, 1976).
Volodin, A. I., Nariakin, Iu. F., and Plimak, E. G., *Chernyshevskii
ili Nechaev?: o podlinnoi i mnimoi revoliutsionnosti v
osvoboditel'nom dvizhenii Rossii 50–60–kh XIX veka* (Moscow,
1976).
Wildman, A. K., *The Making of a Workers' Revolution. Russian
Social Democracy, 1891–1903* (Chicago, 1967).
Williams, R. C., *The Other Bolsheviks. Lenin and his Critics,
1904–1914* (Bloomington, Ind., 1986).

V The war and the February revolution

Burdzhalov, E. N., 'O taktike bolshevikov v marte-aprele 1917',
Voprosy istorii (1956) 4, pp. 38–56.
Burdzhalov, E. N., 'Revolution in Moscow', *Soviet Studies in History*
26 (1987–8), pp. 10–100.
Burdzhalov, E. N., *Russia's Second Revolution. The February
Uprising in Petrograd* (Bloomington, Ind., 1987).
Charques, R., *The Twilight of Imperial Russia* (London, 1958).
Chermenskii, E. D., *IV Gosudarstvennaia duma i sverzhenie
tsarizma v Rossii* (Moscow, 1976).
Dazhina, I. M., *Bol'shevistskie listovki v Rossii perioda pervoi
mirovoi voiny i Fevral'skoi revoliutsii* (Moscow, 1981).
Duggan, W. L., 'The Progressists and Russian Politics, 1914–1917',
(Ph.D. Dissertation, Columbia University, 1984).
Dumova, N. G., *Kadetskaia partiia v period pervoi mirovoi voiny i
Fevral'skoi revoliutsii* (Moscow, 1988).
Florinsky, M. T., *The End of the Russian Empire* (Yale, 1931).
Gleason, W., 'The All-Russian Union of Towns and the Politics of
Urban Reform in Tsarist Russia', *Russian Review* xxxv (1976),
pp. 290–303.
Gleason, W., 'The All-Russian Union of Zemstvos and World War
I', in T. Emmons and W. S. Vucinich, eds, *The zemstvo in Russia.
An Experiment in local self-government* (Cambridge, 1982),
pp. 365–82.
Hasegawa, T., 'The Bolsheviks and the Formation of the Petrograd
Soviet in the February Revolution', *Soviet Studies* 29 (1977),
pp. 86–107.
Hasegawa, T., *The February Revolution: Petrograd 1917* (Seattle,
1981).
Hasegawa, T., 'The Problem of Power in the February Revolution of
1917 in Russia', *Canadian Slavonic Papers* xiv (1972).
Jones, D. R., 'Nicholas II and the Supreme Command: an
investigation of motives', *Sbornik* 11 (1985), pp. 47–83.

Katkov, G., *Russia 1917: The February Revolution* (London, 1967).
Leiberov, I. P., *Na shturm samoderzhaviia. Petrogradskii proletariat v gody pervoi mirovoi voiny i Fevral'skoi revoliutsii (iul' 1914-mart 1917g.)* (Moscow, 1979).
Longley, D. A., 'The Divisions in the Bolshevik Party in March 1917', *Soviet Studies* 24 (1972), pp. 61–76.
Longley, D. A., 'The *Mezhraionka*, the Bolsheviks and International Women's Day', *Soviet Studies* XLI (1989), pp. 625–45.
Melancon, M. S., 'The Socialist Revolutionaries from 1902 to February 1917. A Party of Workers, Peasants and Soldiers', (Ph.D. Dissertation, Indiana University, 1984).
Melancon, M. S., 'Who Wrote What and When?: Proclamations of the February Revolution in Petrograd, 23 February–1 March 1917', *Soviet Studies* XL (1988), pp. 479–500.
Milligan, S., 'The Petrograd Bolsheviks and Social Insurance, 1914–1917', *Soviet Studies* XX (1968–9), pp. 369–74.
Pearson, R., *The Russian Moderates and the Crisis of Tsarism, 1914–1917* (London, 1977).
Siegelbaum, L. H., *The Politics of Industrial Mobilization in Russia, 1914–1917. A Study of the War-Industry Committees* (London, 1983).
Stone, N., *The Eastern Front, 1914–1917* (London, 1975).
Tokarev, Iu. S., *Petrogradskii Sovet rabochikh i soldatskikh deputatov v marte – aprele 1917 g.* (Leningrad, 1976).

VI The Provisional Government, the liberals and the moderate socialists

Basil, J. D., *The Mensheviks in the Revolution of 1917* (Columbus, Ohio, 1983).
Fleishauer, J., 'The Agrarian Program of the Russian Constitutional Democrats', *Cahiers du monde russe et sovietique* XX (1979), pp. 173–201.
Galili y Garcia, Z., 'The Menshevik Revolutionary Defencists and the Workers in the Russian Revolution of 1917', (Ph.D. Dissertation, Columbia University, 1980).
Galili y Garcia, Z., *The Menshevik Leaders in the Russian Revolution. Social Realities and Political Strategies* (Princeton, N.J., 1989). (This study, which appeared after I had completed the manuscript, is based on Galili's valuable doctoral dissertation.)
Getzler, I., *Martov: A Political Biography of a Russian Social Democrat* (London, 1967).
Gusev, K. V., *Partiia Eserov: ot melko-burzhuaznogo revoliutsionarizma k kontrrevoliutsii* (Moscow, 1975).

Heenan, L. E., *Russian Democracy's Fateful Blunder. The Summer Offensive of 1917* (New York, 1987).

Katkov, G., *Russia 1917: The Kornilov Affair. Kerensky and the Break-up of the Russian Army* (London, 1980).

Kochan, L., 'Kadet policy in 1917 and the Constitutional Assembly', *Slavonic and East European Review* XLV (1967), pp. 83–92.

Maier, C. S., *Recasting Bourgeois Europe* (Princeton, N.J., 1975).

Munck, J. L., *The Kornilov Revolt: A Critical Examination of Sources Research* (Aarhus, 1987).

Osipova, T. V., 'Vserossiiskii soiuz zemel'nykh sobstvennikov (1917)', *Istoriia SSSR* (1976), 3, pp. 115–29.

Radkey, O., *The Agrarian Foes of Communism. Promise and Default of the Russian Socialist-Revolutionaries, February–October, 1917* (New York, 1958).

Roobol, W. H., *Tsereteli – A Democrat in the Russian Revolution. A Political Biography* (The Hague, 1976).

Rosenberg, W. G., *Liberals in the Russian Revolution. The Constitutional Democratic Party, 1917–1921* (Princeton, N.J., 1974).

Rosenberg, W. G., 'The zemstvo in 1917 and its fate under Bolshevik rule', in T. Emmons and W. S. Vucinich, eds, *The zemstvo in Russia. An experiment in local self-government* (Cambridge, 1982), pp. 383–422.

Spirin, L. M. and Gusev, K. V., eds, *Neproletarskie partii Rossii. Urok istorii* (Moscow, 1984).

Ulam, A., *Russia's Failed Revolutions* (London, 1981).

Volobuev, P. V., *Proletariat i burzhuaziia Rossii v 1917 godu* (Moscow, 1964).

Wade, R., *The Russian Search for Peace. February–October 1917* (Stanford, Cal., 1969).

White, H. J., 'The Ministry of Internal Affairs and Revolution in the Provinces', unpublished research seminar paper (CREES, Birmingham, 1988).

White, J. D., 'The February Revolution and the Bolshevik Vyborg District Committee, Soviet Studies XLI (1989), pp. 602–24.

Zhilin, A. P., *Poslednee nastuplenie (iun' 1917 goda)* (Moscow, 1983).

Znamenskii, O. N., *Vserossiiskoe uchreditel'noe sobranie. Istoriia sozyva i politicheskogo krusheniia* (Leningrad, 1976).

VII The Bolsheviks, the masses, and October

Astrakhan, Kh. M., *Bol'sheviki i ikh politicheskie protivniki v 1917 godu* (Leningrad, 1973).

Avrich, P., 'The Bolshevik Revolution and Workers' Control in

Russian Industry', *Slavic Review* 22 (1963), pp. 47–63.

Avrich, P., 'Russian Factory Committees in 1917', *Jahrbücher für Geschichte Osteuropas* (1963) 11, pp. 161–82.

Berkman, A., *The Russian Tragedy* (Montreal, 1976).

Blank, S., 'The Bolshevik Party and the Nationalities in 1917: Reflections on the Origin of the Multi-National Soviet State', *Sbornik* 9 (1983), pp. 9–14.

Chase, W. and Getty, J. A., 'The Moscow Bolshevik Cadres of 1917: A Prosopographical Analysis', *Russian History* 5 (1978), pp. 84–105.

Daniels, R. V., *Red October* (London, 1967).

Elwood, R. C., ed., *Reconsiderations on the Russian Revolution* (Cambridge, Mass., 1976).

Ezergailis, A., *The 1917 Revolution in Latvia* (Boulder, Cal., 1974).

Ezergailis, A., 'The Thirteenth Conference of the Latvian Social Democrats, 1917: Bolshevik Strategy Victorious', in R. C. Elwood, ed., *Reconsiderations on the Russian Revolution* (Cambridge, Mass., 1976), pp. 133–53.

Ferro, M., *October 1917. A Social History of the Russian Revolution* (London, 1980).

Ferro, M., *The Russian Revolution of February 1917* (London, 1972).

Ferro, M., 'The Russian Soldier in 1917: Patriotic, Undisciplined and Revolutionary', *Slavic Review* 30 (1971), pp. 483–512.

Frenkin, M., *Russkaia armiia i revoliutsiia 1917–1918* (Munich, 1978).

Frenkin, M., *Zakhvat vlasti Bolshevikami v Rossii i rol' tylovykh garnizonov armii. Podgotovka i provedenie Oktiabr'skoi miatezha* (Jerusalem, 1982).

Getzler, I., *Kronstadt, 1917–1921. The Fate of a Soviet Democracy* (Cambridge, 1983).

Gill. G., *Peasants and Government in the Russian Revolution* (London, 1979).

Golub, P. A., *Partiia, armiia i revoliutsiia: Otvoevanie partiei bol 'shevikov armii na storony revoliutsii. Mart 1917–fevral' 1918* (Moscow, 1967).

Hogan, H., 'Conciliation Boards in Revolutionary Petrograd: Aspects of the Crisis of Labor-Management Relations in 1917', *Russian History* 9 (1982), pp. 49–66.

Kaiser, D. H., ed., *The Workers' Revolution in Russia, 1917. The View From Below* (Cambridge, 1987).

Keep, J. L. H., *The Russian Revolution. A Study in Mass Mobilization* (London, 1976).

Koenker, D., *Moscow Workers and the 1917 Revolution* (Princeton, N.J., 1981).

Koenker, D. and Rosenberg, W. G., 'Skilled Workers and the Strike Movement in Revolutionary Russia', *Journal of Social History* 19 (1985–6), pp. 605–29.

Maliavskii, A. D., *Krest'ianskoe dvizhenie v Rossii v 1917g. Mart-Oktiabr'* (Moscow, 1981).

Mandel, D., *The Petrograd Workers and the Fall of the Old Regime* (London, 1983).

Mandel, D., *The Petrograd Workers and the Soviet Seizure of Power* (London, 1984).

Mawdsley, E., *The Russian Revolution and the Baltic Fleet* (London, 1978).

Maximoff, G. P., *The Guillotine at Work. Twenty Years of Terror in Russia* (Chicago, Ill., 1940).

Miller, V. I., 'K voprosy o sravnitel'noi chislennosti partii bol'shevikov i men'shevikov v 1917g.', *Voprosy istorii KPSS* (1988) 12, pp. 109–18.

Mints, I. I., *Istoriia Velikogo Oktiabria* (3 vols, Moscow, 1977–79, 2nd edn).

Pethybridge, R., *The Spread of the Russian Revolution. Essays on 1917* (London, 1972).

Rabinowitch, A., *The Bolsheviks Come To Power. The Revolution of 1917 in Petrograd* (New York, 1976).

Rabinowitch, A., *Prelude to Revolution: The Petrograd Bolsheviks and the July 1917 Uprising* (Bloomington, Ind., 1968).

Raleigh, D. J., *Revolution on the Volga: 1917 in Saratov* (Ithaca, 1985).

Raleigh, D. J., 'Revolutionary Politics in Provincial Russia: The Tsaritsyn "Republic" in 1917', *Slavic Review* 40 (1981), pp. 194–209.

Rosenberg, W. G., 'The Russian Municipal Duma Elections of 1917: A Preliminary Computation of Returns', *Soviet Studies* xxi (1969), pp. 131–63.

Rosenberg, W. G., 'Workers and Workers' Control in the Russian Revolution', *History Workshop* 5 (1978), pp. 89–97.

Schapiro, L., *1917: The Russian Revolutions and the Origins of Present-Day Communism* (Hounslow, 1984).

Shukman, H., *The Blackwell Encyclopedia of the Russian Revolution* (Oxford, 1988).

Slusser, R., *Stalin in October. The Man Who Missed the Revolution* (Baltimore, 1987).

Smith, S. A., 'Craft Consciousness, Class Consciousness: Petrograd 1917', *History Workshop* 11 (1981), pp. 33–58.

Smith, S. A., 'Petrograd in 1917: the view from below', in D. H. Kaiser, ed., *The Workers' Revolution in Russia, 1917. The View From Below* (Cambridge, 1987), pp. 59–79.

Smith, S. A., *Red Petrograd. Revolution in the Factories 1917–1918* (Cambridge, 1983).

Suny, R. G., *The Baku Commune 1917–1918. Class and Nationality in the Russian Revolution* (Princeton, N.J., 1972).

Suny, R. G., 'Toward a Social History of the October Revolution', *American Historical Review* 88 (1983), pp. 31–52.

Ulam, A., *Lenin and the Bolsheviks* (London, 1969).

Wade, R. A., *Red Guards and Workers' Militias in the Russian Revolution* (Stanford, Cal., 1984).

Wildman, A. K., *The End of the Russian Imperial Army* (2 vols, Princeton, N.J., 1980, 1987).

VIII The aftermath of October

Anweiler, O., *The Soviets: The Russian Workers, Peasants and Soldiers Councils, 1905–1921* (New York, 1974).

Arshinov, P., *History of the Makhnovist Movement 1918–1921* (London, 1987).

Carrere d'Encausse, H., *Lenin: Revolution and Power* (London, 1982).

Daniels, R. V., *The Conscience of the Revolution: Communist Opposition in Soviet Russia* (Cambridge, Mass., 1960).

Figes, O., *Peasant Russia, Civil War. The Volga Countryside in Revolution (1917–1921)* (Oxford, 1989).

Flenley, P., 'Workers' Organizations in the Russian Metal Industry, February 1917–August 1918', (Ph.D. Dissertation, University of Birmingham, 1983).

Helgesen, M. M., 'The Origins of the Party–State Monolith in Soviet Russia. Relations between the Soviets and Party Committees in the Central Provinces, October 1917–March 1921', (Ph.D. Dissertation, State University of New York, 1980).

Keep, J. L. H., *The Debate on Soviet Power* (Oxford, 1979).

Koenker, D., 'Urbanization and Deurbanization in the Russian Revolution and Civil War', *Journal of Modern History* 57 (1985), pp. 424–50.

Leggett, G., *The Cheka: Lenin's Political Police* (Oxford, 1981).

Mawdsley, E., *The Russian Civil War* (London, 1987).

Medvedev, R., *The October Revolution* (London, 1979).

Pipes, R. E., *The Formation of the Soviet Union: Communism and Nationalism, 1917–1923* (Cambridge, Mass., 1964).

Rabinowitch, A., 'The Evolution of Local Soviets in Petrograd, November 1917–June 1918: The Case of the First City District Soviet', *Slavic Review* 46 (1987), pp. 20–37.

Radkey, O., *The Election to the Russian Constituent Assembly of 1917* (Harvard, 1950).

Radkey, O., *The Sickle under the Hammer: The Russian Socialist*

Revolutionaries in the Early Months of Soviet Rule (New York, 1963).

Radkey, O., *The Unknown Civil War in South Russia. A Study of the Green Movement in the Tambov Region, 1920–21* (Stanford, Cal., 1976).

Renehan, T. J., 'The Failure of Local Soviet Government, 1917–1918', (Ph.D. Dissertation, State University of New York, 1983).

Rigby, T. H., *Lenin's Government: Sovnarkom 1917–1922* (Cambridge, 1979).

Rosenberg, W. G., 'Russian Labor and Bolshevik Power after October', *Slavic Review* 44 (1985), pp. 213–38.

Sakwa, R., *Soviet Communists in Power* (London, 1988).

Schapiro, L., *The Origin of the Communist Autocracy* (London, 1977, 2nd edn).

Service, R., *The Bolshevik Party in Revolution. A Study in Organizational Change 1917–1923* (London, 1979).

Voline, *The Unknown Revolution 1917–1921* (Montreal, 1974).

INDEX